# TELEVANGELISM RECONSIDERED

# ÆR

## American Academy of Religion
## Studies in Religion

Editor
David E. Klemm

Number 68
TELEVANGELISM RECONSIDERED
Ritual in the Search for Human Community

by
Bobby C. Alexander

# TELEVANGELISM RECONSIDERED

## Ritual in the Search
## for Human Community

by
Bobby C. Alexander

Scholars Press
Atlanta, Georgia

# TELEVANGELISM RECONSIDERED
## Ritual in the Search
## for Human Community

by
Bobby C. Alexander

© 1994
The American Academy of Religion

**Library of Congress Cataloging in Publication Data**
Alexander, Bobby Chris, 1950-
    Televangelism reconsidered / by Bobby C. Alexander.
        p.    cm. — (American Academy of Religion studies in religion ;
no. 68)
    Includes bibliographical references.
    ISBN 1-55540-906-7 (cloth : alk. paper). — ISBN 1-55540-907-5
(paper : alk. paper)
        1. Television in religion—United States. 2. Evangelistic work—
United States—History—20th century. 3. Fundamentalist churches—
United States—History—20th century. 4. United States—Church history—
20th century. I. Title. II. Series: AAR studies in religion ; no. 68.
BV656.3.A43    1994
269'.26'0973—dc20                            94-19987
                                             CIP

Printed in the United States of America
on acid-free paper

For David A. Martin, Bernice Martin,
and Richard P. DeLong

# ⊰ Table of Contents ⊱

Preface      p. ix

1. Introduction: Televangelism As Redressive
   Ritual within A Larger Social Drama      p. 1

   **[Part One]** Behind the Scenes, or The Bigger Picture      p. 17

2. Televangelism in Caricature and Its Human Face      p. 19

3. Viewers' Marginalized Religion and Social
   Standing within American Society      p. 31

4. The Religion of Televangelism and Its Viewers      p. 49

5. The Emergence of Televangelism As
   Distinctive Religious Programming      p. 57

   **[Part Two]** Televangelism As Ritual      p. 63

6. Viewers' Ritual Participation in the Telecasts      p. 65

7. Ritual in the Service of Legitimation and Adaptation      p. 73

8. Ritual in the Search for Human Community      p. 85

   **[Part Three]** The Television Programs      p. 95

9. "The Old-Time Gospel Hour":
   Ritual in the Service of Legitimation      p. 97

10. The "700 Club": Ritual in the Service of Adaptation      p. 113

11. "Jimmy Swaggart": Ritual Community on the Offensive      p. 125

12. The "PTL Club" and "The Jim and Tammy Show":
    Ritual Community As Refuge                          p. 141

13. Conclusion: The Recent Shift in Ritual Roles:
    Televangelism's New Emphasis on Community           p. 157

    Appendix: Survey of Viewers                         p. 163

    Endnotes                                            p. 185

    Bibliography                                        p. 201

# ᵈ Preface ᵇ

I would like to extend my thanks to many people who read the manuscript for this book and offered helpful comments and criticisms. I would like to offer special thanks to David A. Martin and Stewart M. Hoover, who read drafts of the manuscript in all of its various stages. I would also like to thank Lonnie D. Kliever, Polly A. Smith, E. Richard Knox, Richard W. Cogley, and Ida Louise Noblin, who also helped tabulate the results of my survey of viewers. My thanks also go to Tom F. Driver, who gave me good observations and criticism in response to a couple of papers he heard me give on my research and after reading the introductory pages of the manuscript.

I would also like to thank the members of several groups who gave me their comments and criticisms in response to various papers I presented as my book took shape: the Ritual Studies Group and the North American Religions Section of the American Academy of Religion, as well as participants in two Roundtable discussions sponsored by the AAR, the Society for the Scientific Study of Religion, especially members of the session on "Current Issues in Televangelism," and the Southwest Commission on Religious Studies. I would like to express special thanks to the organizers of the first international conference on "Media-Religion-Culture" held at Uppsala University, in Uppsala, Sweden, for the invitation to present a paper on my research, especially Alf Linderman, Sigbert Axelson, and Stewart Hoover. I would like to thank as well the other presenters attending the conference for their comments and questions.

Several groups provided grant funds to undertake my research. I would like to express my gratitude to them: the American Academy of Religion, the Southwest Commission on Religious Studies, Southern

Methodist University's University Research Council, and the University Lecture Series of Dedman College at Southern Methodist University.

I would also like to thank several other groups and persons who aided my research: People for the American Way—with special thanks to David Crane, who invited me to make use of the extensive video tape archives on television religion held by this organization; International Telecharge, Incorporated—with special thanks to Peter Buonaiuto, John Kutyba, who oversaw the telephone survey of viewers, and the telephone operators who conducted the survey; and Dawson/Duncan Communications—with special thanks to Roslyn R. Dawson, who secured from ITI the service of its operators *pro bono*. My thanks also go to Chuck Elder of the Liberty Broadcasting Network for opening its video tape archives to me.

My thanks go as well to Gina M. Tansley of Scholars Press for preparing and producing the pages of the book. Needless to say, I am thankful to the American Academy of Religion for publishing the book.

Bobby C. Alexander

The University of Texas at Dallas

Dallas, Texas, summer, 1993

# 1

# Introduction:
# Televangelism As Redressive Ritual
# within a Larger Social Drama

*Televangelism Reconsidered:*
*Ritual in the Search for Human Community*

The recent revelation of fraudulent and illegal fundraising methods and use of funds solicited from viewers to support the lavish lifestyle of Jim and Tammy Bakker, two of the more prominent televangelists, along with revelations of the sexual escapades of Jim Bakker and Jimmy Swaggart, another widely known televangelist, have rocked televangelism to its foundations. This has not been the first time televangelism has been embroiled in controversy. Televangelism has also received bad press for another of its controversial sides: the narrow moral or social agenda promoted in its role as a platform of the Religious Right, whose coming to flower during the 1980s was significantly aided by the television venue. Televangelism has played a major role in mobilizing large numbers of conservative Christians to enter the political arena and there press for the legislation of their religious morality within American public life.

There is good reason for the scrutiny recently given televangelism. But the attention given televangelism's controversial or darker side has obscured other dimensions. Emphasis on controversy has helped create the impression that televangelism has won its audience entirely by deception and manipulation. While deceit and manipulation are part of the phenomenon, they do not define televangelism. Nor do trickery and manipulation adequately account for televangelism's relatively large following. The impression stereotypes televangelism.

The stereotypic view of televangelism turns viewers into caricatures. It reduces viewers to passive spectators or victims of fraudulent religion. It obscures the active participation in the television programs of viewers who are already committed to the religion promoted there. Televangelism's viewers are fundamentalist and Pentecostal Christians for the most part.[1] The stereotypic view obscures viewers' religious interest in the telecasts, as well as ways in which the programs address viewers' religious interests. The stereotype of televangelism also hides the religious commitment of the television ministers. They share viewers' religious beliefs. While the televangelists have fallen to temptation and sin or human weakness, they, too, are conservative Christians. Also obscured are other important interests viewers bring with them to their viewing as well as ways in which the telecasts address these interests. These interests are illuminated by this book.

Few studies of televangelism have inquired about the attraction or of the telecasts for viewers. Most have tended to focus on the televangelists, the television ministries and their operation, as well as on controversy, giving little attention to viewers. Those that have focused on viewers have not gone far enough. This book reconsiders the attraction of televangelism for its conservative Christian audience at the height of its popularity during the 1980s.

The book casts a spotlight on the role or potential role of the television programs in helping viewers address and attempt to resolve a larger social drama or social conflict in which they are caught up: their struggle with mainstream American society as a marginalized social group for greater inclusion within it. The holy war waged by televangelism and its followers against highly secularized American society is obvious, as is their battle to gain greater political power and influence within American society as members of a conservative religious group. Not as obvious is the battle waged by televangelism's followers against mainstream American society for greater inclusion.

Viewers live along the edges or borders of the social mainstream. Televangelism's conservative Christian viewers are committed to narrow religious beliefs and morality, and, correlated with these, a narrowly conservative position on social and political issues. These conflict with the highly secularized and pluralistic character of mainstream society as well as its religious tolerance and democratic ideals, putting conservative Christians on a collision course with secular society. Consequently, mainstream society holds the religious conservatives at arm's length as a social group. Commitment to their anti-secular, world-condemning religion also leads televangelism's conservative Christian viewers to keep some distance between themselves and the secularized mainstream, widening the gap between them. Their marginalization leads viewers to struggle for greater community with mainstream American society.

Individual viewers watch the programs in hopes of meeting personal needs and resolving personal crises. They turn to the telecasts to request prayer for physical healing and financial miracles, and to receive guidance during times of domestic and marriage crisis. And they watch out of religious interest. Viewers seek spiritual renewal as well as religious support and guidance in dealing with moral issues.[2] The initial attraction of the television programs is the religious and moral interest they hold for those who watch. The news media, the American public, and many scholars have not given adequate recognition to the religious motivation for watching televangelism. They have not adequately acknowledged the religion of televangelism or the religious commitment of televangelism's viewers as a motivation for tuning in.

Nor have the social and human interests that also motivate viewers been fully recognized, or, bound up with these, the humanity of televangelism's viewers. Viewers see themselves as citizens of heaven or religious conservatives first. They are also members of the society of women and men, and of the wider American society, however. They bring to their viewing of the religious telecasts social and human interests that stand alongside their religious and private interests. They bring to their viewing their interest as a marginalized social group in overturning their marginalization. Viewers do not consciously engage in televangelism in order to address their social struggle. Hidden to viewers is the bigger picture or social drama of their struggle against mainstream society for greater inclusion. They nevertheless experience the effects of their marginalized social standing. The televangelists and programmers share these interests, since they are also members of this marginalized group.

This book spotlights a feature of the television programs that gives them the capacity or potential to play a redressive role within the social drama in which viewers are caught up, namely their ritual nature. All of the programs are ritual performances. Televangelism's viewers actively participate in these as they ritualize their viewing. This book shows how viewers tap various capacities of televangelism in its role as ritual to attempt to rectify their social marginalization. I am modifying the conventional understanding that ritual involves immediate participation as well as face-to-face interaction among participants. Televangelism's viewers do not participate in the performances taking place in the television studio or other broadcast venues in any immediate way. Nor do they interact with one another directly. Their participation and interaction are mediated by the medium of television. They are active participants in ritual nonetheless.

Defined in basic terms, ritual is a performance, planned or impro- vised, that makes a transition away from the everyday world to an alter- native context, within which the everyday is transformed. Religious ritual makes a transition to an ultimate context or framework of action. Ritual has a life of its own. It is also a response to the everyday world. Ritual is transformative of everyday experience, especially everyday human encounters. Ritual is a transformative experience that leads participants to see themselves, others, and the world in a new way and to act in new ways in their everyday encounters. As rituals, televangelism's transformative capacity lends itself to viewers' religious interest in spiritual renewal in the service of making the world Christian. This book focuses on how televangelism's conservative Christian viewers tap ritual's transformative capacity to attempt to rectify their marginalized social standing.

Televangelism has the capacity as ritual performance to help viewers legitimate or validate in their own eyes their religion, religious identity, and religious group in the face of threats and opposition by mainstream American society, which is highly secularized. Conservative Christianity and conservative Christians are not given a new legitimacy in the eyes of mainstream society. Self-legitimation nonetheless has a concrete impact on the social mainstream. Establishing the legitimacy of their religion and their religious group for themselves supports the efforts of the conservative Christians to mobilize themselves within the public sphere, especially within the political arena, and there push for their religious interests. Televangelism has played an obvious role in communicating the militant message of conservative Christianity. Not as obvious is televangelism's role as ritual in legitimating the message. Mobilizing in the interest of religion has the added effect of helping conservative Christians as a social group push for a more significant place and role within mainstream society as they force themselves and their moral and political agenda upon it under the label of the "Religious Right."

As ritual, televangelism also has the capacity to help viewers adapt to the outlook and lifestyle of the very society their religion opposes and which threatens and challenges their religion, because the social mainstream is highly secularized, and yet which they want to be included in more fully. The conservative Christians are not just flirting with the secular lifestyle and outlook, because they find these enticing or have become worldly. Adopting some of the ways of secular society is an adaptive strategy undertaken to win greater acceptance and inclusion by the social mainstream. As viewers adopt features of secular, mainstream dress, speech, aesthetic sensibilities, attitudes, and outlook they accommodate their religion and become more mainstream, moving closer to social acceptance and inclusion.

Ritual legitimation and ritual adaptation are opposite sides of the same coin. They are both strategies for gaining greater inclusion within mainstream society, one by force, the other by accommodation to some of the demands of the social mainstream.

Televangelism's viewers bring their struggle for greater social inclusion to their viewing all the more since televangelism's ritual capacities support their struggle. Viewers are not aware of televangelism's role as ritual within the larger social drama or of what gives televangelism its capacity or potential as ritual to aid them in their struggle for inclusion. Viewers discover televangelism's capacity to aid their struggle as they experience the concrete results it provides as ritual in support of their efforts toward inclusion.

The ritual nature of televangelism has been virtually overlooked. Turning a spotlight on televangelism's role as redressive ritual within a larger social drama, however, casts televangelism, its viewers, and its attraction for them in a whole new light. As ritual, televangelism offers viewers the opportunity to participate in a communal activity that addresses their common social dilemma and holds the capacity or promise to help them overturn together their marginalization as a social group. As ritual, televangelism offers viewers a means or potential means of empowering themselves as it supports their efforts toward inclusion. By "empowerment" is meant a form of social power that includes political power and influence but is more basic. The term is used here to refer to the enlargement of opportunities and freedoms made possible by social inclusion or human community. These begin with a greater role in shaping public or common life and greater freedom to determine one's own life within it.

In the final analysis, this book shows, the effort of televangelism's followers to engage the telecast performances to work toward greater social inclusion are undermined by the contradiction between televangelism's ritual roles. Legitimation and adaptation undercut one another, as we will see. As ritual, televangelism nonetheless helps followers take action to attempt to overturn their social marginalization, which is itself empowering.

This book shows how televangelism as ritual also offers viewers the potential to create among themselves the open and supportive community they seek with mainstream society but do not enjoy. The point is also made that the indirectness of interaction among viewers, forced upon them by the medium of television, restricts community among them. The medium works against the embodiment of community provided by ritual in face-to-face, direct, and open-ended human encounter. The possibility of community is also limited by the authoritarian, top-down organizational interests of the television ministers and ministries, along with the interest in personal, political and economic gain of the televangelists, interest that has led to some manipulation of viewers. Programmers do give consideration to the religious views and opinions of the audience, who send mountains of correspondence to the television ministries. The inclusion of the audience in the planning and design of the telecasts, and in the actual programs, is limited, however. The personal interests of the televangelists, religious and otherwise, restrict audience inclusion.

Four television programs that were prominent during televangelism's heyday are presented in this book as illustrative of one or another of televangelism's roles or potential roles as redressive ritual: Jerry Falwell's "The Old-Time Gospel Hour" (legitimation), Pat Robertson's "700 Club" (adaptation), Jimmy Swaggart's evangelistic telecasts (conservative Christian community on the offensive against secular society), and Jim and Tammy Bakker's "PTL Club" and its replacement, "The Jim and Tammy Show" (conservative Christian community as refuge from the secular world).

The book concludes by noting the shift in emphasis in the television programs' roles as ritual: away from legitimation and adaptation to building up a nurturing community among viewers following the defeat of the Religious Right and the rebuff of conservative Christians by mainstream society in the late 1980s.

### Conservative Religion and Secular Society in Conflict

To be sure, televangelism's viewers are secularized in many ways. And they participate in secular society. They engage in politics. They vote. They enjoy the entertainments, etc. But they are only partly secularized. Their commitment to their religion prevents them from plunging headlong into the secular world view or the secular lifestyle. The religious beliefs of televangelism's fundamentalist and Pentecostal viewers have not changed significantly from those of viewers of televangelism in its infancy during the 1950s.[3] They believe the Bible is literally true, since, they believe, it has been given by God himself. They believe in prayer and in miracles. And they hold to the anti-secular, millenarian outlook of Christian scripture.[4]

Viewers believe they are living in the final days of an ongoing cosmic battle between God and Satan for ultimate rule over God's creation, which has fallen into sin. They believe they are caught up in the battle as redemptive agents of God in the world. They believe the sinful world can be won back to God through moral regeneration. This is achieved, they believe, by practicing biblical morality, which they believe expresses God's purposes for his creation. Viewers believe they are being "persecuted" by the secular world for militantly promoting their biblical beliefs and morality. Persecution is believed to have been masterminded by Satan himself, who, they believe, is seeking to defeat God by defeating God's people. They believe the secular world is allied with Satan. Persecution is also thought to be a fulfillment of biblical prophecy concerning the last days. Viewers believe they will be rewarded for their faithfulness to God and his purposes in the face of persecution by sharing in God's rule over the world, which they believe God will redeem shortly. Viewers' anti-secular outlook is fed by their millenarian belief.

Neither the message of televangelism nor its audience is monolithic. There are significant differences among the religious messages of the various programs and among beliefs held by viewers. These run along the lines of fundamentalist and Pentecostal beliefs. Pentecostal programs include the practice of speaking in tongues, or glossolalia, and emphasize the Holy Spirit and the "spirit-filled life," while fundamentalist programs do not. Speaking in tongues divides Pentecostals and fundamentalists. The latter do not share the view that the practice is a sign that Pentecostals have been sanctified by God, and thus have had their salvation completed.

Televangelism's fundamentalist and Pentecostal viewers hold in common, however, the fundamentals of conservative Christian belief.

Both groups of viewers are "fundamentalistic" in a broad sense.[5] Both hold the Bible to be literally true. Both believe in Jesus' virgin birth, his bodily resurrection, and imminent return. Both hold that the only way to salvation is through belief in Jesus, in his death as salvific, and in his resurrection. Both hold the millenarian, world-opposing outlook of Christian scripture. Both groups believe they are living during earth's final days. And both believe that the practice of biblical morality, which both groups practice fervently, will help bring about the final redemption of the world.

Sharing the biblical fundamentals encourages some crossing over from fundamentalist to Pentecostal programming or vice versa by televangelism's viewers.[6] Falwell, an outspoken advocate of fundamentalist Christianity, primarily draws fundamentalist viewers. Robertson draws fundamentalist and Pentecostal viewers. He bridges both traditions but supports speaking in tongues and emphasizes the Holy Spirit. Swaggart and the Bakkers are well-known Pentecostal leaders and draw Pentecostal viewers primarily.

Mainstream society is itself religious. Religion has long played a role in shaping American society, and Americans continue to look to religion to help shape public values. But mainstream society does not permit any single religion to be the sole arbiter or legislator of public values and public life. Mainstream society views the exclusivist and judgmental religion of conservative Christians as incompatible with its democratic ideal. The effort of conservative Christians engaged in the Religious Right to impose their belief and morality upon the public sphere is viewed as hostile. Consequently conservative Christians are not included fully in shaping public life.

Mainstream society is actively engaged in battling the efforts of the Religious Right to hold sway over the public sphere through punitive court decisions, restrictions imposed through State House legislation, media scrutiny and criticism, and opposition campaigns by civil liberties organizations. Prayer in public schools was banned some time ago. More recently, Christian schools that have defied state accreditation laws have been closed. The teaching of "Creation science" in public school textbooks has been outlawed. "Pro-life" demonstrations have been restricted. Demonstrators have been arrested, etc.

The relatively small number of conservative Christians accentuates their marginal status. They make up only 16% of the American population.[7] The same is true of the small number of conservative Christians who watch televangelism. They make up around only 5% of the population.[8]

Conservative Christians have been highly visible within American politics since the late 1970s, when they began pushing for the legislation of their political agenda as the Religious Right. The high visibility encouraged the assumption, held by the news media, the American public, and many scholars, that the Religious Right had become a political force with enough power to alter American society through the legislation of its moral agenda. The Religious Right has not succeeded by and large, however, in seeing its agenda enacted, at least at the federal level.

The visibility of the Religious Right was increased when its was embraced by the Political Right, which was coming into political power at the same time and gearing up to help put Reagan in the White House in the 1980 Presidential election. But the Religious Right was never included in the power base of the Political Right, which was faced with its own struggle for power with the base of power within the Republican Party. Nor was the Religious Right included in any significant decision making by the Reagan administration. Lack of real support by the Reagan and Bush administrations was one reason the Religious Right failed to see its agenda enacted at the federal level. The Religious Right was co-opted by the Political Right to promote its own conservative social agenda and power interests within the Republican Party and within national politics. The Religious Right has enjoyed some success at the grassroots level. But success there has been limited.

Evidence that the Religious Right has not been brought into the bases of political power is found in the overwhelming defeat of Robertson's bid for the Republican Party's nomination as President in 1988, and in the collapse of Falwell's Moral Majority around the same time for lack of support outside the Religious Right.

## Televangelism As Redressive Ritual

My study of ritual and of the social and human interests it promotes, especially human community and social empowerment, has led me to question the prevalent stereotype of televangelism as sheer manipulation of passive viewers. Televangelism's viewers are anything but passive. My survey of viewers who watch the programs mentioned earlier, the results of which are given elsewhere in the book, shows that they are highly engaged in the television programs. These viewers report that ahead of turning on the programs they undertake ritual routines on their own to prepare themselves for participating in the telecasts. They read the Bible, pray, etc. They also report that they participate in the ritual activities undertaken by the telecasts. They follow along in their Bibles when scripture is read, pray along with those offering prayers, and phone in prayer requests or financial pledges. I also spoke to viewers about their involvement and interest in the programs on visits to the headquarters of all of these television ministries, where they had gone to attend a taping or broadcast of a show.[9] Viewers' active participation puts them in the position to tap the telecasts' capacity as ritual to help them attempt to redress their social marginalization.

"Rituals are expressive of human agency, the power of human beings to act," as Tom Driver has observed.[10] Televangelism empowers its viewers even further as it helps them take action to overturn their social marginalization.

Ritual is a "showing *of a doing*."[11] What is demonstrated or displayed is that participants are engaged in actions that transform themselves and their world. Participants show that they are engaged in the act of making themselves and their world over. "In [ritual] performance we come upon something quite basic about human beings—that we constitute ourselves through our actions," as Driver has noted.[12] "When we perform ourselves, we do not simply express what we already are. We perform our becoming, and become our performing."[13]

Ritual transformation is not symbolic only. As "lived experience," ritual alters human experience itself.[14] Ritual leads to new experiences of oneself, others, and the world. The life-changing experiences made possible by ritual alter the experiential base out of which people live their everyday lives, leading them to live in new ways. While ritual often symbolizes everyday experience, it does not replicate daily experience. Ritual reshapes experience.[15]

Above all else, ritual is socially transformative. It alters everyday social experience. Ritual is a communal act and a communal experience that has consequences for those engaged in it as well as for society as a whole. As ritual alters participants' experience of one another, it transforms how they relate to one another within the everyday world, as well as how they relate to others. Ritual transforms everyday social actions and social relations.

In its role as a "cultural performance," ritual generates experiences that lead people to model their everyday encounters after the social ideal found in a society's established cultural world view and the style of life correlated with it. As a society's world view is dramatized, the ritual performance generates emotional experiences that support it. The emotions aroused are in keeping with the view of the world that is presented. These provide firsthand, experiential evidence of the authenticity and effectiveness of a society's view of the world. In the process of being made an authentic "model of" the world, a world view is made an authoritative "model for" everyday life, especially everyday social relations. Ritual mirrors the established order in its role as a cultural performance; it also shapes it.[16] The chapter concerning televangelism's role as ritual legitimation draws from Clifford Geertz.

Televangelism's conservative Christian viewers exploit its capacity as ritual performance to authenticate and make authoritative in their own eyes their religion, their religious style of life, and their religious group. Their interest in ritual legitimation is keen, since their religion and religious subculture are under challenge and under siege by mainstream, secular society. By giving new legitimacy to their religion and religious group, viewers transform their identity and standing in the world. Seeing themselves in possession of absolute truth as well as God's special favor, they transform their status from that of insignificant citizens of the wider world to that of a special people. The new status they give themselves is symbolic. The symbolic transformation in status has a concrete impact, however. Their enhanced status, in addition to reinforcing their religion, helps galvanize the conservative Christians into doing battle with secular society. As they fight their religious battle, they also fight for themselves as a social group. The effects of self-legitimation upon the wider society are very real.

Ritual does not always confirm or help keep in place an established social order. Ritual is socially transformative in a second and radically different sense. Ritual also brings about social change. Ritual transition away from the everyday world to an alternative context suspends the established order and relaxes obligations to it. In the process, ritual provides an opportunity to entertain new ways of thinking about the world and new ways of living in it and to experiment with these, especially through new social identities, social arrangements, and social encounters. Experimentation creates new experiences that alter everyday practice.[17] The chapter on televangelism's role as ritual adaptation draws from Victor Turner's insights about ritual's role in social change.

Televangelism's viewers take advantage of its role as ritual transition to an alternative context to experiment with and experience the secular outlook and lifestyle of mainstream society. As the telecasts make a transition to an alternative context and suspend the everyday world in their role as ritual, they invite viewers to relax their commitment and obligation to the narrowly conservative religion and morality by which they identify and define themselves within the everyday world. Viewers hold their religious identity in place as they defend themselves and go on the offensive against secular, mainstream society. Transition to the alternative context invites viewers to open themselves to ways of conceiving the world and their identity within it along with ways of living in the world that compete with their religion. As ritual, the telecasts present viewers an alternative, nonthreatening context within which to explore ways of looking at the world and of living in it that have been traditionally opposed by their conservative religion but are more in keeping with the secularized views and lifestyle of a changing American society.

The ritual context invites viewers to lower their guard against a threatening and hostile secular world and to experiment or familiarize themselves with the dress, language, aesthetic sensibilities, and attitudes of mainstream society. All of these are introduced by hosts and guests who appear on the programs. The ritual context also invites viewers to open themselves to learning about social issues and political events within the secular world as well as learning about views that compete with those of conservative Christianity. If viewers are already familiar with these, they are invited to learn even more. In the process, viewers transform their identity from that of misfit citizen of the wider world to that of a citizen who is at home within it. The transformation is not merely symbolic. Viewers become more comfortable with the secular outlook and lifestyle as they familiarize themselves with these. As viewers adopt a more secular outlook and lifestyle, they also accommodate their religion to the secular world and move closer to winning acceptance by mainstream society.

The role of television as public ritual is well known.[18] Also widely known is the centrality of television within a society and culture, given its capacity as mass, ritual communication to create a common culture through conveying a common world view and shared values and presenting these as normative.[19] Television's capacity as ritual to alter viewers' world view has also been observed.[20] Stewart Hoover's is the only study, however, that has taken note of televangelism's ritual nature, and of televangelism's capacity as ritual to adapt viewers, as well as its potential as ritual to create community among them. He has other interests, however, and does not pursue the discussion of how the telecasts adapt viewers or build community. Nor does he take up televangelism's role in legitimation.[21]

Most important, ritual promotes change in the direction of greater human community. As ritual makes a transition away from the everyday world, it suspends the social categories and other social distinctions in place within the everyday world that divide people and hold them apart, along with participants' obligations to these distinctions. In the process, ritual makes it possible for people to experience one another more directly and to discover their common humanity and equality. The experience of human community infuses everyday human relations with communitarian values and purpose. It promotes humanity, human freedom, and the common good. The experience of community also leads people to alter social arrangements that limit human community by failing to promote communitarian values. Ritual's community-building capacity places it at the center of public life.[22]

Televangelism obviously cannot directly create community between its followers and mainstream society. It is the ritual of a marginalized social group, after all. Televangelism's other capacities as ritual help viewers work toward greater community or social inclusion, however. As ritual legitimation, televangelism supports their effort as conservative Christians to mobilize themselves and push for greater inclusion as a social group within the public sphere. As ritual adaptation, televangelism helps the conservative Christians come closer to winning the acceptance of mainstream society as they become more like the social mainstream.

While televangelism cannot create community between viewers and mainstream society, as ritual it has the potential to help viewers create among themselves the open and accepting relations they seek with the social mainstream. The chapter given to this potential draws from Turner's observations on ritual community.

## Concrete, If Limited, Social and Human Benefits to Viewers

Legitimation or revalidation of conservative Christianity and adaptation or accommodation to secular society are contradictory ritual roles. The contradiction expresses the cross-pressures of competing religious and social or human interests that pull televangelism's viewers in opposite directions. Expressed in the contradiction is viewers' ambivalence toward secular society, given its threat to their conservative religion. The contradiction also expresses the ambivalence of viewers toward their religion, given its preventing them from gaining full acceptance by the social mainstream.

Adaptation is at cross-purposes with conservative religion and its rejection of the secular world. It contradicts the efforts of viewers to legitimate their conservative religion for themselves and undercuts their efforts to mobilize themselves as conservative Christians and push their religious interests. On the other hand, legitimation undercuts viewers' efforts toward accommodation. Legitimation for viewers of a religion that is suspicious and condemning of the wider society, and legitimation in the eyes of viewers of their conservative Christian community as an exclusive community of the saved puts in place "we-versus-they" distinctions that close off conservative Christians from the social mainstream. Legitimation encourages viewers to keep their distance rather than engage in more open-ended encounters, keeping in place the gulf between the two groups and winning the disapproval and rebuff of mainstream society. In the end, the contradiction between televangelism's ritual roles cross-wires televangelism, short-circuiting the efforts of its conservative Christian viewers to gain greater inclusion within mainstream American society.

As ritual, televangelism nonetheless affords the conservative Christians an opportunity to respond to their social marginalization rather than remain entirely subject to the forces of secularization or completely at the mercy of the dominant society. As ritual, televangelism puts viewers in the position to become active agents who can adjust to their social circumstances rather than allow these to determine them completely. Ritual, and televangelism as ritual, offers viewers a means to address the struggle for social inclusion in which they are engaged. As ritual, televangelism also offers viewers a concrete means by which to attempt to resolve their struggle.

Televangelism's ritual capacities and ritual roles help viewers make their struggle concrete. Televangelism gives viewers a platform from which to protest against their exclusion from mainstream society. Ritual legitimation of their religion and of conservative Christians as a significant social group in their own eyes helps viewers make their protest concrete. Furthermore, ritual legitimation helps viewers mobilize themselves to push their religious demands and at the same time force themselves upon society as a social group. Adaptation is an inverted form of protest against social exclusion. The demand for greater inclusion is made concrete as viewers partially adopt some of the outlook and lifestyle of the social mainstream and actually become more like the mainstream. The attempt to create among themselves the open community they do not find with the social mainstream is also a form of protest against exclusion by mainstream society. Viewers concretize their protest as they attempt to create community among themselves, since open, human community affirms their humanity, and together with it, their equality as well as the freedom to determine their own lives.

As ritual, televangelism provides its conservative Christian viewers with strategies for gaining greater community with the wider American society and, along with human community, greater empowerment within it. While televangelism's contradictory ritual roles undermine their struggle, as ritual, televangelism nevertheless allows conservative Christians to become active subjects of their own lives.

# ⫷ Part One ⫸

# Behind the Scenes, or The Bigger Picture

Part One takes us behind the scenes of the television programs examined later in this book. It introduces televangelism's viewers, their religion, their positions on social and political issues, and their standing in relation to mainstream American society. In the process, Part One provides an overview of the larger social backdrop against which televangelism is played, namely the social marginalization of its conservative Christian viewers and their struggle to gain greater inclusion within mainstream society. Part One moves from stereotypes of televangelism to the human face of televangelism and its viewers.

# ⊰ 2 ⊱

# Televangelism in Caricature and
# Its Human Face

## *Scandal and Politics*

Televangelism has been part of the American landscape almost since the advent of television. In the beginning it did not dominate the religious airwaves, as it does now, but was overshadowed by mainline Protestant programming. A brief history of the emergence of televangelism as the distinctive programming of conservative Christians is given in a later chapter. Recently televangelism has come to hold a greater place within the American consciousness, especially with its entry into politics in the late 1970s.

During the 1980s, the American public grew increasingly worried by routine reports from the news media on the successes of televangelism in its role as a platform for the Religious Right. Conservative ministers like Jerry Falwell and Pat Robertson, then coming into prominence as leaders of the Religious Right, began using television to mobilize conservative Christians within the political arena. Televangelism drew viewers out of relative isolation and into the public square to press their conservative social and moral agenda on the rest of the nation. Public interest in televangelism waned with the defeats eventually suffered by the Religious Right toward the end of the decade. Robertson failed in his bid to win the Republican Party's nomination as its candidate for President in 1988. Around the same time, Falwell closed down the political lobby of conservative Christians he had headed—the "Moral Majority"—for lack of sufficient support.

More recent revelations by the media of questionable and illegal fundraising practices and sexual misconduct by Jim Bakker, one of the most prominent televangelists, made televangelism a national fixation. The Bakker ministry had been in the news since its beginning in the 1970s, its finances the subject of continuous charges of illegality by the press. Ted Koppel's interview with Jim and Tammy Bakker shortly after the PTL scandal broke in March 1987 drew the highest audience in the history of ABC's "Nightline" news program. New revelations of sexual misconduct by Jimmy Swaggart along with his dramatic televised confession in February 1988 kept televangelism in the fore of the nation's consciousness. At the time, he was the most watched televangelist. The public's interest in the scandals may have had as much to do with wanting reassurance that the conservative Christian threat to the public order had been set back as it had to do with curiosity about the television ministers' clay feet.

Tammy Bakker has now divorced Jim Bakker, who is serving a federal prison sentence for fraud. She has also left the new television ministry the former couple started up in December 1988 in Orlando after being forced to leave their former PTL ministry and the "PTL Club," their popular television program, by the Assemblies of God denomination to which they belonged. The Bakkers' daughter is in charge of the new ministry while Jim Bakker serves time in prison. Swaggart continues to broadcast, after refusing an order by the Assemblies of God elders responsible for his ordination to stay out of the pulpit until he had met their conditions for rehabilitation. Swaggart has also resigned from the denomination. His following has plummeted in the aftermath of the disclosure of sexual impropriety. In late 1990 Falwell dropped most of the stations carrying his program in response to a drop in audience and out of the need to generate revenue.[23] Falwell has redirected his ministry's efforts and resources. He has backed away from politics and toward training future Christian leaders at his Liberty University, formerly Liberty Baptist College, which he founded over twenty years ago. Robertson has told the large audience he continues to draw that he has left politics to return to pastoring his television flock. He has not retired from politics entirely, however, keeping up an association with the political lobby he founded, the Christian Coalition.

In spite of scandal and political defeat, televangelism remains alive and well. The audience for televangelism as a whole has actually grown. Between November 1987 and January 1989, televangelism's share of TV viewers watching during the times the programs aired grew by three percent.[24] The initial reaction to the revelation of the Bakker scandal, however, was a sharp drop off in viewers of all forms of religious television, including moderate and mainline programming. Television ministers like Robert Schuller, the moderate and extremely popular Reformed Church television minister, also suffered a decline in audience.

The television ministries involved in the scandal lost the most viewers. The Bakkers, as mentioned, were forced to leave the "PTL Club," which continued to air without them. Swaggart fell from his position as the most watched television minister, which he held in November 1987.[25] In November 1988, following the news of the Swaggart scandal, he drew 1.23 million viewers, down from the 3 million viewers he drew in February 1987 just ahead of the breaking of the Bakker scandal. At the same time, Robertson drew .29 million viewers, down from .62 million. Falwell drew .54 million, down from .86 million. Oral Roberts, who introduced the scandals that plagued televangelism in the late 1980s through controversial fundraising methods, saw his audience fall from 1.6 to .9 million viewers.[26] The decline in viewers is attributable in part to the decision by some television stations to pull controversial personalities or those involved in controversial politics off the air.[27] As the audience for televangelism declined, donations also fell off sharply.[28]

## Continued, If Slight, Growth Following Scandal and Political Defeat

By January 1989, almost two years after news of the Bakker scandal broke, television religion showed signs of recovering audiences and contributions. Many stations had returned controversial personalities to the air. The number of organizations producing religious television had increased. And contributions were holding steady.[29, 30] Viewers' confidence was being restored. And new requirements for greater financial and ethical accountability to viewers of member television ministries had been put in place by the National Religious Broadcasters, the umbrella association for religious broadcasting. New guidelines included audits and divestment of controlling interest by family members of the television ministries. Much of the growth shifted from the large television ministries to smaller, less well known but emerging superministries. James Kennedy, Charles Stanley, both fundamentalists, Paul and Jan Crouch, Fred Price, Kenneth Copeland, and Robert Tilton, all

Pentecostals, built up large followings. Tilton and Crouch have since been embroiled in controversy over fundraising, expenditures, and other practices and have been under investigation.

Television religion is "here to stay."[31] "Although viewers now have a healthy skepticism regarding specific major TV ministries, they have not given up on the medium or the message. The future is far from bleak for television religion."[32] Clearly the televangelists' actions, in or out of the pulpit, do not alone create a following for television religion. The third generation of televangelists, including sons of prominent television ministers—like Richard Roberts—is already making a name for itself.

### Manipulation and Magic: An Incomplete Picture

The negative image of televangelists as opportunists who promote their own political ambitions or business and economic interests has created the general impression that televangelism is a supply-side phenomenon, religion sold over the airwaves to feed the ministers' interests. The impression is supported by reports on the controversial tactics used to maintain an audience and its financial support. Televangelism is enormously expensive, because of the high cost of the technology and the air time. The various television ministries could not stay afloat or expand without devoting a great deal of air time to soliciting contributions from individual viewers, who supply most of the funds.[33]

The controversy that has recently plagued televangelism has come in waves, the first coming in early 1987. Oral Roberts told viewers that God would "call me home" if he did not raise funds to keep his ministry solvent. Roberts held viewers hostage while he claimed that God was holding him hostage.

All of the television ministers making headlines in the 1980s have been investigated by the federal government for misappropriation of funds. Investigations into fundraising by various television ministries have shown that some have appealed for funds to keep programs on the air by claiming that the programs have been in danger of being pulled off the air when there has been no shortage of funds to pay bills. Some ministers have solicited funds for one phase of the ministry that have been spent on other divisions or interests, including expansion. Some have spent funds raised for personal use. Television ministers routinely solicit funds through letters that appear to be personal, but are electronically generated by staff who make use of data bases of computer information about viewers' prayer requests, personal concerns, and patterns of giving. Many of the television ministers have encouraged contributions by creating the impression of a ground swell of support through inflating the numbers of viewers.[34]

There is truth in the supply-side view. After all, there would be no televangelism or expansion without the force of will exercised by the televangelists to mount the television programs and raise the funds needed to keep them on the air.[35]

Televangelism's negative image has led some to doubt that it offers anything positive to viewers. The negative image has left the impression that televangelism must win viewers by presenting false images, or false promises. It is often assumed that viewers only tune in and give their financial support because the televangelists manipulate their audiences, holding them hostage to promises of pie in the sky by and by or promises of heaven on earth. Viewers are often reminded of the promise made in Christian scripture that a gift to God, especially a "sacrificial gift," will be rewarded many times over. It is assumed that televangelists merely prey upon viewers by selling a quick-fix religion of magic and wish fulfillment.

Such promises are said to blind viewers to the televangelists' political ambitions, business interests, and ego interests. Viewers have not examined as carefully as they might the controversial, questionable, and even illegal fundraising and operational practices of the television ministers and ministries. The problem with the assumption that televangelism wins its audience only by manipulation is that it reduces viewers to grist for the televangelists' mill. The assumption renders them passive consumers of a prepackaged and phony religion. On the contrary, viewers do not accept everything the televangelists say. They bring their own perceptions and understandings of conservative Christianity to their viewing, as well as their own predispositions, filtering what they hear through their own personal faith. They also make their own, independent judgments about what is presented, evaluating the message in light of their own faith or opinions.[36]

## Viewers' Religious Commitment

At the outset it should be noted that viewers are not converted to the television ministers' brand of religion. They are already committed to it. The outstanding characteristic of televangelism's followers is their commitment to their conservative religion.[37] Viewers are "already predisposed or self-selected" to seek out the message of televangelism,[38] which reflects viewers' conservative Christian beliefs.[39] Televangelism's viewers are deeply loyal. Their loyalty stems from their deep commitment to their religion.[40] Regular viewers are "extremely devout: they just cannot get enough religion...."[41]

Television allows viewers to bring religion into their homes, and to do so on a daily basis. Viewers introduce the telecasts as a topic of conversation with family, friends, and at church. In addition, viewers support and participate in the television ministries' outreach and counseling programs. Watching the programs is "so heavily integrated into the religious lives of its viewers that it should be seen as an expression of conventional belief and behavior...."[42]

Televangelism's viewers turn to commercial or public, secular television far less. It is not religious enough for them. Commercial and public television reflect outlooks and values that conflict with the religious beliefs and values of televangelism's viewers. They turn to televangelism as an alternative to secular television. Televangelism's viewers are drawn by content they do not find elsewhere.[43] "Christians have been complaining about the fare on [commercial and public] television," observes the handbook on how to start up a religious program or station published by the association of National Religious Broadcasters.[44] Televangelism addresses a demand for religious fare.[45]

The commitment of televangelism's viewers to their conservative religion and to the religion of televangelism is underscored by a key difference between them and those who watch nonreligious television programming. Heavy viewers of nonreligious television are less religiously oriented than viewers of religious television.[46] Nor do most viewers of other forms of television hold conservative or even moderately conservative religious beliefs.[47] Heavy viewers of nonreligious television who are college educated are less likely to hold conservative religious beliefs than light viewers who are college educated. Only 24% of viewers of nonreligious television identify themselves as "born-again" Christians, i.e. fundamentalists, Pentecostals, and other evangelical Christians. Seventy-one percent of those who watch nonreligious television switch channels when they run across a religious telecast. They express dislike for or disinterest in the programs and rarely watch them.[48] In addition, viewers of nonreligious television have little loyalty to the programs they watch.[49]

Televangelism's viewers have less education,[50] earn less,[51] and are older than viewers of nonreligious television.[52] Light viewers of religious television are better educated, earn more, and are younger than heavy viewers. They also give less importance to religion.[53] The socio-economic profile of today's audience has changed little from that of the earliest audience for televangelism.[54]

The high religious commitment of televangelism's viewers is not surprising. Seventy-seven percent identify themselves as churchgoers, as compared to 66% of viewers of nonreligious television. Viewers of televangelism are members of local church congregations, to which they give financial support. Heavy viewers of nonreligious television are less likely to participate in a local church or to contribute. Forty-eight percent of televangelism's viewers attend church weekly, as opposed to only 33% of viewers of nonreligious television. The latter are also less likely to read the Bible; only 28% do. Televangelism's viewers consider watching religious television a complement to churchgoing. Televangelism is not a substitute for church. On the contrary, it extends viewers' religious commitment. Viewers report that the only thing they find in attending their local churches that they do not find in watching religious television is closeness to members.[55]

The overwhelming majority of viewers of televangelism are members of independent fundamentalist and Pentecostal churches or denominations.[56] And viewers are by and large the most conservative members of these denominations.[57] Ninety-eight percent of televangelism's viewers are Protestant. Of this group, seventy-two percent are members of independent fundamentalist and Pentecostal churches or denominations. Viewers of nonreligious television are members of mainline Protestant denominations or Roman Catholic primarily.[58] More of televangelism's heavy viewers belong to Baptist churches than to any other group: 40%. Nineteen percent of this group are Southern Baptists. Ten-and-a-half percent of viewers are charismatic Christians, including Pentecostals. Ten percent are Roman Catholic. Eight-and-one-third percent are United Methodists. Other Methodists make up 7.1% of viewers. Fewer than 2% of viewers are Presbyterian. Fewer than 2% of viewers come from each of the following denominations: Lutherans, Disciples of Christ, the United Church of Christ, and the Episcopal Church. The remainder come from other groups.[59,60]

Fifty-eight percent of televangelism's viewers believe the Bible is literally true. They believe in miracles and believe they occur today. Viewers pray frequently. And they believe the earth is in its final days and that Christ will return soon to judge the wicked and deliver the saved. These are hallmarks of fundamentalist and Pentecostal belief. Viewers are also conservative on social and political issues. They identify themselves as political conservatives.[61] Viewers of nonreligious television are less conservative on social and political issues than televangelism's viewers. Those who watch nonreligious television identify themselves as political moderates.[62]

The commitment of viewers to their religion is illustrated by the fact that after the Bakker scandal broke, the following for the "PTL Club" did not decline among "ritualized viewers," highly religious individuals who watch out of religious conviction and a predisposition to watch religious, particularly conservative programming.[63] Other viewing patterns underscore viewers' commitment. Seventy-five percent of televangelism's viewers watch more than one television minister.[64] And they often cross over fundamentalist and Pentecostal lines, watching ministers from both camps of conservative Christianity.[65]

### Televangelism As a Human Drama

Manipulation and magic are as much a part of the technology of televangelism as they are of the religion of televangelism. But these do not define televangelism, or conservative Christianity for that matter. To equate televangelism with coercion that plays upon magical interests reduces its viewers to caricatures. They are far more complex, as are their religion and their attraction to televangelism. The stereotypic view overlooks televangelism's human face. Viewers' interest in televangelism is not only a religious one. They also bring with them to their viewing needs and interests they do not completely recognize. As creatures of flesh and blood, they also have very real social and human needs and interests. Viewers bring to televangelism needs and interests that grow out of the larger social drama in which they and televangelism are engaged, looking to it to help them redress a larger social conflict in which they are caught up. Televangelism brings together the religious and social interests held by viewers.

As religious conservatives, viewers stand in conflict with mainstream American society, which is highly secularized, committed to religious tolerance and to a democratic ideal, and highly pluralistic in make-up. Viewers' commitment to a religion that claims to be the only truth, rejects all other positions, and makes war against the secular world leads mainstream society to keep them along its edges rather than include them fully.

Televangelism's holy war against secular society is obvious to the casual observer. Televangelism has declared war on the moral front in defense of biblical morality and the millenarian vision it serves. Public morality is viewed as a battleground on which God and his people are battling to defeat Satan. The moral regeneration of secular society, bringing public morality in line with God's moral laws, is considered decisive to winning the world back to God. Televangelism identifies the cherished religious beliefs and moral values that are at stake in the religious conservatives' battle with the enemy, as well as the consequences of victory—sharing in God's rule over a redeemed world. Televangelism rallies the troops, sounds a call to action, and serves as a staging ground for launching an attack on the secular world. Conservative Christians believe they are being persecuted by the secular world for their commitment to their religious beliefs and their crusade for morality. They believe secular society is in alliance with Satan to defeat God by defeating God's people.

Conservative Christians' battle against secular society is twofold, however. It is both a religious war in defense of conservative religious belief and morality and a battle for greater recognition and inclusion within mainstream society by a marginalized social group. Televangelism is a religious response by conservative Christians to a society whose secularity increasingly squeezes out their conservative religious view of the world and its moral guidelines. Under threat and under fire by the social mainstream, these conservative Christians turn to televangelism to reassure themselves that the religion and morality they live by are authentic. Televangelism offers viewers legitimation in their own eyes of their religious beliefs and morality.

Televangelism is also a social response by a marginalized social group. Reconfirmation of their religion and of their religious group allows conservative Christians to see themselves as a significant social group and not a marginal one. The claim that God is on their side serves to enhance in their own eyes their social standing in relation to the secular world. Self-legitimation mobilizes them to push for their interests as a significant social group while they push for their religious interests. Self-legitimation helps them push for a greater presence and place as a social group within the public arena, particularly the political sphere.

The battle for inclusion also leads viewers to turn to televangelism because it helps them adapt or accommodate themselves to the outlook and lifestyle of the secularized social mainstream. Televangelism helps them learn more about social and political issues within the wider secular society. It also provides them an opportunity to experiment with the secular lifestyle and outlook of mainstream society as they take in the dress, language, and attitudes of hosts and guests who have adopted some of the sensibilities of secular society. Becoming more like those out there in the secular world makes viewers less suspect, in addition to helping them become more comfortable within that world. Incentive for adapting grows out of the recognition that the social mainstream promises greater inclusion to those who become more mainstream, more secularized.

Conservative Christians have been roundly criticized as hypocritical by the social mainstream for embracing a secular lifestyle, especially the embrace of creature comfort and material wealth, as exemplified by the Bakkers. This is in part an adaptive strategy, however, undertaken to win the acceptance of mainstream society.

Understanding televangelism's role in the human drama in which its conservative Christian viewers are players humanizes it, its viewers, and their engagement in it. Televangelism offers viewers an opportunity to do something about their marginalized standing within the wider society. Viewers report feeling pained about their lack of status in American society. They report feeling awkward, embarrassed, and ill at ease about their lack of social standing.[66] Robertson's viewers report that, as a model of the urbane, contemporary Christian, he has helped them gain a new self-esteem. They see Robertson as having moved conservative Christians out of the American backwaters as he moved them into the mainstream political arena.[67]

Living in the sacred and the secular worlds simultaneously adds to viewers' pain. They do not feel comfortable or confident in a highly secularized and pluralistic society that presents views of the world and lifestyles that conflict with those of their conservative religion. The gap between their traditional views and values and those of a society they perceive to be "out of control" produces "cultural dissonance."[68] Viewers also experience the wider society as "hostile" to them, intellectually, socially, and spiritually.[69] They are pained by society's vote of no confidence in their religion and by its rebuff of them as a conservative religious group. They are also made to feel anxious by an "age of uncertainty" and "dissolution."[70] Viewers turn to their religion for answers that help remove the complexities and ambiguities of the larger world and the anxiety these produce, by providing certainty.

Accommodation to the secular world comes at a great price, however. It adds to their pain. Accommodation brings inner conflict as it requires making concessions to the secular world at the expense of viewers' religious identity, which forms a large part of their self-identity.

The ambivalence of conservative Christians toward secular society leads them into self-contradiction. They are torn by the need to authenticate their religion and their religious identity and to participate more fully in mainstream, secular society and be accepted by it. They are torn between choosing a conservative religion that has traditionally given them a sense of higher purpose and place in the face of threat and rebuff by a hostile world, and choosing the secular world, which promises them a more significant place within the society of women and men. Straddling two worlds, conservative Christians face the difficult task of learning how to maintain the integrity of their religious commitment and at the same time of facing up to the demands and challenges of a world undergoing change, a world that is becoming ever more pluralistic, ambiguous, and complex.

Threatened and challenged by mainstream society, conservative Christians turn to the telecasts for a sense of community. The awareness that they hold "a minority worldview"[71] contributes to the sense of community viewers gain by watching the programs. Viewers also turn to the telecasts and to the community it creates for support in their dealings with secular society. Their community provides the support needed to battle against secular society, and the support needed to experiment with secularity.

Conservative Christians' interest in greater inclusion within mainstream society, and their effort to create inclusiveness among themselves, are expressions of a basic need for human community. The interest in community is an interest in a bond that runs deeper than group identification, or membership in a particular group, and deeper than like-mindedness in ideology or belief. It is an interest in a bond that is free of labels, the recognition of common humanity and human equality. With these come the affirmation of human value and worth, and support for the freedom to determine one's own life in concert with other humans. Viewers bring to televangelism their interest in community with mainstream society in an indirect way. Their interest in self-legitimation expresses an interest in forging community. Their interest in adapting to the social mainstream is an interest in winning community with it.

# ⊰ 3 ⊱

## Viewers' Marginalized Religion and Social Standing within American Society

### *The Claim to Power*

A few short years ago, many feared that the Religious Right threatened the balance of power within American public life. The fear was that as conservative Christians aggressively entered the political arena as a new lobbying and voting block, they would refashion American society in the mold of their narrowly conservative religion and morality through the ballot box and the legislative process. Conservative Christians had announced their intent to stop the spread of liberal, "laissez-faire" values and policies in place in American society and government.[72] They announced their programmatic strategy of electing candidates to office who would vote for legislation that would promote their conservative social and moral agenda, targeting for defeat those candidates who did not support their views or agenda. Conservative Christians, some feared, had the potential "to take over the country."[73]

Televangelism played a major role in the revitalization of the Religious Right beginning in the late 1970s.[74] The militant message communicated brought conservative Christians "out of the closet," as televangelist James Robison put it, and into the public square in large numbers, mobilizing them on the political frontlines. Televangelism's programmers and promoters had learned the effectiveness of television in communicating a movement's message and mobilizing a response during the Civil Rights era and the era of the Vietnam War, when television news gave exposure to civil rights and antiwar activists.[75] Televangelism's programmers mounted their own media campaign believing the liberal bias of the news reports of commercial television would not communicate their message faithfully.

Falwell's program has dwelt on social and political issues, as has Robertson's. Both have informed viewers on social and political issues and events in American politics, commenting on newsbreaking developments. And both have suggested political strategy. While Swaggart has given time to discussion of social issues, he has given virtually no time to discussion of political strategy. The Bakkers have talked about social issues far less and only in general terms. The difference in emphasis given the world of politics by the Bakkers and Swaggart reflects Pentecostalism's historical emphasis on personal piety and morality over social and political issues.[76]

Televangelism was one among several media used in the mobilization of conservative Christians. Publishing was another. Scores of books, newsletters, and mass mailings on social and political issues were printed and distributed to religious conservatives. Television ministries distributed many of these to their viewers.[77]

Early claims of the size of the audience for televangelism were greatly exaggerated. The television ministries claimed to have an audience of 25 to 50 million viewers, 10% to 20% of the American population of 250 million. They also claimed the numbers indicated a ground swell of support for the Religious Right.[78] The news media tended to take the claims at face value in their reports on televangelism and the Religious Right. Claims of massive support were intended to win a following among conservative Christians as well as their support for the Religious Right. The rhetoric and images of power and success that have been a prominent feature of the telecasts—including talk of having the ear of President Reagan and other political leaders and people of influence— were designed to do the same.

The images of power given the Religious Right as communicated by televangelism are idealized images. They mask the relatively weak power and influence of conservative Christians at the level of national politics. The images compensate for real power. Conservative Christians have used "the reality-establishing force of mass communications to convince themselves—and many others, apparently—that they are a real presence in American public life. They have transmitted their images into the 'show windows of modern publicity.'"[79] Religious conservatives along with many others see the resurgence of conservative Christianity as well as the growth of televangelism as a sign of the continued vitality and prominence of conservative Christianity within American society. The resurgence of conservative religion can be attributed more perhaps to the need to defend it. Conservative Christianity faces tremendous challenges and opposition from mainstream American society, as we will see.

Televangelism has not won huge numbers of new converts as viewers. While it did undergo a boom during the 1980s,[80] it did not win new audiences outside of the ranks of conservative Christians.[81] And the market for televangelism has reached the saturation point.[82]

The audience for religious television in general is very limited. The number of viewers who regularly or weekly watch some form of religious television, including conservative programming, has been put at 13.3 million, making up only 6.2% of all television viewers,[83] and only 5% of the American population. The audience for televangelism is even smaller. Not all viewers of religious television identify themselves as "born-again" Christians,[84] the hallmark of evangelical Christianity, including fundamentalist and Pentecostal Christianity, and the hallmark of televangelism's viewers.

Conservative Christians are in the minority among the American population, making up only about 16% of the total population. Moderate Protestants make up just over 24%. Liberal Protestants make up almost 9%. Black Protestants make up 9%.[85] The conservative Christian churches have grown, while the mainline denominations have suffered a decline in membership.[86] But the rate of growth for conservative churches has fallen off steadily since 1960.[87] In the late 1950s, conservative Christians made up one-third of the members of the twelve largest Protestant denominations, two-thirds of which were mainline. Two-thirds of all Protestants at the time were affiliated with the moderate and liberal Federal Council of Churches, now the National Council of Churches. In 1987, about the same number, 33.6% of American Christians, belonged to conservative denominations unaffiliated with the NCC.[88] The number of conservative Christians engaged in televangelism is even fewer.

## The Limited Power of the Religious Right

Conservative Christians became highly visible within American politics beginning in the late 1970s, when they began pushing for the legislation of their political agenda. Although the Religious Right was sizable enough to be taken seriously, it failed to implement its political and social agenda at the federal level. None of its central planks was ever legislated as public policy at the time. The Religious Right even failed to win the full support of the Political Right or that of President Reagan, whom it had supported in its effort to promote a "Christian America."

> Even with eight years of the most sympathetic president the NCR [New Christian Right, or Religious Right] is liable to see, there have been few changes which the politically involved conservative Protestants could claim as victories. Not one piece of legislation promoted by the NCR was placed on the federal statute books. There were a number of successes at the level of state legislatures and more at the level of school board but significant decisions on fundamental constitutional issues get referred upwards by the centripetal legal system and come in the end to be judged by the higher courts and the Supreme Court. The NCR has tried to pass laws requiring that any time given to evolution in school biology classes or texts must be matched by equal time for 'creation science'; it has failed. The NCR has tried to have 'secular humanism' defined as a religion so that it can be expelled from classrooms and textbooks; it has failed. The NCR has tried to overturn the ruling that public prayer in schools is unconstitutional because it amounts to the state promoting a religion; it has failed.[89]

The Reagan administration gave no significant support to the Religious Right, contributing to its failure to enact its national agenda. The Religious Right was never included in any significant decision making by the Reagan administration. Nor was it given any real support by the Bush administration or included in it in any significant way. The Reagan administration paid only lip service to the Religious Right and its agenda.[90]

Clearly conservative Christianity and the Religious Right were co-opted by the Political Right during its rise to power during the late 1970s and early 1980s to win over religious conservatives in support of its own conservative social agenda and struggle for political power. It was then gearing up to help put Reagan in the White House in the 1980 Presidential election. The Religious Right was never included in the base of power of the Political Right. The visibility enjoyed by the Religious Right was in large measure a visibility made possible by the Political Right, which promoted conservative Christianity for its own political purposes.

While the Political Right did penetrate the power base of the Republican Party, it did not win complete control of the Party, one of the centers of power in mainstream American society. This was reflected in the ongoing struggle for power between the two factions of the Religious Right and the Party Regulars during the Reagan administration.

Robertson's defeat in his 1988 bid to win the Republican Party's nomination for the Presidency is evidence of the failure of the Religious Right to penetrate these bases of power. Robertson supporters had fought their way into state party caucuses and had elected delegates for Robertson to the convention. The battle between Robertson supporters and party regulars in caucuses in Michigan was particularly bitter, drawing national attention.

Falwell and Robertson, two of the principal architects of the Religious Right, have routinely appeared standing alongside Reagan and other prominent leaders of the Political Right. And they have appeared alongside Bush and other leaders of the Republican Party. They have appeared on the platform during the last several National Conventions of the Republican Party. The Religious Right has also been visible as a participant on the committee drawing up the Party's platform to be presented at its national convention. The Religious Right was instrumental in promoting the anti-abortion plank as well as the plank supporting the use of public funds to support parochial schools adopted by the 1992 Republican Convention.

The visibility of the Religious Right within the Republican Party has been largely window dressing. It has been made highly visible by the Party in order to win the votes of religious conservatives. Bush's embrace of the Religious Right during his Presidential campaign, consummated at the 1992 Republican National Convention, produced different results from the embrace given it by Reagan. The embrace, which came as a last minute strategy for votes once Clinton and Perot showed themselves as strong Presidential contenders, may have cost Bush a second term. Already tired of Reaganomics and of Bush's failure on the domestic front, the American electorate was also tired of the Religious Right. Even Republican Party regulars deserted Bush once he began supporting some of the agenda of the Religious Right, particularly its anti-abortion stance. In some respects, the defeat of Bush's bid for a second term in office was a repudiation by the American electorate of the Religious Right he had begun to court.

The Religious Right continues to fight to move into a more prominent place within the Republican Party. Members of the Religious Right have recently pulled a coup within the Harris County (Houston) GOP, Bush's home caucus. Seizing control of the organization's executive committee after winning the precinct chairmanships that put them on the committee, they rewrote bylaws and stripped power from the Chairwoman who had been elected by the county's Republican voters. She had earlier moved out of Party offices after being pressured by the religious conservatives to exclude abortion rights advocates and homosexuals from the organization. The takeover is being fought by the Harris County GOP mainstream.[91]

The Religious Right has been more successful at the grassroots level. After a push for power at the local and state levels, in 1992 it won hundreds of races for school board seats, as well as seats in city councils and state legislatures, spearheaded by Robertson's Christian Coalition and other groups identified with the Religious Right. A large number of races was won, however, by candidates who had not revealed to voters their identification with the Religious Right, using a method widely practiced by the movement—"stealth candidacies." The tactic did not work for most of those candidates whose affiliation had been exposed during the elections in San Diego County, where most were defeated.[92]

The Religious Right recently helped to overturn a gay-rights city ordinance in Florida—the vote to remove the ordinance in Portland, Oregon, was narrowly defeated—as well as a state ordinance in support of gay rights in Colorado. It also helped defeat an Equal Rights Amendment in Iowa. The defeat of gay-rights legislation followed scare campaigns waged by the Religious Right. Distorting issues is another tactic commonly used by the Religious Right.

In spite of these successes, the Religious Right has not convinced the American public to implement its conservative morality as policy. Nor has it convinced the general electorate whose views on morality are conservative or those who are sympathetic with conservative Christian morality to implement conservative morality as policy. Public opinion polls show that while many among the American public hold views on morality that are similar to those held by the Religious Right, these same people disagree with the policy position of the Religious Right. Many, for example, view homosexuality as wrong. But they do not support policies that make homosexuality illegal. They are less conservative on policy issues.[93] The American public did not shift toward a "blanket conservatism" during the Reagan years. What did shift were attitudes about economic matters. Americans bought Reagan's conservative economics, but remained moderate on social services and libertarian on personal freedoms.[94]

The response to Falwell's political lobby, the "Moral Majority," is revealing. It raised more opposition than it won supporters.[95] The eventual collapse of the Moral Majority—for lack of support outside the ranks of the Religious Right—is further evidence of the Religious Right's failure to penetrate the bases of political power, including that of the Political Right.

Nor did the Religious Right win over all conservative Christians. Not all of them voted for or would have voted for Ronald Reagan in 1984 or for Pat Robertson in 1988. Many conservative Christians are more interested in economic issues. And some like the country just as it is, including the wall of separation between church and state. The conservative Christian vote was splintered by diversity of political opinion among religious conservatives. Even if every conservative Christian had voted for candidates and agenda of the Religious Right, it would not have had enough votes to win.[96]

There is also diversity of political opinion among the conservative Christians who watch televangelism. Not all of them identify with the Religious Right. Those who do, make up a "sub-section" of televangelism's viewers.[97] Robertson, Falwell, and others devote air time to politics. But not all of their viewers are in agreement with their politics or political strategies. Many of Robertson's viewers, for example, have difficulty reconciling political activism with their conservative Christianity, given the apolitical leanings of its recent past. They continue to view political involvement as worldly and as a diversion from the mission of the church, namely preaching the gospel.[98]

There is a different degree of political activism among the two camps of conservative Christianity. Pentecostals are political activists to a far lesser degree than fundamentalists. For Pentecostals, the main battlefield for reshaping the public sphere is the moral regeneration of the individual. Pentecostalism places greater emphasis on the private and inner, the individual heart and soul. Pentecostals nevertheless make their influence felt at the ballot box. Activism is growing among Pentecostals, aided by the efforts of Robertson's Christian Coalition among other groups. Until recently, Pentecostals have not had the organization or machinery, including televangelism, to engage in activist politics in an effective way.

Fundamentalists have taken the lead among conservative Christians in reshaping public and civic life through the election and legislative process. They have organized major political lobbies and voting blocks, for example, Falwell's Moral Majority.[99] The activism of fundamentalists reverses the condemnation of politics by fundamentalists living earlier in

this century. The latter considered politics worldly activity. Falwell himself once held this view.[100]

Diversity and even mistrust and hostility among conservative
Christians also makes forging a political alliance among themselves
difficult. Fundamentalists and Pentecostals are engaged in a running
battle over doctrinal issues.[101]

### Mainstream Society As Player in the Televangelism Drama

The number of conservative Christians committed to the Religious
Right was too small to effect the sweeping changes it had hoped for
within the political arena and American society.[102] The defeat of the
Religious Right can be attributed in large measure, however, to
American society's commitment to its democratic ideals, as well as to the
pluralistic make-up of American society.[103] Steve Bruce has argued that

> ...The price conservative Protestants will have to pay to achieve political
> leverage in a pluralistic democracy is the abandonment of almost all of the
> distinctive platform that initially motivated them to get involved in politics.
> Any movement which remains seriously 'conservative Christian' will fail;
> any movement which succeeds will have abandoned its distinctively
> conservative Christian issues.[104]

Mainstream American society is itself deeply religious.[105] Eighty-six-
and-a-half percent of Americans identify themselves with the Christian
religion. Of these, the overwhelming majority are Protestant: 60%. Forty
percent are Roman Catholic. Americans who identify with Judaism
number under two percent. Muslim Americans make up one-half of one
percent of the population (.5%). Only 7.5% of Americans do not identify
with any religion.[106]

Religion has long played a role in shaping American society.
American society is still influenced by religious values that were part
and parcel of its early history.[107] Americans continue to look to religion
to help shape public and civic values and civic and public life. But mainstream society does not permit any single religion to be the sole custodian or arbiter of civic values or civic life. Public and civic life include
religion but are not defined or dominated by it. Groups like the
conservative Christians are encouraged. But they are not permitted to
impose their religion and morality as the law of the land. American
society upholds freedom of religion. It also upholds freedom from
religion. While religion is included within the public or civic arena, it is
allowed expression in only the most generalized form, including the

dominant, Protestant tradition.[108] Laws separating church and state—the disestablishment laws—prevent the hegemony of any single religion. American society and the Christian and Jewish religions are intermeshed. They are not coextensive, however.

Its commitment to democracy and religious freedom has made mainstream society a major player in the drama of conservative Christians' defense of their religion and morality. Mainstream society holds little tolerance for exclusivist and judgmental religion and morality, viewing the narrow religion of conservative Christians as incompatible with its democratic ideal, and the effort of the religious conservatives to impose their beliefs and morality upon the public sphere as hostile. Conservative Christians promote and defend a democratic American society. They believe that American society has gone too far, however. They are militant in their opposition to mainstream society, which they perceive as preventing the free expression of religion or as throwing out religion entirely in its radical separation of church and state. Conservative Christians believe American society is committed to secularism, the rejection of a role for religion in shaping public values and civic life. They confuse secularism with secularity, which does not necessarily stand opposed to religion. Conservative Christians fail to see that the separation of church and state is designed to protect the freedom of religion.

The opposition of mainstream society to conservative Christians and especially to the Religious Right is a response to the militancy with which conservative Christians seek to impose their religious morality through legislation and the ballot box. Mainstream society has opposed the religious conservatives in defense of its democratic way of life as well as freedom of religion. The religious conservatives have attempted to make their religious morality normative for everyone else, depriving others of the freedom to decide for themselves and in concert with the body public what course of moral action to take. That American society is suffering a crisis in morality as conservative Christians charge is not in question. At issue for the wider society is what values to promote and who should promote them.

What conservative Christians call acts of "persecution" by society—court decisions barring Bible-study groups from public schools, police arrests of "pro-life" demonstrators, etc.—are actions undertaken to insure the separation of church and state. Courts have closed Christian schools that have defied state accreditation requirements and have ruled against teaching "Creationist science" in public school biology classes.

State legislatures have rejected the teaching of "Creation science" in public school textbooks. And police have arrested Christian pro-life activists blocking abortion clinic doors. Conservative Christians and the Religious Right have been heavily scrutinized and criticized by the news media. And civil liberties and watchdog groups—People for the American Way, for example—have lobbied aggressively against the Religious Right. While mainstream society's opposition is not conspiratorial, as the conservative Christians claim, it is nevertheless real. At times, the opposition has been hard hitting. The sentence delivered Jim Bakker has been recognized as excessive by the federal agency that monitors and enforces guidelines for judicial sentences.

The militancy of conservative Christians is fueled by the belief that their effort to bring about the moral regeneration of American society is part of God's plan to defeat Satan, who wins people away from God through encouraging immorality. Conservative Christians believe they are living during the final days of Satan's ongoing battle to defeat God, as indicated by the "persecution" of Christians by the secular world prophesied in the Bible as a sign of the end times. They believe their persecution is masterminded by Satan, who has won over the world as an ally. The effort to establish conservative Christian morality and thereby win over the secular world is viewed as critical to the defeat of Satan.

Mainstream society's opposition is not only a response to the militancy with which conservative Christians have sought to legislate their religious morality. Its opposition is also fed by its interest in protecting its role as chief custodian of religious piety and morality within American public life, and along with this, its interest in the benefits due the guardian of American piety and morality. Mainstream society is committed to a secularized version of Protestant values, viewing democracy and freedom as critical to America's role as divine agent in the world. Conservative Christians engaged in the Religious Right and mainstream society are engaged in a family quarrel. They are diverse members of a religious family making rival claims to custodianship over public piety and morality. Needless to say, the quarrel also involves a dispute over which beliefs and values are to be promoted.

Both groups claim custodianship of America's most sacred, or transcendent public and civic value: freedom. Each group puts its own spin or twist on the mythology of America's beginnings as a free nation and its role as divinely appointed agent of freedom in the world. Conservative Christians equate a free America with "a Christian America," a recurring theme of televangelism. In order for America to remain free, they argue, it must remain a "Christian nation." They believe God made America a free nation in order to promote Christian beliefs and values. Conservative Christians argue that the nation's "founding Fathers" were Christians who established the new nation on biblical and Christian beliefs and values and who were led by divine guidance. The argument freely engages in revisionist history. Religious conservatives see themselves as following in the footsteps of the nation's "Christian fathers." They promote themselves as rightful inheritors of the founders' mantle and of their position of leadership as they remind the nation of its "Christian heritage" and call it back to its Christian roots. By claiming the lineage of the nation's so-called "Christian fathers," conservative Christians also promote themselves as representative of the American mainstream.

Religious conservatives view the promotion of secular beliefs and values by mainstream American society as a threat to freedom. They believe that God will take away America's freedom as punishment for the failure to keep the nation Christian. If America is to remain free, they believe, it must be restored to its original, divinely ordained path of Christian belief and morality. Conservative Christians also view a free America as critical to promoting freedom around the globe, which, they believe, provides the opportunity to choose God and his purposes for the world. This is another recurring theme of the television programs.

The mythology to which mainstream society subscribes—manifest destiny—holds a similar, although less extreme view. The mainstream speaks of freedom as a divine capacity and divine right more than it expresses an interest in freedom as an instrument of promoting the godly life, or Christianity, the interest of those in the mainstream who are less ecumenically minded. The recent challenge to or erosion of American dominance around the globe has led to the reinvigoration of the myth of America as divine agent in the world by mainstream society, as illustrated by the invocation of God and the claim to represent God during the recent Persian Gulf War.

Each group also has its own version of the benefit due it of sharing in God's rule over the world as chief guardian of human freedom. Conservative Christians view the benefits in millenarian terms. Mainstream society is more interested in the geo-political, military, and economic benefits due it in this present world as guarantor of freedom. The view of America as divine agent played out during the Gulf War served as a rationale for the promotion of American interests. The rival claims to custodianship of American piety and morality and to the benefits due the guarantor of freedom are mixed into the opposition between the conservative Christians and mainstream society over religious and public values.

## A Marginalized Subculture

The militancy with which conservative Christians defend their religion and their religious group is not entirely born out of religious commitment. The aggressive defense of their religion is also born out of their interest in standing up for themselves as a "marginalized"[109] social group. Conservative Christians make up a "dispossessed segment of American society."[110] They are "outsiders."[111] Their status stems from their commitment to a "minority worldview."[112] Conservative Christians live along the ideological borders of American society.[113] They are a religious "sub-culture."[114] Their commitment to their religion wins rebuff and outright opposition by mainstream society.

Televangelism measures and expresses the conservative Christians' feelings of disenfranchisement.[115] It has provided a platform from which to serve notice of their demands of the larger society. It has offered a venue within which to mirror and shape the social and political agendas of conservative Christianity.[116]

Televangelism has given its religious constituency, with its long history of disfranchisement, social visibility and a voice, things it had not enjoyed previously.[117] It has given "a minority with a distinctive culture" a voice "to express its beliefs and values and to strive for increasing acceptance and respectability."[118] Televangelism has played a major role in "serving notice to the nation that evangelical Christians are no longer content to be treated as a peculiar and obscurantist minority, but are a force with which to reckon, socially, politically, and theologically."[119] It has mobilized a new "counterculture" and restored traditionally conservative religion as a social movement, giving it powers it had not previously enjoyed.[120]

In the process of increasing contact among a group, members of which had previously been isolated from one another, and helping to build a mass movement,[121] televangelism has raised morale among those who have had a "sense of inferiority." In this role it has helped its constituents "feel better about themselves and their place in modern America."[122] "Folk to whom a medium has meant so much will not readily abandon it in time of trouble."[123]

## Struggling Citizens of the Secular World

To be sure, conservative Christians participate in secular American society. They are citizens of the wider society, after all. They vote,[124] appeal to courts of law, and compete in business. They put science and technology to work. They have also adopted a secularized lifestyle and outlook, some with a vengeance. This is especially true of the younger generation, who have more liberal attitudes than their elders toward sex, alcohol, dancing, popular music, and films.[125] They see nothing wrong with material success. Nor do they see anything wrong with creature comforts, leisure and entertainment, or just plain fun, if these are not carried to excess.

Today's conservative Christians have modified the hard-line condemnation of the "secular" world and separatism identified with the revivalist traditions of their nineteenth- and early twentieth-century forebears. They have relaxed the old condemnation of the secular world, signified by their increased participation in it.[126] This is especially true of the younger generation, who have relaxed even further the world-condemning theology and morality of the older generation, taking less of a hard line on social issues such as abortion and prayer in public schools.[127] There is a new acceptance of personal success, self-improvement, self-esteem, and psychological gratification.[128]

These changes in outlook have come with the help of greater economic mobility. Conservative Christians have come up in the world. The socio-economic gap between conservative Christians and the American middle class has shrunk. Today, most of televangelism's fundamentalist and Pentecostal viewers are lower middle class.[129] Economic mobility has helped them move closer to the center of mainstream society as it has helped them afford the lifestyle enjoyed by the middle class. Material success and its rewards are signs that conservative Christians "have arrived." The gospel of "prosperity theology" rationalizes conservative Christians' success and new wealth as signs of God's blessings. Still, those who go too far are criticized. Swaggart and Falwell have been highly critical of the Bakkers' lavish lifestyle, denouncing them for making an unholy alliance with the secular world.

It has been suggested that the restrictive attitudes of an earlier generation were cultivated as a coping strategy. The early conservative Christians did not enjoy the creature comforts afforded those who had made it in industrial American society and condemned the comforts of urban society in order to dull the pain of desire. Pentecostals generally remain less well off than fundamentalists. Pentecostals who remain poor condemn the lifestyle adopted by more successful brothers and sisters.[130]

### The Pull between the Sacred and Secular Worlds

In many respects the lifestyle and outlook of conservative Christians are no different from those of mainstream American society. Religious conservatives are only partly secularized, however.[131] Their commitment to their millenarian religious vision and to the narrow interpretation of biblical morality at its center requires them to keep their distance from the rest of secular society, placing them a world away in an important respect. Conservative Christians live in two worlds simultaneously. They are pulled by the conflicting demands each world places upon them, since the two worlds stand in opposition to or in tension with one another.

Steve Bruce has argued that it is difficult to support the view that televangelism is radically "world-rejecting," since it has "*accommodated* to the modern world almost every bit as much as the liberal Protestantism which [the televangelists]...disdain for its compromises with the secular world."[132] And yet he goes on to point out that the religion of televangelism requires a fundamental separation from the world.

> Although...most conservative Protestants are on rather comfortable terms with the material world, in one sense they are clearly divided from it. ...the conservatives wish, in rhetoric at least, to distance themselves from the surrounding culture. They talk of being 'in the world but not of it.' The logical extension of the liberal Protestant position [which holds that God's word can only be understood in relation to the Christian's position within society and culture] is to reduce the things that separate him from the rest of his culture. Indeed, one often finds liberals arguing that the truly Christian thing to do is to embrace the secular world and secular struggles. /.../ If the evangelical [conservative] Protestant wishes [however] to do something evangelical, he tries to convert people to his values and beliefs....[133]

Distinction from the world is an important part of conservative Christians' self-identity or self-definition. Their religious world view "requires separation, even isolation, from a debased, secularized society"[134] as a form of judgment against it. They are to love the "lost" world, but not to tolerate it or fraternize with it, since its humanistic interests deviate from God's laws and serve Satan's purposes. Fraternizing with the secular world is viewed as weakening commitment to biblical morality and the millenarian future it serves. Loss of commitment would undermine God's effort to redeem the world, as well as reduce one's stake in God's future rule over a redeemed world. Unswerving belief and morality are considered the best defenses against the secular world, since they instruct in the ways of God.

Conservative Christians narrowly define God's friends. Those "out there" in the secular world are labeled deviant or the enemy because they are perceived as having replaced God's interest with human interests and God's "revealed truth" with finite human understanding, which is considered flawed. "Secular humanists" are held up as an extreme case. They are said to leave God and morality out of the picture altogether. (Never mind the ethical and even spiritual interests of humanists!) The term "secular humanists" was coined as a catchall word to refer to liberals. The phrase is now used to refer to any group whose position on morality stands in disagreement with that of conservative Christians. "Secularists" or "liberals" are said to have replaced absolutism in belief and morality with relativism. The attitude that "anything goes" is seen as an open invitation to Satan to step in and confound the ways and purposes of God. Relativism and liberalism, which are said to stand for nothing, cannot stand for God, it is held.

The same charge is made against pluralism, including religious pluralism. Secular society is also said to have gone too far in its tolerance of diversity of values and religion, and even tolerance of lack of religious belief. The state is considered the greatest threat to conservative Christian morality, since it is said to be run by "secular humanists," and since its power or control over public and civic life is said to be growing—through restrictive court rulings and legislation.[135] Falwell's Moral Majority and Robertson's Freedom Council were formed specifically to counter the "humanistic" policies of the state.

Conservative Christians draw the battle lines between themselves and the secular world in clear, "either/or" terms, making their opposition strident. Narrow belief and morality are lines of defense against a society that appears to be growing even more secular and to be in the process of moral and spiritual breakdown.

Conservative Christians also hold mainline Christianity suspect. Its liberal outlook is viewed as compromising or abandoning biblical fundamentals. For conservative Christians, these are considered the only basis on which to judge truth, live the moral life, and hold the line against the secular world. Liberal Christians are viewed as worse than secular "relativists," because they are thought to give false witness to what Christianity stands for. What liberal Christians see as an attempt to make the Bible relevant to a complex and changing, pluralistic world, conservative Christians see as the watering down of biblical truths, which they consider unalterable and relevant for any age. Conservative Christians eschew and outright oppose the ecumenical movement, wanting no dealings with liberal Christians who they believe make a mockery of the Christian religion.

Although the tension between the secular and religious worlds experienced by conservative Christians has eased, it still remains high. Religious conservatives do not move back and forth from secular society to the world of their religion freely. They feel the constant pull of their religion, which is their center of gravity. The comprehensive scope of their religion and its claim on their lives encourages them to see themselves as citizens of heaven first, leading them to act within the wider world in accord with their religious beliefs. Their religion does not allow them to compartmentalize the world or their lives within it. The movement for Christian schools illustrates the point. Christian schools were founded as an alternative to public schools, which are said to indoctrinate students in "secular humanism," since they are run by the secular state. Biblical belief and biblical morality together make up the cornerstone of Christian education.

### Preaching to the Choir

It has been observed that televangelism is short on doctrine and does not dwell on discussion of theology. The religious message presented by televangelism is highly generalized,[136] blurring distinctions between fundamentalist and Pentecostal doctrine.[137] Televangelism's message is presented in the fashion of a morality play.[138] To be sure, televangelism does condemn sin and the sinful or immoral world.[139]

"Sin" is a synecdoche for the whole of the religious message of conservative Christianity, which is shared by fundamentalists and Pentecostals alike. Sin is linked to the cosmic battle between God and Satan, beginning with the sin of Satan: the sin of Adam and Eve and the introduction of sin into the world, the alliance of the sinful world with Satan and its opposition to God, to salvation, God's redemptive death on the cross, the persecution of conservative Christians by the sinful or immoral secular world, the immediate return of Christ to judge the world, the defeat of Satan, the redemption of a sinful world, the final victory of God and of God's people over sin and Satan, and the establishment of God's perpetual rule. Even when televangelism does not communicate all of the elements of the message of conservative Christianity in its rhetoric, the message is still conveyed in its entirety through images and symbols, such as the Bible or the cross. The whole of the conservative Christian message is ever-present in the telecasts as a theological backdrop against which discussion of sin and immorality takes place.[140]

The television ministries have attempted to attract a wider audience, one beyond the traditional audience of conservative Christians. Toward this end, they have made use of state-of-the-art technology and production values that match those of commercial television and have introduced new formats. Robertson was the first to experiment with a talk-show format. The "PTL Club" imitated the format Robertson introduced with the "700 Club." The "700 Club" and the "PTL Club" have done more in the way of innovation and experimentation with format than any of the other television programs.

Despite efforts and claims to attract a younger, better educated, less religiously conservative audience, the television ministries have failed to do so.[141]

> ...In spite of...much-touted new formats, new appeals, technological sophistication, and prominence in the 'secular' world, the audience for religious television today is what it always has been—older, less educated, more rural, and more conventionally religious than its nonreligious-viewing cohort. There is little reason to believe that many outside of the traditional audience are actually viewing. Further, the new genres of religious programs that are specifically intended to increase the size of the audience seem to be ineffective at doing so.[142]

"A more moderate, 'upscale' audience seems not to be the dominant pattern."[143]

Televangelism has not won converts outside the ranks of conservative Christianity[144] because its message, expressed both overtly and implicitly, is the message of conservative Christian religion and morality. Televangelism is conservative Christian in its heart and soul. It expresses and confirms viewers' own religious beliefs and religious view of the world.[145] These have not changed significantly from the beliefs of televangelism's viewers in its infancy.[146] The audience for televangelism is made up of those who already subscribe to its conservative Christian message.[147]

What those in mainstream society who live in a pluralistic and changing world find unattractive, obnoxious, and even dangerous about the religion of televangelism, its conservative Christian viewers gravitate toward. The religious message of televangelism offers conservative Christians ready answers that are both straightforward and absolutistic.

Certainty helps viewers face a society and world undergoing rapid social and cultural change and along with it, growing complexity, tension, and ambiguity. Certainty helps them face the social and cultural dissonance created by the conflict between their religion and the secular world, as well as a society and culture in crisis.[148] The conservative Christian religion resolves all complexity, tension, and ambiguity as it presents its simple understanding of biblical morality, and its millenarian vision of transforming a confusing and threatening world through the practice of biblical morality.

The same promise of certainty in the face of growing dissonance and social and cultural crisis that lies behind the recent growth of conservative Christian churches[149] is a large part of televangelism's attraction for the religious conservatives. Televangelism makes the conservative Christian religion even more available, and along with it, the company of other viewers who face the same dissonance and uncertainty and seek the same religious answers. Televangelism presents another comfort. Viewers recognize that other viewers have also met with opposition and persecution from the secular world and can offer their support.

# ⊣ 4 ⊢

# The Religion of Televangelism
# and Its Viewers

### A Bible-believing Religion

Televangelism's viewers are "fundamentalistic" in outlook.[150] They are "Bible-believing" Christians. They hold to biblical fundamentals, beginning with the belief that the Bible is literally true. They believe that all of the other beliefs they hold are true, since, they claim, they are rooted in the Bible. Literalism hinges on the belief that the Bible is "God's revealed word." The Bible is held to be "inerrant" or "infallible," since it is believed to be God's own word. To doubt the scripture is to doubt God himself. Anything that contradicts the Bible is believed to contradict God.

The Bible is held to be the only truth. And the truth discoverable there is believed to be unchanging. The Bible is regarded as historical and scientific fact, from its account of the creation of the world, to its account of the events that will take place as the world comes to an end. The doctrine of inerrancy is used as a litmus test of true faith, separating true believers from nonbelievers. Viewers also hold biblical morality as fundamental to belief. They believe the Bible reveals how God wants believers to act. The practice of biblical morality is considered further evidence of belief. As God's authoritative word, the Bible is held to be authoritative in every area of life.

Because of its meaning for conservative Christians and its value in orienting their lives, the Bible is the central symbol found in televangelism. The telecasts began as Bible oriented preaching, and although sermonizing has changed greatly with shifts in format, televangelism has never taken its emphasis off of the Bible or Biblical fundamentals as authoritative for conservative Christians. All of the television programs make reference to it in one way or another, often reading directly out of it, selling it, or giving it away. The television ministers or others tirelessly quote it, preach out of it, or display it. Bible passages are frequently displayed on the screen. Ninety percent of the telecasts read from, show, or mention the Bible.[151] A great deal of the music on the program makes reference to it. The Bible, and fundamentalistic belief, are the bedrock of televangelism.

Viewers believe that God created the world, exactly as recounted in the book of Genesis, in six twenty-four-hour days. They believe in Adam and Eve. They believe God miraculously or supernaturally intervenes in human history, moving all events in accord with his divine purpose—the redemption of the world—which is necessitated by human sin. They believe that Jesus was God incarnate, as testified by his virgin birth, and to a lesser extent his miracles. They believe Jesus died on the cross to bring salvation from sin, that salvation comes only to those who believe that Jesus was the son of God whose sacrificial death overturns sin, and that Jesus rose from the dead. They believe in Jesus' bodily, physical resurrection. And they believe that the resurrected Christ will return to earth in the very near future to judge the living and the dead.[152]

All of televangelism's viewers are fundamentalists in a broad sense. "Fundamentalist" viewers, who make up most of the audience for televangelism, are fundamentalistic in a narrower sense. They do not accept the Pentecostal doctrine of sanctification or completion of salvation by the pouring out of God's spirit on the believer, manifest in "speaking in tongues." Fundamentalists believe that salvation comes instantly to those who "profess Jesus Christ as personal savior." They also view speaking in tongues as unruly, going against church discipline. Pentecostals view noncharismatic traditions as less "spirit-filled," as stifling the Holy Spirit.[153] Speaking in tongues divides fundamentalists and Pentecostals. The fundamentals of belief they hold in common, and the fierceness with which they hold them unites them in belief, however.

Falwell's viewers are fundamentalists. Robertson draws both fundamentalist and Pentecostal viewers. He straddles both traditions, supporting the practice of the charismatic gifts. Swaggart and the Bakkers draw Pentecostal viewers. Robert Schuller is the only television minister among the most watched television personalities who has not said that he is a fundamentalist in the strict sense of the word.[154]

## Fundamentalism

"Fundamentalism" emerged earlier in the century as a movement among Bible scholars and other Christian thinkers who were interested in reasserting the authority of the Bible in the face of the challenge of modernism, especially the challenge of theological "modernism" or liberalism being practiced within the mainline churches, and along with this the practice of "demythologizing" the Bible.[155] "Fundamentalists" took their name from the biblical fundamentals they believed to be the authoritative word of God, and authoritative for the modern world. Fundamentalism was originally a defense against and challenge to the increasing liberalization of the historic Protestant denominations in biblical teaching, theology, and church polity. These had embraced the historical, scientific, and critical study of the Bible as practiced by religious scholars in church seminaries, uncovering its historical and cultural roots.

Fundamentalists oppose the view of liberal Christians that the Bible is human interpretation, and therefore culture-bound, constructed in the light of changing historical and social situations and expressing a variety of world views, and therefore producing contradictory and ambiguous interests and claims. Fundamentalists argue that the Bible is a timeless declaration of God's full truth for all people of all ages. Fundamentalists also oppose the view of liberals that God's revelations to earlier peoples as reported in the Bible are not necessarily God's revelation for today, the view held by Luther. Fundamentalists oppose the liberal view that the Bible does not contain the whole of God's revelation, which is continually changing.

Fundamentalists reject the liberal view that the Bible is symbolic, including the accounts of miracles, and must be read for its philosophical or existential and psychological insight about human limitations, human potential, and the search for well-being—a view that can be traced back to Origen. Fundamentalists oppose the de-emphasis of divine miracles by liberals, especially the miracles of Jesus, along with the view of many liberals that the resurrection is an image of inner transformation and new life. Liberals look for encounters with God not in a burning bush, but in women's and men's spiritual search for well-being and in the search for social justice. "Modernist" liberals practiced a "social gospel," which saw social justice as essential to the gospel of salvation and essential to salvation itself.

In the eyes of fundamentalists, theological modernism challenged the centrality and authority of the Bible, while the emphasis on social justice took the emphasis off of sin and salvation, heaven and hell. The objection to theological modernism was also an objection by fundamentalists to the modern, secular society with which the mainline denominations were meshed. The battle waged against the mainline churches and their liberalizing of the Bible, along with the battle against the modern world among early fundamentalists, continues among fundamentalists and among televangelism's fundamentalist and "fundamentalistic" viewers today.

### Pentecostalism

While fundamentalistic in belief, Pentecostals distinguish themselves by emphasizing the "spirit-filled life," along with the "gifts of the Holy Spirit," or the "charismatic gifts": "speaking in tongues," and interpretation of tongues, prophecy, etc. They hold speaking in tongues to be a sign of sanctification, or the completion of their salvation by the pouring out of God's Holy Spirit upon them. The spiritual gifts are regarded as evidence of God's spiritual presence in the life of Pentecostals and of God's blessing and favor. Pentecostals believe they stand within the tradition of the apostles, on whom the resurrected Christ is said to have poured out his spirit at Pentecost following his death. They believe they have inherited the mission the resurrected Christ assigned the apostles, namely, preaching the gospel throughout the world, made possible by the gift of tongues. Pentecostalism emerged just after the turn of the century, indebted to the revivalist tradition of the Holiness movement out of which it sprang, and to its early African-American adherents, for whom spirit possession was part of their heritage. [156]

### A Millenarian, World-opposing Religion

As fundamentalists and Pentecostals, televangelism's viewers, subscribe to the millenarian view of the Christian Bible. According to this view, the world is an arena within which God and Satan are engaged in an ongoing cosmic struggle. God is engaged in a struggle with Satan to win his creation back to himself. Satan steered creation off of its divine course by seducing Adam and Eve, whose fall brought sin into the world. Viewers believe they are living during the concluding stage of the cosmic struggle, evidence for which they find in their "persecution" by the secular world, especially by the secular state and "secular humanists." Further evidence is found in wars, particularly those in the Middle East, the scene of the biblical Armageddon, the war to end all wars, as well as in economic and natural disasters, pestilence, and other crises.

The secular world is believed to have been enlisted by Satan to help defeat God's purposes for his creation in order to rule it himself. The millenarian view divides all men and women into two agonistic camps.[157] One is either for God, or for the Devil. It is believed that the persecution of conservative Christians by secular society is a strategy masterminded by Satan himself to defeat God by defeating his people. Viewers see the hand of Satan at work in the negative judgments handed down by courts against Bible study or prayer in public schools as well as in court-ordered closings of Christian schools. They see Satan at work in decisions by state legislatures against textbooks teaching "Creationist science" for public school use. They see the hand of Satan at work in police arrests of "pro-life" demonstrators. They also see Satan behind the close scrutiny given the televangelism ministries by the news media and in the organized opposition to television ministries by civil liberties groups, and the like. Bakker's defeat and Swaggart's controversy are also seen as the work of Satan.

While viewers believe that God will come out the victor in the end, being Lord of the universe, they also believe that they themselves have a critical role to play in the defeat of Satan. They believe that God has enlisted them to help defeat Satan by bringing the secular world back to God. They believe that they are called upon to bring about no less than the moral regeneration of society, bringing public morality in line with God's moral laws. Moral reform is not viewed as an afterthought but as an imperative. Nothing short of militancy is required, it is believed, since the stakes are high: the ultimate defeat of Satan. The moral regeneration of the secular world is believed not only to rob Satan of an ally and of an instrument through which to thwart God's purposes, but to bring back sinners to the ways of God, winning the immoral world back to God.

Viewers believe that God will be victorious in the end and that he will vindicate his people, who are persecuted for their efforts, by including them in his rule over a redeemed world. They believe in the imminent return of Christ, who will judge the wicked. In the interim, viewers believe, God will sustain them as they face persecution at the hands of the secular world.[158]

### A Religion of Morality

For televangelism's fundamentalist and Pentecostal viewers, departure from the old, immoral or sinful life is demonstrated by the salvation experience. They believe they are "born-again," having died to a life of sin or immorality. For them, the born-again experience distinguishes them as moral men and women from the secular world in need of moral regeneration.

For televangelism's fundamentalist and Pentecostal viewers biblical morality is best represented by "family values." Holding "pro-family" values as the moral ideal, they denounce the liberalizing of gender roles, the alternative family, alternative lifestyles, especially homosexuality, abortion, pornography, etc. Viewers promote "family values" in the belief that these values will "restore" America as a "godly" or "Christian" nation. They believe that America must be restored to the path of moral righteousness if it is to serve as agent through which God will redeem the world.[159]

Half of all viewers of religious television, including televangelism, say they are dissatisfied with the present moral climate in America. Only 31% of those who watch nonreligious television say they are dissatisfied with the prevailing moral climate. The latter group of viewers is less "fundamentalistic."[160] Thirty-nine percent of viewers in my survey of viewers of televangelism indicated that they watch the telecasts primarily to learn the biblical position on social issues. This was the second highest reason given after wanting a spiritual boost (43%). Seventy-four percent indicated that they watch because the programs stand up for Bible-believing Christians, whose position on social and moral issues, they believe, are not taken seriously in America today. Fifty-one percent said that they watch because in speaking out, the programs increase the influence of Bible-believing Christians.[161] The more popular programs give a great deal of air time to discussion of social issues.[162]

Sixty-eight percent of viewers of religious television of all forms oppose legalized abortion, while 39% of viewers of nonreligious television are opposed.[163] Ninety percent believe extramarital sex is always wrong, as compared to 79% of those who watch nonreligious programming. Sixty percent believe premarital sex is wrong, as compared to 29% of viewers of nonreligious programming. Sixty-nine percent object to divorce. Only 21% are divorced or widowed. (The national average for divorce is roughly 50%.) Eighty percent believe women are happiest when at home with their children, as compared to 63% from the other group of viewers. Fifty-six percent believe the wife should not work if she is supported by the husband. Only 33% of the other group of viewers agree.[164] Thirty-two percent of those who took part in my survey object to equal rights for women.[165] Ninety percent of viewers of religious television view homosexuality as wrong. Seventy percent of viewers of nonreligious television do. Eighty-one percent favor stricter anti-pornography laws, while 76% of those who watch nonreligious television do.[166] The morality of conservative Christians avoids social justice issues, however. They associate social justice with the liberal outlook of the mainline churches.[167]

### An Activist Religion

The millenarian vision of conservative Christianity is not strictly escapist. Certainly, the religious vision opens up a heavenly world. The other world serves, however, as a backdrop against which everyday life is lived, judged and recast. The heavenly vision of the world also offers a vision for it. The religious vision offers an idealized model for the world by which the everyday world is evaluated and realigned. Televangelism and the millenarian religion promoted there scrutinize the everyday world in the light of a heavenly model. The world-transcending or earth-shattering features of the conservative Christian religion are finally world-confronting and world-transforming. The religious vision of an alternative world leads conservative Christians to make the world over in the image of a heavenly reality, their idealized vision.

The millenarian religion of conservative Christians has escapist elements in conjuction with its otherworldly and world-opposing interests, particularly the promise of supernatural intervention and deliverance. The rosy vision of a world transformed by God in the future nevertheless requires some action on their part in order to achieve it. Their religious vision for the future requires religious conservatives to lay the groundwork for the transformed world through militant action. The millenarian religion of conservative Christians bends back upon the world in a concrete way as their religious vision leads to political activism in the service of conservative Christian morality.

The religious vision of the world and vision for it held by conservative Christians are linked to the real world in yet another way. The religious vision is rooted in the actual world, even if some of their beliefs about the world are misinformed. Their millenarian vision is rooted in conservative Christians' experience of the world as hostile and as placing limits on the value and significance of their lives. Their vision is in large measure a response to their social marginalization.

The millenarian vision held by conservative Christians is also influenced by the very real crises in values and morality facing American society. The solutions proposed by conservative Christians are shortsighted, however. The social problems confronting an American society undergoing rapid social change are bewilderingly complex and new. There are no simple or easy solutions. Democratic, mainstream society looks upon the moralizing judgments of conservative Christians as obnoxious because they are repressive, and even oppressive. Conservative Christians equate their morality with a divine order. They ignore the fact that the social mainstream is deeply spiritual and moral and also committed to addressing America's crisis of morality.

# ⊰ 5 ⊱

# The Emergence of Televangelism As Distinctive Religious Programming

## *An Alternative to Mainline Religious Television*

The narrowly conservative orientation of televangelism is reflected in its history.[168] Conservative religious programming was originally kept off the air by the national networks because it was too risky to air to their national audience. "Being 'born again,' speaking in unknown tongues, tent revivals, witnessing for Christ, and other hallmarks of evangelicalism and pentecostalism were identified...with being uneducated and poor" in a post-war America with a mushrooming middle class. Conservative Christians suffered from an image problem.[169] There were no opportunities for conservative religious programming, since there were no independent religious television stations or networks as there are now.

In the early days of religious broadcasting, the television networks as well as their local affiliates were highly selective in choosing the religious groups to which they granted air time. Not every religious group could put its programs on the air. The national networks were required by the Federal Communications Commission to air religious broadcasting as a public interest. An arrangement was made to air the programs of the mainline Protestant denominations along with a Roman Catholic and a Jewish program free of charge. Religious broadcasts were confined to the early Sunday morning time slot. These were often taped Bible lessons, or sermons. Programming was staid in comparison to the televangelism that would follow.

A new policy put in place by the FCC in 1960 mandated selling air time to anyone wishing to put religious programming on the air. The new ruling opened the airwaves to conservative Christian programming. Today televangelism enjoys a virtual monopoly of Christian television, reversing the early dominance of mainline programming. Conservative Christians were interested in gaining access to the airwaves in order to preach the gospel. They were also interested in producing a distinctive programming. They demanded an alternative to the liberal programming sponsored by the mainline churches. The religious conservatives were of the mind that the religious programming then dominating the airwaves had watered down the Christian message by abandoning the fundamentals of biblical belief and morality. The religious fare then available was thought to have accommodated the secular world. Conservative Christians produced religious programming that did not give up what to their minds was distinctive about the Christian religion. To do so, however, they had to buy their way onto the air.[170]

Religious radio was also originally dominated by mainline programming. The first religious radio broadcast was an Episcopal church service heard over a local station in Pittsburgh in 1921. "National Radio Pulpit," broadcast in 1924 by the National Council of Churches of Christ, the national organization of mainline Protestant denominations and forerunner of today's National Council of Churches, did not include the conservative and evangelical churches. Programs featured theologically liberal Protestant ministers. Harry Emerson Fosdick of the Riverside Church in New York was heard regularly.

The first radio network, the National Broadcasting Company, looked to the National Council of Churches of Christ to oversee its national religious programming. NBC and the NCCC struck an agreement that groups not in league with the council would not be given or sold air time. The agreement blocked conservative Christian programming from the air. NBC also gave time to Roman Catholic programming, which was coordinated by the New York Diocese, and to Jewish broadcasting, coordinated by the New York Rabbinical Council. In 1930, CBS sold air time to the first nonmember of the NCCC: The Lutheran Church Missouri Synod. The Lutheran program attracted a massive audience.

In the 1940s a coalition of mainline denominations and advocates of the separation of church and state lobbied the national radio networks not to sell time for religious broadcasts. The intent was to keep conservative programs off the air, or at least restrict them. An agreement was struck. Conservative Christians formed the National Association of Evangelicals in 1942, forerunner of the National Religious Broadcasters (formed in 1944), to mount their own broadcasts and to defend their right to have access to the airwaves through donated and paid air time. Through the 1950s, radio stations continued to give or sell air time to organizations representing mainline religious groups.

The first national religious series broadcast over television was aired by ABC in 1949. The program featured prominent theologians discussing the place of religion in daily life. Rival CBS dramatized Bible stories in a puppet series and in 1951 began a dramatic television series. Religious programs remained predominantly Protestant, Bishop Fulton Sheen, the Roman Catholic, being an exception among the hosts of the various television shows.

Pioneers of conservative religious television also took to the air during the 1950s: Oral Roberts, Rex Humbard, and Kathryn Kuhlman, all Pentecostals. They appeared on local stations from which they purchased air time. Billy Graham, an evangelical Christian, enjoyed national coverage.  Although conservative theologically, he was considered acceptable by the national networks.

The amount of paid religious programming—primarily evangelical and fundamentalist and Pentecostal programming—soared between 1959 and 1977, moving from 53% of all religious programming to 92%. Through the paid-time arrangement, conservative religious programming came to dominate religious television programming.[171] The number of syndicated conservative religious programs purchasing air time from several local stations rose from 38 in 1970 to 72 in 1978.[172] Paid-time programming, dominated by conservative Christians, all but eliminated religious programming provided as a free public service by local television stations. Conservative religious programming proved more profitable for local stations. Much of the paid-time, conservative religious programming aired in smaller television markets than mainline religious programming and aired at more off-times than mainline programming. The growing domination of religious programming by conservative religious broadcasts on local affiliates of the national networks eventually pressured the national networks to reexamine and reprogram the mainline religious programming they offered.[173]

Most religious programs aired on commercial stations are scheduled on Sunday morning, known in the television industry as "The Sunday Morning (Religious) Ghetto."[174] The religious fare provides filler for air time that is unattractive to secular audiences as well as to program sponsors, who keep commercial television afloat. Advertisers pay to air commercials on programs that draw larger audiences. Religious programs also generate revenue for commercial stations. Religious sponsors can afford air time on Sunday mornings. The cost of air time is lower then because audiences are smaller. Exorbitant production costs force independent television ministries that do not have denominational support or draw little support to devote time on the air to raise money. "Donor-based broadcasting" is necessary if they are to stay afloat. Televangelism fits into this category.

In 1961 a new development began within conservative religious television: the purchase of independent television stations and the organization of independent television networks. Pat Robertson started the first, the Christian Broadcasting Company, in Virginia Beach, Virginia, in 1961. By 1978 there were approximately 30 religious television stations, and 30 applications for a television license with the FCC by religious groups. By 1979 half of all religious programming aired was taken up by only ten major conservative Christian programs.[175]

The 1970s saw the addition of other, large, independent conservative religious television networks. The Bakkers, who originally worked for Robertson, producing and starring in their own popular puppet program for children, got the PTL Network off the ground. Paul Crouch started Trinity Broadcasting Network. These television networks provided exclusively religious fare or combined Christian programming with "family" oriented programs made for commercial television, for example, "The Little House on the Prairie" or "The Merv Griffin Show." The new networks pioneered the Christian talk-show and news-magazine format. United Methodists, the Southern Baptist Convention, and Roman Catholics also organized television networks.

The rush into television is underscored by the publication of numerous "how to" guides addressing the practical problems of starting up and managing or leasing a television station and mounting programming. These publications discuss the process of applying to the FCC for a license, FCC regulations, including the "Fairness Doctrine," ratings, "good neighbor" policies and politics in relation to the community, start-up and ongoing expenses, and technological and aesthetic considerations. The handbook provided by the association of

National Religious Broadcasters notes: "'Above all else, brethren,' broadcasting is a business." The handbook also includes a chapter on "Management From a Biblical Perspective."[176] It has been observed that

> These broadcasters [National Religious Broadcasters], who once could not get enough time, have been so effective in their struggle that they now hold a virtual monopoly over air-time used for religious programming, having forced most other religious programs off the air by their cut-throat purchase of time. Yet they show none of the consideration for other types of programming which they originally sought for themselves.[177]

The "Statement of Faith" by the National Religious Broadcasters reads:

1. We believe the Bible to be inspired, the only infallible, authoritative Word of God.
2. We believe that there is one God, eternally existent in three Persons: Father, Son, and Holy Ghost.
3. We believe in the deity of Christ, in His virgin birth, in His sinless life, in His miracles, in His victorious and atoning death through His shed blood, in His bodily resurrection, in His ascension to the right hand of the Father, and in His personal return in power and glory.
4. We believe that for the salvation of lost and sinful man regeneration by the Holy Spirit is absolutely essential.
5. We believe in the present ministry of the Holy Spirit, by whose indwelling the Christian is enabled to live a godly life.
6. We believe in the resurrection of both the saved and the lost, they that are saved unto the resurrection of life and they that are lost unto the resurrection of damnation.
7. We believe in the spiritual unity of believers in Christ.[178]

In harmony with its statement of belief is the NRB's statement of purpose, which heads its "Code of Ethics":

> Recognizing the vital and increasingly important role played by broadcasting as an agency of mass communication—vastly extending the potential audiences of the church and the classroom—National Religious Broadcasters believe the propagation of the Gospel by radio and television is essential to the religious inspiration, guidance, and education of the public, to the enrichment of national life and to the full use of this blessing of modern civilization in the public interest.[179]

Included in the document is a reference to maintaining "high standards with respect to content, method of presentation, speakers' qualifications, and ethical practices."

The statement of purpose provided in the Broadcasting and Film Commission handbook circulated in the late 1950s by the National Council of Churches of Christ, today's National Council of Churches, helps to illustrate the contrast between the religious orientation and motivation of mainline Christian programming and that of conservative Christians. Its language, which today would be considered archaic, is far more general, since it is far less doctrinally oriented and is ecumenically minded.

> To win listeners and viewers to the Christian faith—
> By instruction in Christian living.
> By presenting programs for those who are unfamiliar with the forms of worship, the life and the language of the Church. /.../
> To build a stronger Christian family—
> By strengthening the local church.
> By creating a better understanding of the local and world-wide services of the Church.
> To make known the Christian Gospel to every person everywhere—
> God as the One to whom the listener or viewer belongs.
> Jesus as the continuing Saviour.
> The Bible as the bearer of eternal truths.
> The Church as the family of believers around the world.
> To help the different religious groups to understand each other.[180]

The handbook includes a statement on the recognition by the NCÇC of the need "To bring the judgment of Christ to bear upon our culture, and to speak to the condition of modern man," and

> To bring people into the fellowship of other Christians, in worshipping congregations that extend the leavening influence of the Gospel into the secular sphere, permeating every walk of life, every community relationship and all the institutions of modern society.[181]

Promoting greater understanding among different religious groups is far from the minds of conservative Christians, who engage in religious television to preach conservative religious doctrine to a lost world.

# ⊰ Part Two ⊱

# Televangelism As Ritual

Part Two calls attention to televangelism's role as ritual in helping viewers legitimate their religion and religious group for themselves in the face
of threats and opposition from mainstream American society.
Televangelism's role as ritual in helping viewers adapt themselves to the
social mainstream is also given attention. In addition, Part Two attends
to the role televangelism plays as ritual in helping viewers attempt to
create among themselves the community they seek with mainstream
society but do not find. Contradictions between and among
televangelism's capacities and roles as ritual are also pointed out. The
following section begins by showing how viewers ritualize their viewing
in order to tap the transformative capacities of the ritual performances of
which the telecasts are made.

## ⚛ 6 ⚛

# Viewers' Ritual Participation
# in the Telecasts

*Active Versus Passive Viewers*

The cliché view of televangelism's viewers is that they are passive recipients of a packaged television religion, mindless spectators who are spoon-fed religious hype. While viewers are on the receiving end of television signals, they are hardly passive. Programmers do not approach viewers as passive spectators. They seek to engage viewers as active participants in the telecasts in order to win their support for the television programs, financial and otherwise. Engaging viewers is also intended to win their financial support for the television ministries as well as the various missions and evangelism programs undertaken by the television ministries: food and medical relief programs, education and literacy programs, counseling, prison ministry, etc. Viewers contribute most of the operating budgets of the television ministries.

The support of viewers is won by engaging them as active participants in the telecasts. Viewers are provided opportunities to join in various activities undertaken during the telecasts. Viewers are invited to read along in their Bibles, pray along with those on the telecasts offering prayers, etc. Live telecasts invite viewers to phone in prayer requests which are taken on the air. Viewers are also invited to phone in pledges for financial contributions. Pledges are taken by phone bank volunteers who are visible on screen, and are then reported on the air.

Viewers are also invited to write to the television ministries and send in their prayer requests, religious questions, and comments on the programs. And viewers do write.

> ...a broadcaster becomes very sensitive to the audience feedback provided by one's mailroom. The daily report on both income and issues from the mailroom becomes an important item in each broadcaster's daily briefing. ...bulk mail is not only the lifeblood of the broadcasters but it also becomes a type of barometer of the broadcaster's performance in relation to his audience. [182]

The television ministries take viewers' feedback seriously and make efforts to meet their expectations of and suggestions for the shows.[183] Programmers know their audiences. In addition to viewers' comments, programmers have detailed demographic information on audiences.[184]

Above all, programmers seek to engage viewers in the religious message of the telecasts, recognizing that if they are to win viewers' support, the message must make an impact. Involving viewers as active participants in the telecasts is intended to open them to the message and its impact. The message presented is not new to viewers. It is the message of the religion to which they are already committed. Televangelism's religious message addresses viewers' own religious interests, which they bring with them to their viewing.

### Viewers' Choice

Viewers watch the religious telecasts and actively engage in them as a way of extending their own religious commitment.[185] Their active engagement, as well as religious commitment, are reflected in the high degree of selectivity with which viewers tune in. Viewers select programs for their messages and inquire about what other programs are available. They watch religious programming as an alternative to commercial and public television, objecting to too much sex, violence, and the liberal cultural and political bias aired there.[186] Televangelism offers viewers a "safe" alternative, and an "antidote" to secular television.[187]

Viewers bring to their viewing the expectation that a particular television program will express their own religious beliefs, will provide information that will help them better express their views, and will give spiritual inspiration, as well as give evidence of care about the viewer.[188] Fifty-four percent of the viewers who took part in my survey reported that they watch the telecasts in order to worship or get a spiritual boost.[189] Eight percent indicated that they watch in order to undergo a religious experience and not just to worship. Thirty-nine percent indicated they watch in order to become informed on the biblical position on moral or political issues. Fifteen percent watch to gain answers to personal problems or crises. Fifty-nine percent watch to get answers to personal problems. Fifteen percent seek marriage counseling or advice. Twenty-five percent seek financial counseling or advice. Thirty-nine percent seek family counseling or advice. And 19% seek advice or counseling related to their jobs.

Sixty percent of these viewers look to the host as a worship leader. Some viewers regard the host as a "spiritual leader" or as a "Christian leader" or Christian educator. Ninety percent believe the program host cares about them personally. Nineteen percent think of the host as a friend. All of these responses reflect the active engagement of viewers in the telecasts.

## Viewers' Ritualized Viewing

Viewers' active participation in the telecasts is also reflected in the regularity with which they tune in. Viewers make watching the programs a ritual. Forty-one percent of the viewers who took part in my survey watch more than seven hours of Christian programming each week. Thirteen percent watch between five and seven hours. Twenty-four percent watch between three and five hours of programming each week. Twenty-one percent watch between one and three hours. Only 2% watch less than one hour. Viewers tune in to Christian programming five hours a week on average.

These viewers spend far fewer hours watching commercial or public television. Twenty-four percent watch less than one hour of commercial or public television each week. Forty percent watch between one and three hours. Twenty-one percent watch between three to five hours. Four percent watch between five and seven hours. Only 7% watch more than seven hours each week. The average number of hours of commercial or public television watched each week is under three, as compared to five hours of Christian television. The average number of hours of commercial television watched *each day* by the typical American television household is now up to six and a half hours![190] These figures reflect the high degree of selectivity and involvement of televangelism's viewers.

Half of the viewers in my survey (51%) watch the programs every time they are aired. Forty percent watch most of the time. Only 10% watch occasionally. Seventy-six percent watch all of the program when it is aired. Seventeen percent watch most of the program. Only 8% watch only part of the program. Fifty percent of these viewers reported that they do nothing but watch when they tune in. They do not do other things while they watch. Other viewers reported that they undertake household or business chores, eat, and get ready for work, or do other things while they watch. Sixty-three percent of the viewers in my survey reported that they attempt to include family when viewing programs. Eighty-two percent discuss the shows with their families, and 86% do so with friends. These viewing patterns suggest that those who watch the telecasts are highly involved in them.

Before turning on the programs, viewers undertake ritual routines that prepare them for engaging in the telecasts. Forty-three percent of the viewers who took part in my survey reported that they pray before they turn on the programs. Seventy-seven percent indicated that they pray after they turn off the programs. Forty percent read the Bible before turning on the programs. Twenty-nine percent do so after turning off the programs. Twenty-three percent reported that the Bible they read out of as they follow along with Bible readings on the program was purchased from the television ministry airing the program. Sixty-three percent reported that they have purchased study materials or mementos advertised on the air from the television ministries. These materials help establish a connection between the viewer and the television personalities and ministries, as well as other viewers.

## Viewers' Participation in the Ritual Activities of the Telecasts

The ritual routines viewers undertake on their own ahead of turning on the television programs are not empty habit, simply going through the motions. Their ritual routines help make viewing a participatory event.

The ritualized viewing habits of televangelism's audience serve as a runway leading up to participation in the activities undertaken by the telecasts. Viewers follow along with the worship activities of the telecasts. They pray along with the prayers offered during the programs, they read along in the Bible, and they sing along. Viewers also phone in prayer requests as well as pledges to pray for a particular cause, or pledges to contribute money. Forty-nine percent of the viewers taking part in my survey phone in financial pledges during the show, 8% of them frequently. All of these activities are rituals in themselves and are intended by programmers to engage viewers in a hands-on way. All are familiar elements of church worship, inviting greater participation of an audience largely made up of churchgoers. Falwell's and Swaggart's telecasts are edited video tapes of actual worship services.

Eighty-two percent of the viewers who took part in my survey indicated that they participate in these activities. Fifty-one percent reported that they do so frequently. Fifty-one percent phone in prayer requests during the shows, 12% of these on a frequent basis, and 39% on an occasional basis. Viewers phone in prayer requests concerning physical healing, financial miracles, marriage problems, children facing problems, etc.

Many viewers reported that they undergo a religious experience while watching. Some reported having "felt God's touch," "God's guidance and strength," or having been "touched by the Spirit" or "uplifted." Twenty-five percent of the viewers in my survey report that they feel the need to rededicate their lives to Christ. Twenty-four percent reported physical healing in answer to pray. Nineteen percent said that they have had a "word of knowledge," or revelation about someone else's need. Seven percent reported "dancing in the spirit." Three percent reported "speaking in tongues." The same number reported prophesying.

Viewers' engagement in the telecasts is reflected in their involvement in various ministries and programs of the television ministries. Viewers contribute money to the missions and evangelism projects of the various ministries. The engagement of viewers is also reflected in their participation in the many seminars and workshops made available to viewers at television headquarters and advertised during the telecast. Many of these are counseling seminars, and range from marriage crisis counseling and counseling on alcohol addiction, to "marriage enrichment" and financial planning.

Viewers also extend their engagement with the telecasts by seeking counseling over the phone with telephone counselors on staff at the various television ministries. Much of the counseling involves praying with a caller. "Go to your phone, pick it up, and call the number that's on your screen. We care about you. We want to be there when you need help. Someone is there waiting to help you," Robertson or a co-host will say to viewers.[191] Robertson's show also airs short commercials inviting viewers to phone the counseling service, which is open for crisis counseling twenty-four hours a day. Viewers are invited to call in and speak to a counselor about drug addiction, depression, loneliness, marriage crises, financial crises, or other problems.[192]

Viewers frequently go on pilgrimage to the headquarters of the television ministries, where they join the studio audience for a taping of the programs or a live broadcast. This also reflects their interest and engagement in the television programs. Twenty-eight percent of the viewers in my survey indicated they have visited headquarters. Seven percent have made plans to visit. Viewers' interest in the programs is also made evident by the fact that they purchase a host of materials made available by the television ministries: Bible-study guides, study aids, devotional materials, counseling materials, audio cassettes, video tapes, and record albums published or printed by the television ministries, as well as mementos provided by the ministries. Many of these as well as the various programs and projects of the ministries are advertised on the air.

### The Telecasts As Ritual Performances and Viewers' Participation in Them

Viewers also participate in the transformations or reconstructions of the everyday world and of their identity within it undertaken by the telecasts in their role as ritual performances. All of the television programs are highly choreographed or ritualized performances. The formats of the performances differ from program to program. Robertson's program is a news-journalism or news-magazine format. The Bakkers' program leans toward a talk-show format combined with that of a variety show. Falwell's and Swaggart's programs are broadcasts of actual worship services. While these programs use different modes of ritual performance, they all engage in ritualized display to dramatize the religious message.

The openings of all of the television programs make use of ritual routine. At the outset of each of the television shows, the logo used by each of the programs appears on the screen while the theme music for each show is played or a congregational hymn or choir anthem is sung. While the music plays, a narrator offers viewers a familiar and personal greeting. The openings often introduce the religious or moral theme or topic for a particular telecast.

The opening for each of the television shows helps viewers make a transition away from the everyday world to an alternative context, where they undergo transformative experiences generated by the telecast performances. The rituals viewers undertake on their own ahead of turning on the programs help them begin to make the transition. As the millenarian message of conservative Christianity is dramatized in the ritual performances, viewers undergo emotional experiences that lend credibility to their religion and its accounting of the world.[193]

Viewers share in the production of religious meaning generated by the telecasts. They already hold to the beliefs presented, bringing these and other religious interests to their viewing. Viewers also bring to the telecasts their unique religious views, filtering and adjusting the religious message presented to them accordingly.[194] It is well known that the general television viewer is not a passive viewer. Television viewers reflect on the ideas or views of the world presented by television and reconfirm or question their own ideas, making the television message meaningful for themselves. There is give and take between television programs and their viewers.[195]

Viewers also participate in the production of meaning that has relevance to the social marginalization of conservative Christians as a religious group within mainstream American society. The meanings generated by the religious telecasts, programmers, and viewers are not strictly those of conservative Christian belief and morality. Viewers may consciously identify themselves as citizens of heaven first. But as flesh and blood creatures who have social needs and interests, they bring to their viewing their interest in overturning their marginalization, even though they may not be aware that they do so. Viewers also seek legitimation of their social group. They find it in the legitimation of their religion and of their religious group provided by the telecasts. They create significance for their social group as they legitimate their religion. They see themselves as significant people because they possess "the truth." They find added significance for their social group as they legitimate their religious group as a people blessed by God and special to him.

Viewers give significance to their social group in yet another way. They raise their social status in their own eyes as they adopt the outlook and lifestyle of the social mainstream presented by the telecasts.[196]

As the ritual performances make a transition to an alternative context, they also help viewers open themselves to the secular dress, speech, aesthetic sensibilities, and attitudes of mainstream society. The alternative context also helps viewers open themselves to learning more about social and political issues of significance to the wider society.

Televangelism's effectiveness as ritual in redressing viewers' social marginalization hinges upon their active participation in the telecast performances. By engaging the telecasts as active participants, viewers put themselves in the position to tap the telecasts' capacity as ritual to provide for themselves legitimation of their religion and religious group in the face of the threat and opposition from mainstream society. They also put themselves in a position to tap the capacity of the telecasts as ritual to assist them in adapting to mainstream society. And they put themselves in a position to tap the telecasts' potential as ritual to help them create among themselves the community they seek with the social mainstream but do not find. Viewers do not set out to use televangelism in these ways. They discover televangelism's capacities as ritual as they engage actively in the telecasts.

# ⊰ 7 ⊱

# Ritual in the Service of
# Legitimation and Adaptation

## Televangelism As Ritual Legitimation

As mass communication, television offers a natural and important vehicle for the masses of televangelism's conservative Christian viewers to express, communicate, and reinforce their religious beliefs and morality in the face of challenge and opposition by mainstream, secular American society. All of these are critical to the mobilization of conservative Christians in defense of their religion.

Television is also a vehicle by which conservative Christians broaden their horizon. Through the religious television programs, viewers familiarize themselves with social and political issues and developments within the wider, secular world, as well as familiarize themselves with its dress, language, aesthetic sensibilities, and attitudes. All of these capacities of televangelism are capacities inherent to the medium of television.

Television helps build a network among conservative Christian viewers scattered among conservative churches and denominations and scattered throughout the country. Along with electronic mailings, other publications, rallies, etc., television offers a communication link. Television provides information on political organizations and activities in which viewers can participate, for example the Moral Majority and the Christian Coalition, and the political rallies and voting efforts they promote. Televangelism opens up lines of communication among the different subgroups that make up conservative Christianity and creates among them a sense of common identity. These were vital to the revitalization of conservative religion as a social movement and vital to the Religious Right.

> ...Evangelical broadcasts have provided the wherewithal for evangelicals all across America to develop a national, common sense of self. Through the instrumentality of Christian television, the scattered evangelical flock is receiving and accepting the message that it is socially acceptable to be an evangelical. The television not only tells them, it also shows them that they 'are one in the Lord, and [they] are strong in the power of his might.' /.../ Through the melding power of religious broadcasting, evangelicals from Maine to Florida, Alabama to California, Texas to Rhode Island, and throughout all of America, are being told and shown that they are not a small, isolated group of religious eccentrics. Religious broadcasters claim that God has returned to modern society and He is using television to 'gather the remnant of [his] flock (Jeremiah 23:3).' [197]

Televangelism also builds a movement among conservative Christian viewers as it communicates and reinforces the message of conservative Christianity. Television provides reinforcement through "teleconditioning," or the repeated exposure television allows.[198] Reinforcement comes by way of ritual repetition of the message.[199] Another important reinforcement provided by television is its "reality-making" capacity.[200] Television reinforces the message by creating the image that the message communicated is "reality." Television creates the impression that what is seen and heard is objective reality. The "reality" or image of reality created is backed up by cultural myths that grow out of society's definition of what reality is.[201] Television expresses viewers' own views and values.[202] It also provides important reinforcement.

Televangelism's role in communicating and reinforcing conservative Christian belief is well known.[203] Televangelism and the message of Bible-believing, millenarian Christianity are inseparable.[204] Unremittingly and tirelessly presented is the belief that the world is a stage for an ongoing cosmic battle between God and Satan, that conservative Christians are caught up in the final stage of the battle, that Satan has enlisted secular society to persecute conservative Christians, that Christians will play a critical role in the defeat of Satan and his secular ally as they push for the moral regeneration of secular society, and that

God will reward his faithful people for helping to defeat Satan with a share in his rule over a redeemed world.[205] The religious message is presented through a variety of elements which make up the telecasts: songs, prayers, meditations, testimonials, sermons, etc. The message of conservative Christianity is often presented in its entirety in highly dramatic sermons, shorter homilies, testimonials, and prayers. When it is not, the whole of the message is communicated through various images that symbolize it, both verbal images and visual ones: the cross, the Bible, etc. The cross symbolizes God's victory over sin as well as the redemption of the world and final victory over Satan in the near future. Or the message is communicated through symbolic acts, such as praying, giving a testimonial, responding to an altar call, or speaking in tongues.

Conservative Christian belief is reinforced through intellectual argument. The case is made that the religious beliefs and morality communicated are true, because they are based on God's revealed truth, which is found in the Bible televangelism's followers live by. The Bible is prominently displayed in the television programs. Conservative Christianity is thereby made congruent with the divine order.

Televangelism presents images or impressions that reinforce conservative Christian beliefs about the world. A dominant image is the authenticity or authority of conservative Christian belief. Also dominant is the image of the faithfulness or integrity of Bible-believing Christians. Another dominant image is that conservative Christians are persecuted by the world for standing up for their beliefs but are supported by God for their efforts. Conservative Christians are portrayed as a kind of David, facing an overwhelming power: secular society, especially the secular state, a Goliath. The secular courts, legislative bodies, the press, and civil libertarian groups are all portrayed as persecutors of conservative Christians. Actual images or pictures shown on the screen help create these images or impressions: pictures of police arrests of "pro-life" activists, pictures of activists who have been arrested in confinement, etc.

Another dominant image is that conservative Christians are winning some victories in their battle against the secular world with God's help. Conservative Christians are presented as growing in political influence. Falwell and Robertson are presented as cutting a powerful figure within the arena of American politics. They are portrayed as powerful leaders of conservative Christians who enjoy the ear of Presidents, congressional leaders, or powerful political figures. There are frequent pictures of the televangelists standing in front of the Capitol building, leading rallies on the steps of the Capitol. They are shown on the political stump in their role as leaders of the Religious Right. The image of power is reinforced by the use of the medium itself, which by its very presence on the national scene represents power for the conservative Christians.[206] Conservative Christians are portrayed as an unstoppable army whom God is raising up and through whom God is working to accomplish his purposes in the world. They are portrayed as eventual victors over the world.

As conservative Christian belief and its world view is authenticated, the style of life correlated with it, which hinges on biblical morality, is also made authentic. The conservative Christian lifestyle is shown to be a reasonable strategy for negotiating the world, because it is shown to be effective in dealing with the world as described by millenarian belief. The conservative Christian world view is in turn reinforced, when the world is shown to accommodate the life guided by biblical principles. World view and lifestyle are shown to go hand in hand.[207]

Communicating endlessly the message of conservative Christianity, and presenting images and impressions along with intellectual arguments that reinforce it, is only one level on which televangelism reinforces its religious message. Televangelism does not appeal to intellectual argument alone to create confidence in the authenticity and authority of conservative Christian belief. It also elicits emotions that ring true to the view of the world presented. These provide experiential evidence of the rightness of conservative Christianity's accounting of the world and strategy for living within it. Only then can conservative Christian belief and morality become fully authentic and authoritative models for viewing and living in the world. Reinforcement of the credibility and authority of conservative Christian belief and morality at the experiential level is critical to the efforts of televangelism's conservative Christian viewers to mobilize themselves in the attempt to bring the world in line with their religious vision of it and vision for it. Televangelism provides critical emotional and experiential reinforcement in its role as ritual performance.[208]

As a ritual performance, televangelism enhances the dramatic presentation and dramatic effect of the religious message. Introducing the programs are ritualized routines—a show's theme song is played, an announcer or emcee gives a standard greeting—that set the performances off from the everyday world. The routines help viewers undergo a transition away from the everyday world to the world as envisioned by conservative Christianity. The transition helps viewers focus on the religious message and open themselves to its dramatic presentation and emotional impact.

The ritual performances weave together all of the disparate elements of the telecasts, which present the message of conservative Christianity in bits and pieces. The performances also structure the presentation of the message to its most dramatic advantage, pacing the emotional intensity of the presentation and building to a climax. The programs keep up the emotional intensity as they move back and forth from moving testimonies and prayers, Bible readings or Bible lessons, special music or hymns, before building to a short meditation or longer sermon.

As the performances dramatize Satan's presence in the world, they arouse anxiety and even fear. Satan is stalking the earth like a lion, seeking to devour whom he may, Swaggart shouts, citing scripture. He paints a graphic picture of conservative Christians' arch enemy as he grimaces and threatens with his animated body, hurling himself toward the viewer. Swaggart is something of an actor. He uses facial and body gestures as well as inflections of the voice to bring Satan and his diabolical threat alive.

Anxiety and fear reinforce the view that Satan is alive and well and that the cosmic battle between God and Satan is being played out on the earthly stage at this very moment. These emotions make equally real Satan's battle against conservative Christians being waged through his secular ally. The emotions also confirm the view that conservative Christians are living during the last days and must not let down their guard but step up their moral battle against secular society in order to help God defeat Satan.

The attacks of secular society were illustrated in a video clip on a program of the "700 Club" showing Atlanta police dragging to waiting police vans members of "Operation Rescue" who had blocked the entrance to an abortion clinic.[209] The clip later showed the "pro-life" demonstrators incarcerated behind a high, chain-link fence. The clip was shown in conjunction with a report on the "pro-abortion" plank adopted by the 1988 Democratic National Convention, then meeting in Atlanta. The effect was to underscore the threat to "pro-family," biblical morality and its conservative Christian supporters by one of the nation's political parties.

Another program offered as further evidence of the Democratic Party's attack on biblical morality its adoption of an abortion rights as well as a "homosexual rights" plank.[210] The Party's plank in support of the Equal Rights Amendment was also mentioned. A clip showed homosexuals staging a "kiss-in" in protest against a "pro-family" forum and rally sponsored by conservative Christians and held in Atlanta alongside the Presidential convention. Patrick Buchanan, then a speech writer for President Reagan, appeared on the program as special guest commentator on the convention and the Party's Presidential candidate, Dukakis. Robertson asked him why the convention was not using the word *liberal*. Buchanan answered that the convention was "an elaborate charade" to hide the Democratic party's liberal agenda. When Robertson asked Buchanan what Dukakis' position was on "family issues," Buchanan pointed out that Dukakis had repealed Massachusetts' antisodomy law while governor. Buchanan said Dukakis' choice of running mate—Senator Lloyd Bentsen of Texas—was designed to diminish Dukakis' image as liberal.

Robertson suggested that the party was controlled by "the Far Left," noting that Dukakis' campaign manager was formerly on the staff of People for the American Way, the civil liberties advocacy organization. Robertson's co-anchor, Terry Meeuwsen, characterized the convention as "liberalism in full form" in another broadcast on the Democratic Convention aired later in the week.[211] The segment portrayed conservative Christians as defenders of biblical morality, which was said to underlie American values. It portrayed conservative Christians as holding the line against the efforts of "secular humanists" to uproot the Christian principles on which the nation was said to have been founded.

The telecast performances create emotional relief, however, as they dramatize God's protection of the faithful as they battle against Satan and the secular world. Exultation is also elicited as the telecasts dramatize God giving victories to conservative Christians in their effort to bring the nation back to its godly roots in the rule of God. The telecasts also elicit exultation when they dramatize the inevitable and imminent defeat of Satan and punishment of his secular ally. Triumphalism is aroused as God's vindication of conservative Christians and their share in his rule over the redeemed earth is dramatized. All of these emotions make God's presence equally real, reinforcing the belief that God is who he says he is, and that he will protect and bless conservative Christians in return for their faithfulness and commitment to do moral battle against Satan and the secular world.

Televangelism has played an obvious role in communicating the message of conservative Christianity. Not as obvious is televangelism's role as ritual in legitimating the message. This is critical if viewers are to return to the real world with renewed commitment to their religious vision of the world and vision for it as they engage in their holy battle against secular society. While the religious message of the television programs plays an important role in televangelism's power to mobilize viewers for battle, it is the ritual experiences created by the telecasts that activate the power of viewers' religion to move them and put them into action. The experience of their religion as a convincing and powerful vision or explanation of the world and effective and powerful strategy for negotiating it galvanizes viewers. Legitimation of their religion also supports the interest of conservative Christians in standing up for themselves as a marginalized social group as they mobilize in defense of their religion. Viewers find in the millenarian religion that lies at the heart of televangelism support for their effort to give significance to themselves as a religious and social group. They find even greater support for this effort in the legitimation of their religion made possible by televangelism in its role as ritual performance, which makes viewers' religion more convincing.

The routine sign-offs and farewells that end the telecasts help viewers make the transition back to the everyday world armed with renewed commitment to their religion. The closing segment serves as a kind of benediction, offering a prayer that viewers make it through the week, or through the night. The closing segment also reminds viewers that they are in the company of a vast community of fellow Christians whose prayers and support they can count on as they go out to face a hostile world.

## Televangelism As Ritual Adaptation

In its role as ritual legitimation, televangelism gives expression to the conservative religious and social interests of its viewers. It gives expression to their interest in the security provided by their narrowly conservative religion as they face a changing society of increasing complexity, ambiguity, and pluralism, which presents world views and life strategies that compete with those of conservative Christianity. Televangelism gives expression to an additional interest. It also gives expression to the interest of conservative Christians in adapting to a changing society. Sixty-three percent of the viewers who took part in my survey indicated that they watch the television programs in order to help them understand today's changing society. Thirty-two percent reported that they watch in order to help them learn how to fit better into a changing society. These competing interests express the ambivalence of conservative Christians toward mainstream, secular society, as well as their ambivalence toward their religion and religious group.

Televangelism has the capacity to help viewers broaden their horizons. Television's capacity to enlarge viewers' awareness of the world is well known. Television reports on the wider world. The exposure to new content has the capacity to change former views and values.[212] As ritual transition to an alternative context, the religious telecasts relax viewers' commitment to former beliefs and attitudes, allowing them to entertain new possibilities.

Stewart Hoover observes that programs like Robertson's "700 Club" have helped transform the consciousness of conservative Christian viewers. The programs, he notes, have moved viewers away from the "insularity" and "particularism" of traditional or sectarian roots of conservative Christianity. Coming from "outside their [the viewers'] local frames of reference," the telecasts promote a "translocalism" that transcends viewers' own beliefs. The programs introduce a range of perspectives on Christian doctrine, represented by hosts and guests, often during the same telecast. The programs move viewers toward a religion that is more open to the universe of the Christian religion, more aware and accepting of the diversity of religious belief and doctrine within Christianity, and more aware of the parochial character of traditional forms of Christian fundamentalism, which offer limited views. The programs also make viewers more aware of and open to the wider world.[213]

> Coming as they do from the 'right bank' of mainstream American Protestantism and American culture, even so seemingly (to the mainstream) closed and conservative a witness as the *700 Club* serves to open, even liberalize their [viewers'] view of the world, and their faith.[214]

> ...Religious broadcasting has been at the center of reformulation of the fundamentalist worldview.... Religious broadcasting today reflects a universalizing of claims that were once dogmatic. /.../ The electronic church...[is] transforming traditional symbols, structure, and relationships.[215]

Hoover sees the broadening effect of televangelism as vital to the revitalization of conservative Christianity, which won new interest during the 1980s as a response to growing discomfort with the dissonance or gap between the traditional values and beliefs of conservative Christians and a culture in runaway change and crisis. Broadening conservative religious belief and opening it up to respond to social issues and political developments within the wider world helped make it more vital.[216]

Hoover observes that the "broadening and universalizing" of viewers' religious outlook[217] grows out of televangelism's ritual base. He was the first to make this observation. He was also the first to recognize the ritual nature of televangelism.

> ...They [viewers] need to find for themselves a sense of wider possibility,...for reorganization of meaning, in order to move along their life trajectories. This sense of possibility is made real...for them when it emerges from a ritualized experience, the liminal, where they are able to see beyond the restrictive structures and meanings of the past.[218]

Hoover has other interests, however, and does not pursue the point. He draws from Victor Turner's observations of ritual.[219]

The conventional understanding of ritual is that it keeps things in place. Turner has observed that ritual is primarily a vehicle of social change.[220] The capacity of ritual to promote change, Turner has noted, lies in its "liminal" nature. Ritual puts the established world in limbo as it makes a transition away from the everyday world to an alternative context. Ritual transition relaxes, if it never completely annihilates, the seemingly fixed assumptions about the way in which the world is put together as well as the rules and duties that regulate everyday routine and people's obligations to it. In the process, ritual permits and invites participants to open themselves to and to experiment with new ways of conceiving the world as well as their relationships to one another, including those that compete with the routines and norms in place within the everyday world.

As ritual, televangelism offers its conservative Christian viewers a nonthreatening, alternative context within which to open themselves to the wider world and explore ways of looking at the world and of living in it that are more in keeping with the secularized views and lifestyle of a changing American society. The alternative ritual framework invites viewers to relax their grip on their conservative religion and its world-condemning position, by which they identify and define themselves within the everyday world as they battle against secular society.

With one hand, viewers hold onto their conservative religion. As they carry their interest in adapting themselves to the wider world into their viewing, ritual invites them to let go of their obligation to their religion with the other hand. The alternative ritual context invites viewers to lower their guard against the threatening and hostile world, to open themselves to learn more about competing views on social and political issues. Televangelism has helped to make its conservative Christian viewers more interested in the world of politics and has helped them to become more politically involved. It has also helped them open themselves to and experiment with attitudes, dress, language, music, and aesthetic sensibilities of the secular world which fundamentalism and Pentecostalism have traditionally opposed.

Televangelism routinely reports on and discusses social and political issues and developments taking place within American society and the wider world. Robertson's program includes a news segment and discussion and analysis of news, including international developments. Falwell offers extended commentary and some analysis. Swaggart and the Bakkers offer far less commentary and analysis. The reports and discussion are always accompanied by commentary from the conservative Christian perspective and are given new, religious meaning. The events and developments reported are often set against the backdrop of millenarian religion and presented as the workings of Satan in the world. The reports nevertheless provide information about important issues and developments within the wider social and political world, familiarizing viewers with the wider world. The reports also acquaint viewers with points of view on social and political issues that compete with the conservative Christian view. They acquaint viewers with the reasoning behind the opposing views, and with the various parties involved.

Additional exposure to the wider world comes with reports on and discussions of pressures and challenges presented by that world to conservative Christian belief and morality and to its general way of life. There is discussion of pressures on marriage, discussion of problems related to rearing children who face the pressure to experiment with drugs and alcohol, etc. Robertson's program takes the lead in this discussion, but all of the programs touch on these problems in one way or another. Robertson's program also discusses the national economy, financial investment, running a business, and other economic and job-related issues and developments.

The television programs familiarize viewers with aesthetic sensibilities of the secular world as they make use of the aesthetics of commercial and public television. Televangelism often looks like secular television. This is especially true of the "700 Club" and the "PTL Club," which have consciously mimicked the aesthetics of commercial and public television. These programs incorporate upbeat, light-rock and pop music, as well as dazzling, computer generated visuals. The "700 Club" makes the greatest use of background or incidental music. Unlike the other programs, it does not make use of a choir, band, or soloists. All of the other shows regularly program "Christian music," which sets Christian lyrics to upbeat, light-rock and pop music. The same music is played on Christian radio stations. The other three shows also incorporate new gospel music that is more uptempo than the gospel music of yesteryear. The production values of all of the programs are state-of-the-art. The production technology needed to produce them is state-of-the-art as well. These make the programs all the more captivating.

Some of the programs have also mimicked the formats of commercial television. Robertson's program is patterned after the magazine show and talk show. It opens with a news segment, delivered by Robertson, which includes videotaped reporting from the field. His program then moves on to extended interviews with guests on some current social issue or topic of relevance to viewers, both religious and otherwise. Robertson is joined on the program by a co-host, more recently a woman. The Bakkers' program imitated the talk-show and entertainment- or variety-show formats. The Robertson and Bakker ministries have made no secret of wanting to update format in order to attract a wider audience outside of the traditional pool of conservative Christian viewers, as well as younger viewers.

Falwell's and Swaggart's telecasts make use of state-of-the-art production values but mimic secular television far less. Their programs are edited versions of actual church worship services, or in the case of Swaggart, evangelistic crusades.

The telecasts also familiarize viewers with the current dress, hairstyle, make-up, lingo, and attitudes of the secular world. These are introduced by hosts and guests, many of whom are personalities in the entertainment world, sports heroes, successful business entrepreneurs, the occasional politician, or Christian authors, musicians, or entertainers. In the process, the programs familiarize viewers with mainstream American enjoyment, pleasure, and creature comfort.

Televangelism creates the image that conservative Christians are a people who fit comfortably within the wider world. When Terry Meeuwsen was his co-host, Robertson would occasionally remind the audience that she was a former Miss America. Robertson comes across as urbane. The Bakkers come across as fun-loving and feeling right at home in the world. Although Falwell and Swaggart keep their distance from the secular lifestyle, they, too, are shown smartly dressed. All of the audiences shown on the programs look very middle class, helping to establish the impression that conservative Christians are educated, successful, and well-adjusted people.

Use of the medium of television also enhances the image of conservative Christians as comfortable and successful. Use of television, and state-of-the-art technology and programming at that, contributes to the impression that conservative Christians possess the sensibilities as well as technological knowledge, financial resources, and the legal and business acumen needed to keep up with the secular world.

Images of power and success communicate to conservative Christian viewers, "you are somebody." Televangelism has created a new self-image for a social group that has existed "on the lower social edges of middle-class America...isolated from the mainstream of society." The raised self-esteem has helped bring conservative Christians "out of their religious, social and political closets" and into the public square.[221] Along with images of success, the adaptation televangelism as ritual has made possible for televangelism's conservative Christian viewers has helped them cast off the image of backward, social misfits and outsiders and demand that secular society take them seriously as a social group.

The image of citizen of the wider world stands in tension with that of God's righteous opponents of the secular world, however. The effort of televangelism's viewers to adapt themselves to secular, mainstream society is undercut by the legitimation of their religion and religious group. Self-legitimation as a community of the saved promotes an exclusionary stance toward the wider society. The "us-versus-them" distinction encourages conservative Christians to hold themselves separate and apart, closing them off from those outside the fold. Self-legitimation is a strategy of fighting against a society that is closed to their religion and to their religious group by creating another closed society.

The very marginalized social standing of conservative Christians that encourages them to legitimate their religion and religious group for themselves in the face of challenge and opposition by mainstream society also encourages them to adapt to the social mainstream in hopes of winning greater inclusion. Religious conservatives are pulled in two opposed directions at the same time. They are pulled by their religion and by their interest as a social group in overturning their marginalized status. They carry their ambivalence with them into their viewing, simultaneously engaging capacities of ritual that produce opposite results. The adjustments they make to mainstream society are, consequently, tentative.

# ⪥ 8 ⪥

## Ritual in the Search for
## Human Community

### *Televangelism's Community-building Possibilities*

The interest of televangelism's conservative Christian viewers in legitimating their religion and religious group for themselves includes an interest in building community among themselves. A sense of shared belief and purpose and of mutual support helps televangelism's viewers face the threat to their religion and religious group posed by mainstream, secular American society, as well as face its opposition. A sense of common belief and purpose, together with a sense of support from other viewers, are critical to the efforts of these conservative Christians to mobilize themselves in defense of their religion and their religious group. In addition, a sense of community with other viewers fills the need for human community not met in the conservative Christians' relations with mainstream society. They are a marginalized social group. A sense of community with others who are treated as outsiders by mainstream society provides a needed sense of acceptance, as well as support for the efforts of these conservative Christians to stand up for their social group. A sense of community also provides encouragement as they explore and adapt to the wider, secular society in their effort to fit into it more comfortably and gain greater social acceptance.

The television ministries are interested in building a sense of community among viewers in order to build up a following for the television programs as well as gain their financial support. The television ministries tap the interest of viewers in extending their involvement in the community of fellow conservative Christians and in the various missions and outreach projects of the Christian community, including those in which the television ministries are engaged.[222]

To be sure, televangelism's viewers have personal reasons for tuning in to the television shows. The most popular religious programs give a great deal of attention to personal problems:[223] illness, death, the loss of a job, financial worries, marriage problems, problems rearing children who live in a permissive society, and all manner of spiritual crises.[224] A sense of community is also important for these viewers, who look to fellow conservative Christians for a sense of support as they face their personal problems. Conservative Christians often see the crises they undergo as a test of their faith, making all the more attractive the support of other conservative Christians for viewers undergoing personal problems and crises.

Seventy-nine percent of the viewers who took part in my survey reported that they have a sense of belonging to a community of viewers watching the television programs. Seventy-eight percent think about other viewers when they watch.[225] A viewer "may watch alone, but she knows others are watching, she knows others who are watching, and they form an important part of her actual community." She also discusses what she watches with family members, and friends, along with fellow churchgoers.[226]

Stewart Hoover suggests that one of the major interests viewers have in televangelism is the possibility it offers of recovering "authentic community."[227] He suggests that televangelism's viewers are on a "quest" for a sense of "belonging," of "community," now lost in American society.[228] He writes:

> It is tempting to think that such 'traditionalism' (or 'antimodernism')...born of basic fundamentalism is at the heart of the electronic church for most viewers. It is tempting to see the fundamentalism of...[followers] as nothing more than social anomie or dissatisfaction. These viewers do share with many Americans, evangelical and not, a sense that something has gone wrong with the promise of modernity.... There is more going on here, though. There is a...personal dimension that *underlies* the more social or political ones. /.../ In a secular world where meaning is most often sought in therapy, materialistic individualism, or in the artificial communities of work

or vicarious escape, many of these people seem grounded in 'community' of a sort that is only a memory to most Americans.[229]

Hoover suggests that the breakdown of community within American society, which is increasingly marked by social division and cultural crisis, helps lead viewers to look to televangelism because it offers the ideal of universal human community. He sees the interest in universal community as bound up with the efforts of viewers to broaden their religious outlook, which includes taking into account the wider social world.[230] The ideal of universal human community is expressed in the millenarian vision of conservative Christianity. It looks forward to the time when the entire world will be redeemed and united under the reign and rule of God.[231]

The interest of televangelism's viewers in human community is also motivated by their marginalized standing within mainstream American society. They seek to create among themselves the human community they do not experience in their encounters with mainstream American society, which holds them at arm's length, given their commitment to a judgmental and exclusionary religion and morality that runs counter to its democratic ideal and pluralistic make-up. Holding themselves separate and apart, encouraged by their separatist religion, also keeps conservative Christians from enjoying community with the wider society.

Televangelism's viewers also bring to their viewing an interest in a form of community that is not dependent upon or equivalent to agreement in religious belief, or even group affiliation, which are the bases of viewers' sense of religious community and of community with a common social group. Viewers bring to their viewing an interest in a more basic form of community. They also bring their interest in human community, in direct, open, and open-ended human encounter, one that recognizes and supports their full humanity, equality, and self-determination. Viewers' interest in basic human community is accentuated by their social marginalization.

Television offers a natural vehicle for building a sense of community with other viewers. Television builds a sense of "commonality" among its mass audience as it communicates values they share as members of a common society.[232] Televangelism builds a sense of commonality among viewers as it communicates the values and beliefs of conservative Christianity, which they hold in common.

Television helps to create a sense of community among televangelism's viewers in other ways. It gives them an opportunity to see and hear from one another. Viewers who follow one program or another are often brought on a program as special guests. These viewers will have often written to the television ministry about some problem or crisis it helped them overcome by discussing that very problem and giving encouragement to those facing it or similar problems. Or viewers brought on as guests will have written to report a miraculous deliverance from a problem or crisis after requesting prayer support from the ministry.

Calls from those viewing at home are often taken directly on the air. Callers phone in to ask the host or guests questions about social or political issues or about matters related to conservative Christian belief and morality. Hosts frequently speak directly on the air to a caller brought to his or her attention who has phoned in a special prayer request to telephone bank volunteers seated on the stage along with the host. Hosts very often thank viewers who have phoned in financial pledges to the phone volunteers, reading out their names and the amount they have pledged. Piles of prayer request cards, pledge cards, and other communications from viewers are sometimes displayed on the air, making viewers present to one another in an indirect way.

A sense of belonging to a community of viewers is also created as the television programs include frequent shots of the studio audience. Frequent quick shots show the audience's reactions to comments made by hosts or guests. The audience is often shown in prayer, especially when the host prays for those who have phoned in requests. In these cases the host will have often asked the studio audience to join in offering a prayer for the viewer watching at home. There are frequent close-up shots of individual members of the audience as they pray, follow along in the Bible, or listen intently. Often members of the studio audience are invited to ask questions of hosts or guests, who sometimes come out into the audience. The presence of an audience, even when not shown on the screen but made present as they applaud or sing along, provides an important sense of identification for home viewers, who see the studio audience or the audience gathered in the crusade arena as members of their community.

### Ritual Community

Televangelism is also a natural vehicle for helping viewers attempt to create community among themselves in its role as ritual. Hoover recognizes the capacity of televangelism to meet viewers' interest in community in its role as ritual, drawing on Victor Turner's observations of ritual. "Liminality [Turner's term for the openness to experimentation and to new possibilities made possible by ritual suspension of the status quo] and communitas [ritual community] are lenses through which we see the development of contemporary religious consciousness. Liminality helps individuals understand and accept new cultural possibilities [motivated by]...the desire for true, universal communitas."[233]

Turner observes that ritual is put into play in response to the breakdown of human community during times of social conflict, in response to a threat to community, or is periodically put into play to rejuvenate community.[234] He defines community as direct, or open and open-ended, and egalitarian relationships, that is to say, relationships that recognize common humanity and human equality and promote human freedom and the common good. Turner views human community and its several aspects as basic human needs.

Turner also views structured social relations as a basic human need. Women and men rely upon structured relationships—social classifications, roles, and duties—to organize themselves in order to meet their material needs. But for all of its positive benefits, social structure has its drawbacks. It defines people's identity, value, and worth too narrowly. Social structure requires people to deny their full humanity as it forces them to keep to their places within the social system and fulfill their social duties for the sake of maintaining the existing social order. Social structure deprives people of direct and open-ended human exchanges, which recognize their common humanity and equality and support the freedom to determine their own lives. Social structure distances, alienates, and exploits people, Turner observes.

Given the equal need for community and social structure, ritual's primary role, as Turner sees it, is that of creating more communitarian social arrangements within the everyday world, putting everyday social-structural arrangements in the service of human community, human equality, and the common good.

The capacity of ritual to create community and to promote social change in the direction of greater human community grows out of its liminal nature, Turner notes. He observes that ritual puts the established world in limbo as it makes a transition away from the everyday world to an alternative context. Ritual transition relaxes the seemingly fixed assumptions about the way in which the world is put together as well as the rules and duties that regulate everyday routine: "role, status, reputation, class, caste, sex or other structural niche."[235] Ritual is:

> quintessentially, a time and place lodged between all times and spaces governed...by the rules of law, politics, and religion, and by economic necessity. Here the cognitive schemata that give sense to everyday life no longer apply, but are, as it were, suspended.[236]

As a result, participants are "liberated" from social classification and social duty.[237] Transition to an alternative context makes possible more spontaneous and immediate, more direct and open human encounters. There, participants experience a directness and an openness, and along with these a sense of shared humanity and human equality not possible in encounters that are guided by obligation to social status or hierarchy, or by social groupings that divide them. In the process, ritual permits and invites those engaged in it to experiment with new, more communitarian ways of conceiving the world and their relationships to one another, including those that compete with routines and norms in place within the everyday world. The freedom, spontaneity, and directness of ritual liminality give rise to human community.

Stepping back from everyday social structure also allows women and men to reflect on the status quo and to assess the adequacy of the social arrangements in place as instruments of human community. Ritual invites experimentation with alternative social arrangements, ones that better promote community. These can then be put in place within the everyday world.

The use of ritual to restore the existing social order by reinvigorating or imposing established roles, duties, and social divisions is well known, Turner observes. Ritual is often used to step aside from conflict and to remind people of the advantages of sticking to their places within a social system. It is used to recount the benefits of keeping to one's social role, namely a sense of stability or order. But these uses keep tight rein on ritual liminality and on its radically transformative potential.

When ritual is used to reinforce or legitimate an existing social structure, Turner argues, it has been "circumscribed, ...pressed into the service of maintaining the existing order" as over against communitarian ends.[238] Turner goes on to argue that, even when co-opted, ritual remains potentially subversive of the existing social order, since ritual stands essentially opposed to social structure. Ritual, he argues, is basically or inherently "anti-structure," given its liminal and communitarian features. Ritual's relation to social structure is thus a dialectical one.

Ritual emerges in response to the limitations social structure places on human community, transforming an existing social structure as it redirects social relations toward communitarian ends. The experience of human community infuses or has the potential to infuse everyday social roles and duties with communitarian values and purpose, making everyday social-structural relations more communitarian, at least temporarily, until the demands of social structure erode community.

As the ritual of a marginalized social group, televangelism does not have the capacity to create community with those outside the group of conservative Christians who participate in it. Televangelism does have the potential, however, to promote open, human community among viewers in its role as ritual. Viewers are invited to open themselves and bring their full humanity to their viewing along with their interest in human community as they undergo a ritual transition away from the everyday world to the alternative ritual context. Viewers are invited to bring to their viewing their interest in being accepted fully, being treated as an equal, and being supported in their efforts to determine their own lives.

As ritual, televangelism invites viewers to express these interests over the air as they phone in prayer requests or phone in questions for hosts or guests. Many of the requests and questions posed are concerned with lack of full acceptance as conservative Christians and as human beings, and with the need for acceptance and support. Viewers are also invited to express these interests when they appear on the television programs as special guests, or when they ask questions of the hosts or guests as members of the studio audience. As viewers open themselves to their own humanity and interest in being included in human community, they are also invited to open themselves to the humanity and interest in human community expressed by other viewers. In the process of opening themselves to these interests and expressing them, viewers create community with one another, if in limited ways.

## Limits Televangelism Places on Community

Televangelism's role as ritual legitimation of the conservative Christian religion and of their religious group undercuts viewers' efforts to create open community among themselves, however. Conservative Christianity promotes "fellowship" among believers. It also places restrictions or boundaries on relations among believers that work against open and open-ended encounter. Televangelism passes these along.

Conservative Christianity holds believers to strict biblical injunctions that guide their relations with one another. It teaches that these guidelines have been given by God himself in order to promote his purposes for women and men. It also teaches that the injunctions have been given in order to distinguish believers from the members of the secular world. Strict adherence to biblical norms also enables televangelism's conservative Christian viewers to enhance, in their own eyes, their social status as a religious group. Following God's guidelines wins God's special favor, they believe, earning for themselves in their own eyes special status as a social group.

Conservative Christians follow the biblical admonishment that women not fail to subject themselves to male authority, for example. They believe that wives are to subject themselves to their husbands. They reject the ordination of women, or the inclusion of women as church deacons. This attitude is reflected in the relative absence of women as central figures in the religious telecasts and in the lack of leadership roles for women who do appear.[239] The subservient role assigned women is carried over into the conservative Christians' "pro-family" morality.

Conservative religion makes further distinctions among Christians. Fundamentalists distinguish between "spiritual Christians" or those "on fire for the Lord" and less spiritual Christians. They follow the biblical distinction between those who are "hot," "warm," or "cold" for the Lord, warm being the worst, since those who are warm are considered indifferent. Pentecostals distinguish "spirit-filled Christians" from the less spirit-filled. They also distinguish among the various spiritual gifts, in spite of the New Testament admonition not to rank above others those with higher spiritual gifts (speaking in tongues, prophecy, etc.). Those who are spiritually zealous or spiritually gifted drive a wedge between themselves and members of the body of believers who are neither.

"Christian fellowship," or the "family of God," are beloved images of community and support among conservative Christians. The image of fellowship is an ideal. In practice, "fellowship" among conservative Christians promotes keeping to one's place within the community as defined by the Bible, or distinguishing among members. In practice, "fellowship" carries a threat. Those who do not follow the strict guidelines expected of conservative Christians put themselves in the position of receiving the same condemnation reserved for those who live according to the ways of the secular world. The worthiness of those who are less spiritual or who do not follow the biblical injunctions for inclusion in Christian fellowship is called into question. The coerciveness of conservative Christian relations works against open human community.

Open community is also limited by conservative Christianity's hierarchical, minister-centered arrangement of power. The pattern carries over into televangelism. Power is concentrated at the top among the television ministers. It is not shared or spread among followers of the television ministries. This is demonstrated most dramatically in the financial and sexual scandals that recently shook televangelism off of its foundations. The incidents demonstrated a lack of accountability of the television ministers and the leadership of the television ministries to viewers. The incidents prompted the National Religious Broadcasters to put in place more stringent guidelines for financial and ethical accountability of television ministries affiliated with the association.

The medium of television places additional restrictions on community among televangelism's viewers. The distancing of viewers from one another forced by the medium robs televangelism of the immediacy of direct encounter. Viewers cannot engage in direct give and take with one another. They cannot interact spontaneously. Televangelism is missing the spontaneity and free flow or reciprocity of direct, face-to-face, physical encounter, ritual's primary mode. As a result, televangelism robs exchanges among viewers of the openness and open-endedness of direct human encounter. Televangelism puts viewers in indirect contact with one another. Viewers see or hear other viewers on the programs. But they are unable to embody community. As Steve Bruce has observed:

> To a limited degree, televangelism creates a sense of fellowship or communion among its viewers but it is still an impersonal medium and the vital stimulation of actually being part of the mass, the crowd, the living community which in unison sings 'Just as I am' or some such gospel anthem, is missing.[240]

Televangelism also undercuts the effort of its conservative Christian viewers to create greater community with mainstream American society. The effort is undercut by ritual legitimation of their religious community for themselves as a distinctive, exclusive, and exclusionary community of the saved. Self-legitimation encourages them to hold themselves separate and apart, provoking rebuff and outright opposition by mainstream society. The conservative Christians fight a society that is closed to their religion and to their religious group by building another closed society.

The effort of the religious conservatives to adapt to mainstream society gives evidence that they remain interested in greater community with the larger society. The pull of their religion, which is found front and center in televangelism, prevents complete openness toward mainstream society. The cost of joining the secular world is thought to be too high: the weakening of faith, and along with this, loss of acceptance by the community of the saved. In addition there is the cost of the loss of support by conservative Christians needed to face a harsh, threatening, and uncertain world.

The ongoing social struggle between conservative Christians and mainstream society leads them to carry with them into their engagement with televangelism as ritual both their interest in adaptation and in self-legitimation. Ritual does not annihilate the everyday world, or the tensions and cross-pressures participants feel, even if it relaxes them. Unable to create greater human community with secular, mainstream society, televangelism's conservative Christian viewers resort to attempting to create human community on their own. Unable to experience it fully among themselves, and still wanting community with mainstream society, as well as the full acceptance, equality, and freedom made possible by human community, viewers continue to engage in their struggle for social acceptance by the wider society and social inclusion within it.

## ⊰ Part Three ⊱

## The Television Programs

The remainder of this book discusses the television programs. Each of the programs is offered as illustrative of one or another of televangelism's ritual roles: legitimation of conservative Christianity and conservative Christians, adaptation of religious conservatives to mainstream society, and community. All of the programs fulfill these roles. Each, however, emphasizes one or another of televangelism's roles as ritual. Falwell's "The Old-Time Gospel Hour" represents televangelism's role as ritual legitimation. Robertson's "700 Club" represents televangelism's role as ritual adaptation. Swaggart's "Jimmy Swaggart" and the Bakkers' "PTL Club" and "The Jim and Tammy Show" represent televangelism's role as ritual community. Swaggart's program is offered as illustrative of televangelism's narrow interest in community: the banding together of the "saved" in order to go on the offensive against the secular world. The Bakkers' telecasts are offered as illustrative of another narrow interest in community, but one that moves in the opposite direction: the banding together of the "persecuted" who seek refuge from the world.

# ⊰ 9 ⊱

## "The Old-Time Gospel Hour": Ritual in the Service of Legitimation

*Defense and Offense against the Secular World*

A television viewer who accidentally turns the dial to "The Old-Time Gospel Hour" will have no difficulty recognizing that she is watching a broadcast of a Sunday morning church service. The program is an edited video tape of the Sunday morning worship service at Jerry Falwell's Thomas Road Baptist Church in Lynchburg, Virginia. She sees a real church auditorium. She sees and hears an actual liturgy, with prayers, scripture reading, and singing, lots of prayers, scripture, and singing. "Thank God for Gospel music!" the minister in the pulpit declares.[241] And she hears a half-hour sermon, preached by Falwell, pastor of the congregation gathered in worship. If she had any doubts that she had tuned in to a fundamentalist Christian broadcast, she would cease to have them once she heard the sermon, even if she did not know who Falwell was. The sermon, like the message of the music, scripture reading, and prayer, is gospel-centered and emphasizes biblical morality. The sermon is distinguished by its Bible-centered emphasis on sin, salvation, and political activism in the service of moral reform.

"The Old-Time Gospel Hour" is what it says it is. It is the preaching of the gospel. But it is preaching of the gospel according to fundamentalist Christianity. Here no room is given to interpretations of Christian scripture or Christian gospel that compete with its own. Nor is any room given to competing views of the world. The world view presented is embedded in a fundamentalist reading of Christian scripture. While the program allows that there are competing views, it tells the fundamentalist Christian side of things. The program presents fundamentalist Christian belief as the gospel truth, because, it is said, it is rooted in the Bible, God's inerrant word. Likewise, fundamentalist morality is presented as the only possible lifestyle, because it is rooted in biblical morality. The authority of the Bible is transferred to fundamentalist Christian belief and morality. Fundamentalist Christians are presented as righteous upholders of God's Word and of God's ways in the world, and, consequently, as heirs to God's promise of victory over Satan and the world, and to a share in God's future rule, which will extend to the ends of the earth.

The program emphasizes the millenarian, apocalyptic vision of the world and the vision for it found in Christian scripture. There is condemnation of the sinful, secular world. There is also a reminder that the world is an accomplice of Satan and of Satan's effort to defeat God and his plans to redeem a lost world that has turned against God. There is a reminder that conservative Christians are agents of God in the world, that God works to bring the world back to himself through their effort to lead the secular world to moral regeneration and repentance. There is a reminder that the attacks on God's servants by the world are masterminded by Satan as an effort to defeat God by defeating his people. There is a reminder that Satan has stepped up his attacks on God's servants during these last days in the final phase of the ongoing cosmic battle between God and Satan for rule over God's creation being played out on the human stage. Conservative Christians are reminded that God will sustain them in their battle against an immoral world, and that Satan will ultimately be defeated. And they are reminded that they will ultimately enjoy victory over the world. They are reminded that they will be vindicated upon the return of Christ, who will judge the lost, who continue to side with Satan, and who will give Christians a share in God's rule over a redeemed world. And there is a reminder that Christ's return is imminent.

The program also weds the millenarian vision with the vision of and vision for America held by the Religious Right. "The Old-Time Gospel Hour" has been a major platform of the Religious Right and has promoted its political interests. These are found front and center in the program. Falwell, the man in the pulpit, is a chief spokesman for the movement and uses the platform to express its views, especially as they are articulated by the Moral Majority, the political lobby he founded. Viewers are informed of political events, pending and enacted legislation, court decisions, and the activities of various political groups. They are also informed of opportunities to get involved within the political arena. They are told about political rallies sponsored by the Religious Right, "I Love America Rallies" being held across the country, including rallies before the nation's Capitol building, campaign drives, drives to defeat liberal candidates for office or "liberal" legislation, lobbying efforts, political fundraising opportunities, and the like. "We must learn the issues," Falwell tells his hearers.242

The program portrays conservative Christians as standing in the long line of the nation's founders, who are said to have established its foundations on Christian belief and morality. Conservative Christians are portrayed as bringing a nation that has strayed off course back to its "Christian" origins. They are depicted as moral reformers who are restoring the nation to its original role as God's agent in the world. The nation must return to godly morality if it is to remain free, if it is not to be taken over by godless "secular humanists," and if it is to use its freedom to preach the gospel to the world. God will punish America by taking away its freedom if it does not return to its godly roots, the program reminds viewers. Falwell, who refers to the United States as "the greatest nation on earth," is seen wearing an American flag pin in his lapel, just above a "Jesus First" pin. The ministry gives the religious pin to its "Faith Partners."243

The American flag is displayed in video clips or graphics. It is also displayed on the platform directly behind the pulpit, opposite the Christian flag, the two flags flanking the baptistery. The logo that introduces the show incorporates the Liberty Bell, a reference to the name of the television ministry: Liberty Broadcasting Network.

"The Old-Time Gospel Hour" is more than fundamentalist Christian preaching and worship. It is a ritual performance that offers legitimation for conservative Christians of their religion and their religious group. This is critical in the face of threats and opposition from the secular world, and critical to the efforts of conservative Christians to mobilize themselves in order to defend their religion and religious group, especially on the political front.

The religious message provides reinforcement by reminding the audience of conservative Christian beliefs and by presenting intellectual arguments in support of them. The dramatic presentation of the message of millenarianism in scripture reading, song, prayer, testimony, images, and symbols, as well as the sermon, arouses certain emotions among the audience. The picture painted of conservative Christians under siege by Satan and the secular world and of the increasing dismantling of traditional morality by "secular humanists" intent on spreading immorality arouses anxiety and even fear. These emotions support the message that Satan is alive and well and living on planet earth, and that Christians must not let down their guard. The message of eventual triumph and vindication over the world produces a sense of relief and exultation, even triumphalism, making God's presence, support, and promise for the future equally real.

These emotions ring true to the apocalyptic view of the world presented in the religious message, providing experiential evidence for the audience that the message is trustworthy. They experience the world as it is described in the religious message. Anxiety also works together with exultation to win the commitment of viewers to join the holy war against the secular world, especially that being waged by the Religious Right. Ritual legitimation of the message creates the confidence needed to battle the secular world.

### Ritual Legitimation

The opening of "The Old-Time Gospel Hour" helps viewers make a transition away from the troubling world of competing beliefs and confusion in moral purpose or outright immorality to the alternative world constructed along the lines of the fundamentalist vision presented in Christian worship. An aerial shot of the exterior of the Thomas Road Baptist Church is the first image viewers see. The church is a sprawling complex, anchored by a massive auditorium that holds 4,000 worshipers. While the aerial shot is run, an announcer welcomes viewers to the regular Sunday morning worship service of the Thomas Road Church, which, he points out, is already in progress. The congregation gathered in worship is heard in the background singing a rousing opening hymn. The announcer introduces the topic of Falwell's sermon, which addresses some moral theme or social issue. Falwell sometimes appears in the opening in a pretaped clip, makes a short comment on the day's theme, and invites viewers to stay tuned. The opening often introduces the theme through a videotaped teaser. Sometimes the opening will show a clip from national network news of some political event or development.

"In just a little while," Falwell tells viewers in a video clip taped earlier, "four-thousand persons will fill this Thomas Road Baptist Church sanctuary and from that pulpit I'll be preaching to you and to them on 'Christian Crises.'"[244] He gestures out over an empty church auditorium toward the pulpit. "I want you to hear that message...." The opening includes a video clip of gays and lesbians picketing Falwell. A close-up is shown of a sign carried by one of the protesters. It reads, "Falwell Fascist!" The crowd is heard chanting, "Falwell, Schlafly, you will pay. We're angry people, and we're here to stay." (Phyllis Schlafly is founder of the American Eagle Forum, a women's political lobby whose major cause is opposition to the Equal Rights Amendment.) Another sign is shown which reads, "The Moral Majority has got to go." In the sermon that follows, Falwell speaks about opposition he has faced in his ministry and about the need for support among conservative Christians as they attempt to evangelize the world.

As the show progresses, Falwell appears in additional short video clips. Each gives a brief report on some incident illustrating the crisis to traditional morality rocking the nation. As the reports move from town to town, and from one end of the country to the other, the names of each city are superimposed upon the screen. Falwell is shown surrounded by dozens of small American flags. One of the crises identified is the threat of "extinction" of the "monogamous family." The real problem underlying the threat to the American family, "the cornerstone of the nation," is identified later in the program as the threat to "Bible morality." Abortion, described as "mass legalized murder," and pornography are also identified as crises. Last is the threat to the authority of the nation's leaders, who are said to have been "placed over us" by God himself. The video clips help Falwell set up the solution to moral crisis—biblical morality—to which he devotes his sermon. Later in the program Falwell announces his plans to shift his priorities away from leading the Moral Majority to pastoring his flock. The program nevertheless enables Falwell to keep up his political involvement and influence.

The openings of all of the telecasts then cut to the worship service in progress. At the top of the program the congregation is shown singing one of the beloved hymns of conservative Christianity, or a hymn is sung by the church choir: "I will sing the wondrous story of the Christ who died for me, sing it with the saints in glory, gathered by the crystal sea."[245] The format of conservative Christian worship provides an immediately recognizable and familiar context for viewers. The service is occasionally interrupted on the television screen by spots seeking financial support for the activities and opportunities of Falwell's ministry: missions, relief work, Liberty Baptist University, the Liberty Broadcasting Network, etc. Falwell appears in most of these spots.

The attentive and involved congregation gathered in the packed church auditorium is shown throughout the program. The cameras continually cut in to show the congregation looking toward the pulpit, listening, singing, reading the Bible, praying. There are many, many group shots, as well as close-ups of individuals who appear to be deeply engaged in the service. These shots help provide the viewer with a sense of identification with those gathered in worship and a sense that she or he is participating in the event itself. The shots of the teeming congregation also convey the sense that conservative Christians make up a vast army.

Falwell is then seen mounting the pulpit to give an opening prayer and extend a welcome to the congregation inside the church as well as to home viewers. He looks directly into the camera. He is a master at addressing home viewers through the camera and helping them feel included. The pulpit and the podium over which Falwell presides remain the focal point of the program. When Falwell is not seen in the pulpit, he is seen seated in a chair just behind the pulpit on the dais, along with other staff members of the church.

At the outset of the program aired just after the 1988 Democratic National Convention and just ahead of the Republican Convention, Falwell introduced the theme for the program: "What the Bible Says about Man."[246] Holding a Bible up in the air for emphasis, he reminded his hearers that the Bible was absolutely authoritative. "This book, the inerrant, infallible book, is the only one in the universe that is infallible." He congratulated the newly elected fundamentalist leadership of the Southern Baptist Convention on its victory over nonfundamentalist, moderate and liberal candidates, who represented those within the Convention who did not believe in the literal truth of scripture. Fallwell suggested that what was really at issue in the election was the infallibility of the Bible. He commented further on the election "skirmish." "Thank God those who believe this book won!" He acknowledged that the Bible was a "tough" book to accept, because it said that "we all deserve to go to hell." Falwell, Mother Teresa, John Paul the Second, none was deserving, said Falwell. He opened the service with a prayer in which he asked God to bless the telecast and give wisdom in order to turn the nation "back to you." Falwell frequently addresses God in familiar tones, and he prays frequently for God's guidance and wisdom.

Continuing with the day's theme of the authority of the Bible and biblical morality, the "LBN Singers" performed an updated version of a familiar hymn. "Tis so sweet to trust in Jesus," they sang, "just to take him at his word." The uptempo, pop "Christian music" used in the worship services is one of the few attempts made by the show to emulate the aesthetics of the secular world. A jazz band composed of drums, guitar, trumpet, saxophone, and electric organ accompanies the singers. The congregation broke out into applause when the singers and band finished. "Amens!" were heard coming from the congregation and from the staff and pastor seated on the platform. The musical group appears regularly on the show, singing several times over the course of a single telecast. The church choir also sings.

Falwell returned to the pulpit, reiterating for emphasis one of the lines from the choir special: "Oh, for grace to trust him more!" He gave a report on correspondence he had received from viewers around the country who "got saved" by watching the program. He rejoiced that they are now "God-centered" and no longer "world-centered."

The LBN Singers sang another song: "It's real, it's real, Oh, I know it's real. Praise God my doubts are settled, for I know it's real." When they had finished, Falwell called on a member of the congregation to give the offertory prayer. Applause followed the organ and piano offertory. Falwell then delivered church announcements. He again introduced the LBN Singers and commented on the song they were about to sing, quoting the scripture passage from which the song was taken (Isaiah 40:31): "Teach me Lord to wait, down on my knees, wait on thee,...wait for answered prayer." "Keep my eyes on thee. 'They that wait on the Lord shall renew their strength.'" "Every Christian ought to learn to practice this song," Falwell said. He reported that the choir had just returned from singing for the "Family Forum," held to coincide with the Democratic National Convention, and that they would sing at the "Family Forum" planned to coincide with the upcoming Republican Convention. The forums were sponsored by the Moral Majority and other organizations within the Religious Right. Applause and an audible "Amen!" from Falwell followed the special music.

Falwell returned to the subject of the "Family Forum" and invited the congregation and viewers to attend the "free celebration" when it met at the time of the Republican National Convention. He announced that the program would include "national leaders." He named William Bennett,

Secretary of Education; Congressman John Sununu; Phyllis Schlafly; and Paul Weyrick, head of the Committee for a Free Congress, a political lobby of conservative Christians. "We pray the family will win in November," he said. He pointed out that a central issue to be presented at the forum was the "pro-life" stance. Falwell then criticized politicians who supported civil rights and yet would not support "the rights of the unborn," calling their position "gross hypocrisy." He told his audience he lived for the day when both parties would adopt a pro-life position, observing that the pro-life position is already part of the official platform of the Republican Party. "Until then, it's a lot of hogwash. Whether Democrat or Republican, put that in your pipe and smoke it!" he said, drawing applause from the congregation.

Falwell then criticized Senator John Glenn, Democratic candidate for President, whose status as a "great American hero" he called into question. Falwell quoted Glenn's convention speech in which he told delegates that the "Religious Right" was not going to tell Glenn what to do. Falwell noted that Glenn had mentioned him, Jim Bakker, and Jimmy Swaggart by name. Falwell told his listeners that he considered Glenn's "pejorative" comment a personal "put down." He corrected Glenn, arguing that Bakker and Swaggart had never been part of the Christian Right.

Falwell continued to criticize Glenn, noting that two of Glenn's good friends in Congress, Barney Frank and Gerald Studd of Massachusetts, were "avowed homosexuals." "Massachusetts has a lot of things coming out of it," he joked. The congregation laughed. Falwell's joke was an indirect put-down of the Democratic Party's Presidential nominee, Dukakis, then governor of Massachusetts. The joke was also an indirect condemnation of the Democratic Party's gay-rights stance.

Falwell then launched immediately into his sermon. He began with the question, "'What is Man that thou [God] art mindful of him?'" The question, he noted, was posed by the Bible. Falwell's sermons weave together themes introduced by the prayers, testimonies, special music, etc. that have preceded it: the authority of the Bible, the need for redemption and moral regeneration, and the godly life. He began with the biblical account of human origins. The creation account found in Genesis, with its six, twenty-four-hour days, must be taken literally, he said. "Man" was produced directly by "the hand of God." This showed, Falwell argued, that men and women did not appear by accident, as "atheistic," evolutionary theory holds, whether the theory of Darwin or that of Carl Sagan, the popular scientist, whom Falwell described as a modern-day Darwin. "The Bible refutes this." He then read from the book of Genesis, raising a refute to Darwinian theory on several points. Before he reads, the scripture passages from which he reads are flashed onto the screen, along with the page numbers on which the passages appear in the "Faith Partner Bible" made available for purchase through the ministry. Falwell announces page numbers for the benefit of those following along. He is shown in an overhead shot as he reads out of the Bible.

There was a deeper issue at stake in taking the Genesis account at face value, Falwell noted. "Man" was created by God but "fell voluntarily" from a state of grace, he observed. "All are sinners," the Bible said, and as sinners everyone stood in need of moral regeneration and redemption, Falwell continued. The Bible described humans as "sinful, hopeless, hell-bound, no good," and in need of salvation. Evolutionary theory "violate[d]" the Christian understanding of "Man" as a creature sinful "by nature," as "innately bad," who "must have rebirth through faith in Jesus Christ," Falwell argued. "Man" "disobeyed" and listened to "the Devil." There was "no hope" apart from the "shed blood of Christ," which overturns human sin.

Falwell concluded with the account in Genesis of Adam's and Eve's temptation by Satan and the Fall. God gave "Man" dominion over the earth, Falwell observed, but he came under the dominion of things God did not intend him to come under the influence of, namely drugs and alcohol. God also implanted in women and men a "sense of morality," he observed. Morality was consciousness of God and of his purposes. The practice of biblical morality lead back to God and to redemption. Falwell skillfully linked morality, and fundamentalist morality in particular, with the very foundation of the world and with God's plans for the redemption of his creation.

Falwell brought his sermon to a close by returning to the battle within the Southern Baptist denomination. He observed that the recent debate within that body centered on the precise issue now before his hearers, "the integrity of the Word of God." By embracing the Bible as the literal word of God, one came to know who God was and who "Man" was in the mind and will of God: a divine creation, fallen, and in need of restoration from the immoral life and of redemption from sin. Falwell ended by quoting Christian scripture: "Ye shall know the truth, and the truth shall make you free." He again drew a link between biblical inerrancy and biblical morality. In the process he reinforced the legitimacy of fundamentalist belief and the legitimacy and urgency of the moral and political agenda put forward by the Moral Majority and the Religious Right.

Falwell has spoken openly about moral regeneration through political activism since the late 1970s. In 1979 he announced the formation of the "Moral Majority" on a telecast of "The Old-Time Gospel Hour."[247] "I believe there is a moral majority in America," Falwell said on that occasion. "We are trying to rally the moral majority behind family, home, and Bible." "We think the time has come for God's people to stand up and be counted," he declared. "I think it's high time the churches, preachers, and the Christians in America stood up courageously and said we believe in Bible morality and we want to call this nation back to God and back to Bible morality." He promised to "stir up a hornet's nest" of "Left-wingers!" Falwell spoke of God's judgment against America for abandoning biblical morality, evidence for which was found, he claimed, in "internal chaos" in the land, economic inflation, the energy crisis, and America's military inferiority. All of these were "God's way of trying to get our attention, trying to awaken us to the fact that we as a nation are not immune to the judgment of God." "God will bless this nation if we live by this book," he told viewers, holding up the Bible.

On that telecast, Falwell identified three areas targeted for moral reform during the coming year. The first was abortion. Falwell read a proposed "pro-life" amendment over the air. "We need to be pro-life in everything we do." He said there were 300,000 pastors in the country and that it was their duty to teach that abortion is a sin. Falwell later gave a sermon on the biblical condemnation of abortion. The second area identified was pornography, including sex in television and movies and in books used in the schools. The third area was sex education. He reported that specific textbooks would be identified and targeted for removal from schools. Falwell announced that over the next several weeks, telecasts would be given to the pornography issue. He also promoted the "traditional family."

In that telecast, Falwell showed a ballot being mailed out asking for people's opinions on pornography and obscene classroom textbooks, legalized abortion on demand, and sex and violence on television. Viewers were provided information on the screen about how they could write and obtain a ballot to mail back to Falwell. He noted that a display add of the ballot would be carried shortly in *The Washington Post*, the *National Inquirer*, *Star*, *Grit*, *Soap Opera Digest*, and other national publications "asking people to vote their convictions as the moral majority." He announced that the results of the ballots would be provided to Congress, the Supreme Court, the President, as well as key television advertisers, the national networks, and "all opinion makers" and "decision makers."

Falwell also spoke of challenging the threat by the Internal Revenue Service to withdraw tax exempt status from Christian schools. And he announced a "Clean Up America" campaign to be kicked off with a rally that would take place on the steps of the Capitol building. Falwell also solicited funds from viewers to support the balloting and "Clean Up America" campaigns.

"We've decided to enter the political process," Falwell explained in a later telecast, because "a little minority has been jamming their amoral lifestyle down our throats."[248] He quoted a Gallup poll reporting that 84% of all Americans believed the Ten Commandments were valid. Conservative Christians had been a "silent group" that had remained uninvolved, Falwell told his listeners. He pointed out that he had reversed his earlier view that ministers should not get involved in the politicizing of moral issues, explaining that God had "laid it on our heart to challenge the moral decadence in this nation." "God convicted me to involve pastors in bringing the nation back to morality." The conservative Christian stand was not a popular stand, Falwell continued. But it was "the right stand." The conservative Christian position knew "what is right," and "what is wrong." It possessed the "biblical plan" for rebuilding America. The nation could not experience spiritual revival unless it was convicted of sin. And it could not become convicted "if preachers don't say what it is." "All that's needed is a little holy boldness," Falwell declared.

Toward the close of the telecast, Falwell offered viewers a copy of his book, *Listen America*. The book, he told viewers, offered the biblical diagnosis of immorality in America, as well as a cure. The book identified the "cancers that are corrupting" the nation "from within." He named abortion, described as "the national sin," pornography, homosexuality, divorce, and drugs. "Can a country like ours, a superpower, be turned around?" Falwell asked rhetorically. "The answer is in 2 Chronicles 7:14." "America *can* be saved." Falwell gave a mailing address over the air where viewers could write for a free copy of the book and urged them to buy it and pass it around to their families and neighbors. He indicated that he wanted his book to have a reading by a "million or more." He went on to express his desire to see "millions" get involved as "good citizens...in making America again the nation God designed it to be. One nation, under God."

Falwell asked those "watching by TV" "to help me get out the message." He also asked them to call the number flashing on the screen and make a financial contribution to his ministry. "I would like a few million to say we're standing with you." We "can't allow the enemy to put us down." He reminded his hearers of the hard work that lay ahead during "difficult times." He also asked them to pray with him that God would give wisdom to those newly elected to office, pointing out that Christians have a mandate to pray for those in authority, because it is God who has put them in power. (Reagan had just been elected President.) Prayer was "our secret weapon," "a heavenly advantage." Falwell then led in prayer: "Help us somehow, millions of us who love you [God], help us to join hands to bring this nation back to that place where you can once more bless America. Heal our land and help us bless the world for whom your son Jesus died."

Once conservative Christians had mobilized themselves politically, Falwell's program helped them persist and remain hopeful in the face of intense and strongly negative national criticism and opposition. The telecasts addressed the criticism and went on the offensive. In a sermon titled "'No Small Stir,'" Falwell told his hearers of the intense hostility encountered by the Apostle Paul while preaching God's word to the people of Ephesus.[249] Falwell then read from the Bible passage from which the title of the sermon was taken (Acts 19), while the scripture passages were flashed onto the screen. Paul had produced "no small stir," the scripture reported. Those who do not accept the Bible "get mad" when those who take the Bible literally preach it, Falwell told his hearers. He compared the response of the ancient Ephesians to the Apostle to the response of today's "liberal churchmen" toward him for speaking out. He told viewers he received "most of his flack" not from "liberal Democrats" of the likes of Norman Lear and George McGovern but from "the blessed liberal churchmen." Suddenly fundamentalist preachers are speaking out, Falwell told his audience. "That makes the other side mad." "This is America. They can yell and scream and all the rest. But we're gonna yell and scream, too. By the way, there are more Bible-believing Christians than any other variety. We've been quiet." "The time has come when the churches and the preachers and the people of God in this country realize if we're going to change the society there will be 'no small stir!'" Falwell shouted. As he shouted, he pounded the air repeatedly for emphasis, his right hand shaped into a fist.

Falwell also mentioned receiving criticism from the press. He mentioned an item in the *Richmond Times Dispatch*, which he took to be an effort to "demean Jerry Falwell and the Moral Majority." The newspaper had taken a poll asking people, "If Jerry Falwell told you how to vote, would you do it?" "You can make a poll say whatever you want," Falwell said. He went on to say that the vast majority of Americans believed in "moral values."

The members of the press "don't take this lying down," Falwell reminded his audience in an earlier telecast.[250] On that program Falwell pulled press clippings out of a box, held them up to the camera, and read the headlines. "Ayatollahs of Religion," read one headline. "The Political Gospel according to Falwell," read another. "Manipulation of the Bible," "Clergy Oppose Trends of Right-Wing Christians," etc. "All we're trying to do is return to moral principles," Falwell told his audience. "Why are we called 'Right-wingers' when we just believe in the Judeo-Christian ethic, the family, morality?" he asked.

Falwell identified still others who had been upset by the outspokenness of "fundamentalist preachers": those who deal in pornography, drugs, and scams, "the occult," "Satan worshipers," some of whom go under the name of "hedonist," and some under the name "humanist," and along with these, abortion clinics.[251] When you "preach about sin, you get sinners upset," Falwell shouted. The gospel must be preached "without fear or favor," however. Holding up the Bible's "standard of righteousness" did not win popularity, Falwell pointed out. "One must decide whether he wants to be right or popular." Standing with God against the world always went "against the tide." "We're not supposed to be popular. We're not supposed to be attracting the masses in a way that everybody likes us." Falwell offered homosexuals as an example of disapproving hearers. "We're not to tell people what they want to hear. We're to tell them what is written in this book, the Bible," he said, holding it up for all to see. "America is not far from having 'no small stir.'" "I want to go on record saying that's good. We need to be redirected. I believe the nations of the world need to be stirred up." As he spoke, he pounded the air with his fist.

"What is the real conflict in today's world?" Falwell asked. It was not the world's hatred of the Christian; it was the conflict between Satan and Christ, he observed. "We just happen to be caught in the middle. We are God's agents. We are Christ's servants. And therefore the servants of the other leader [Satan] are aiming all of their pellets at us, because we represent him. Jesus, Lord," Falwell called out, looking upward and extending his arm into the air, his index finger pointing heavenward. "And it is a pleasure to suffer for Christ."

Falwell explained away the "assaults" and "vicious attack" on conservative Christianity by the secular world as temporary setbacks. The attacks were to be expected, he reminded his audience, since conservative Christians were fighting a divine cause. The world's "wrath" was motivated out of the recognition that conservative Christians were on the side of God, whom the world did not serve. Falwell also reminded the audience that they were not alone in fighting their battle against the world; they had God's support. And he reminded them that they would win in the end. "Knowing we have God...behind us, we'll return the nation to moral and to biblical principles." "Let's lead the way and under God turn the country around."

"Biblical fundamentalism today is coming to the forefront," Falwell had told his hearers on an earlier telecast.[252] "Bible-believing Christianity is becoming prominent. America is about to turn around, back toward God." Much later Falwell told his audience that the conservative Christian message had received an unexpected response from the "highest levels."[253] He went on to claim that there was a new "spiritual consciousness" that had not existed two years earlier. "This nation is not too far from a spiritual awakening!"

In spite of criticism and opposition to conservative Christians, the future will see the "triumph of the church," Falwell promised his audience in another telecast.[254] In the end, conservative Christians would be victorious over the world. Helping create the mood of expectancy, hope, and a spiritual high is the special music sung during the telecast. Falwell's message of triumph was followed by a stirring rendition of the song, "Triumphantly, the Church Will Rise," performed by the LBN Singers. The piece began softly and gradually built in volume and in emotional intensity. As the song progressed, it moved through several changes in key, moving to higher and higher pitches as the stanzas moved toward a climax. The trumpets accompanying the piece also grew louder. The opening stanza painted a picture of the entire universe eagerly awaiting Christ's return: "The stars dance in anticipation" as Christ "welcomes his bride." The imagery is drawn from Christian scripture, which refers to the church as the bride of Christ. The choir had earlier sung a song referring to the universe as God's throne and to the "master plan" God had for the universe he ruled.

"Triumphantly, the church will rise! Victoriously with the skies. The Father will welcome his bride. Triumphantly the church will rise!" The lead singer raised his hands in a salute to heaven throughout the piece. There was a change in key. "From every nation, souls tired from the race they've run, bruised and battered, wearied ones. Lord we shall be changed in that resurrection morn. Triumphantly the church will rise!" The singers raised their hands toward the heavens as the key changed again. "All nations will bow down, proclaiming him King. We're laying our trophies and crowns at his feet. This trip has been paid for by God's precious Lamb. Triumphantly the church will rise!" The pitch climbed even higher as the singers again raised their hands. "The Father is ready to welcome his bride. Triumphantly, the church will rise! Victoriously, up in the skies. The Father is ready to welcome his bride. Triumphantly, the church will rise!" Thunderous applause from the congregation greeted the singers as they concluded.

Every program closes with an altar call, during which Falwell asks for a "show of hands" of those who are "lost" or need prayer.[255] While the invitation continues, the program announcer returns to the air: "You have been watching 'The Old-Time Gospel Hour' originating from the Thomas Road Baptist Church in Lynchburg, Virginia." The announcer invites viewers to become a "Faith Partner" in support of the television ministry. "Join us next week for another telecast of 'The Old-Time Gospel Hour.'" The camera cuts back to the church service while he concludes. "And until then, may God richly bless you is our prayer."

"The Old-Time Gospel Hour" presents and reinforces the fundamentalist Christian view of the world and vision for it. The ritual setting, a fiery fundamentalist Christian worship service, creates distance from the world, allowing the world to be restructured along the lines of fundamentalism. How the world is presented is carefully controlled. Something of the larger world still slips in, however, in the discussion of social issues and political developments. The safety of the distance made possible by the ritual setting also allows these fundamentalist Christians to familiarize themselves with the threatening and hostile secular world reported on in the discussion of issues. The distance provided by the setting also allows them to entertain the diversity and complexity within the larger society, as they take in the diversity of moral and political points of view and choices. While the fundamentalist consciousness is legitimated anew, and fundamentalists are once again fired up to go head to head with the secular world, the consciousness of the audience for the program is challenged, and even changed. The other, secular world is presented to them through political discussion. Ritual self-legitimation stands in tensed relation to the everyday world. This ritual performance self-consciously stands over against the secular world, which never completely disappears but presents itself ever anew in opposition to it.

# ⊰ 10 ⊱

## The "700 Club": Ritual in the
## Service of Adaptation

*A Tentative Entry into a Brave New World*

The television viewer who accidentally tuned in to the "700 Club" would at first glance think he was watching a news and entertainment magazine show on commercial or public television. The show follows the typical magazine-show format. The show opens with a news report given by the host, Pat Robertson, before moving on to human interest stories, interviews with guests appearing on the program, and discussion by hosts or guests on practical and topical information, on everything from how to invest and run a business, to domestic and marital relations.

The impression is aided by the sets. One set looks like the command center of a powerful news program. Robertson is surrounded by high-tech equipment, rows of television monitors and control panels. Another set looks like a comfortable sitting room. The music used also helps create the impression. The light-rock music that opens and closes the show and brings on and off the various segments sounds like the music heard on commercial or public television.

The program looks like secular television. It is fresh and contemporary looking. The presentation is captivating, visually and aurally. It is fast-paced and entertaining. The program employs the latest in television technology and the latest in television production values. The professionalism and attractiveness of the telecasts are the result of a combination of twenty-first century technology and the careful and thoughtful planning by a young, educated, forward-looking staff and crew. The programs are extremely well made.[256]

News items are always current social issues (gay rights, for example)[257] and political events on both the national and international fronts, from developments in the Middle East[258] and in revolutionary Nicaragua,[259] for example, to Party politics[260] and the Presidential election.[261] There is reporting on Congressional legislation (for example, the military budget),[262] and on judicial decisions (judgments made on the separation of church and state).[263] There is reporting on the national budget (President Bush's trip to Europe to discuss the European economy and Third World debt).[264] During one broadcast the former chief economist with Merrill Lynch discussed federal laws on protectionism and the Federal Reserve's new strategy to deal with the national recession. Viewers phoned in questions on how they might invest in light of the recession.[265] Commercials also invited viewers to phone financial counselors employed by the television ministry. There is reporting on developments in science—the space probe was a topic on one program—and in health care (eating disorders, for example),[266] and reporting on education (the Carnegie Commission, etc.).[267]

"Straight Talk," also produced by Robertson's Christian Broadcasting Network and hosted by Scott Ross, discusses controversial social issues (abortion, for example,[268] or "values clarification" in public school)[269] or personal problems.[270] Guests holding opposite opinions and positions are invited to appear in order to debate the issues. Government legislators and administrators, and professionals—lawyers, educators, etc.—frequently appear as guests.

Two state senators appeared on a "Straight Talk" program given to new developments in laws on abortion. One represented the "pro-life" position, and the other the "pro-choice" position. Faye Wattleton, head of Planned Parenthood, appeared in a video clip speaking against legislation outlawing abortion at the state level. (The "700 Club" has frequently addressed the abortion issue and the Roe versus Wade Supreme Court case.)[271] An attorney with People for The American Way and a public school teacher appeared on the program on values education, speaking in favor of teaching values in the schools. They made the argument that diversity, pluralism, and complexity in American society require that children learn how to make value judgments. Norma and Merland Gabler, conservative Christian activists in the area of education, appeared on the same program. They spoke about their efforts to stop the use of textbooks in public schools they feel promote moral relativism. Patrick Buchanan, then a speech writer for Ronald Reagan, appeared on one edition of the program. He commented on the Democratic Convention meeting that week, its platform, and its candidate.[272]

Segments aired later on the "700 Club" addressed personal problems and crises. Guests interviewed on the show, very often "700 Club" viewers, spoke about the stresses and strains they live under in a complex and rapidly changing society. They spoke, for example, about marriage crises, the crisis of losing a job, drug or alcohol addiction, and bringing up children who live in a drug and alcohol oriented society.

Many of the guests interviewed on the "700 Club" are celebrities from the entertainment industry or from the world of sports. Isaiah Robertson, former all-pro linebacker with the Buffalo Bills, appeared as a special guest to talk about his fight to overcome drug addiction.[273] The "Doublemint Twins," who appeared in the television commercial for the chewing gum, spoke about their experience of sexual stereotyping in the fashion and advertising industry and the pressure to follow the sexual mores of the industry.[274] Other celebrities appear on the show to help raise funds. On one telecast, Miss California helped raise funds, along with Mr. Universe and Mr. South Africa.[275] Another Miss California was interviewed on another edition of the program.[276] (Terry Meeuwsen, once co-host on the program, is a former Miss America.) The viewer will also occasionally hear an appeal for funds to help support hunger relief, literacy, counseling, and other programs.

The "700 Club" is far from the traditional, conservative Christian worship seen on "The Old-Time Gospel Hour" or the other religious telecasts. There is no gospel singing or congregational singing. There is no sermon. (There is no pulpit.) There is no shouting. There is no altar call. Where is conservative religion? It is ever-present. Conservative Christian religion is found in the content of the program. It is introduced through commentary, short homilies or meditations, testimonials given by guests on the program, and prayers. Even when it is not referred to directly, conservative Christian belief serves as a backdrop for all of the other elements of the program.

"The '700 Club' [is] TV journalism with a different spirit," says a commercial for an upcoming edition of the show.[277] When the program reports on the news, it does not simply give a news report. The program presents the news in order to put the news in perspective and "get to the truth."[278] The events reported are analyzed from the biblical perspective, or from conservative Christian interpretations of the Bible. Conservative Christian beliefs guide the selection of news items as well as analysis of the news. They also guide the choice of topics for discussion, the choice of personalities or guests to be interviewed, as well as the choice of personal problems to be discussed. All of these are placed within the context of conservative Christianity.

Robertson or a co-host frequently prays for the salvation of the world and frequently asks viewers in need of salvation or rededication in the Christian life to pray along with him.[279] Viewers who prayed are then asked to write to the ministry to report salvation or rededication and request more information or counseling from the ministry. Robertson is sometimes shown praying over the tens of thousands of prayer request forms phoned or mailed in by viewers. He places his hands on the forms while he prays, making contact with viewers.

When religion is not the topic of conversation, it is visible in the symbolic elements of the program. A large "prayer clock" serves as a reminder of the need to pray around the clock. Scripture verses routinely appear on the screen between the different segments of the program.

The "700 Club" gives conservative Christian religion a fresh face. Conservative Christianity is not just presented as timely, but as up-to-date; not just intellectually defensible but intelligent; not just applicable to today's world, but practical; not just accommodating of a faster lifestyle but uptempo; and not just respectable, but fashionable. It is not simply presented as fitting right in with all of the other latest interests and outlooks of the contemporary individual or complementing them, but as completing the contemporary outlook. Conservative Christians are not simply presented as fully functional within or adjusted to the modern world, but as those in the best position to live happily within it.

The "700 Club" is illustrative of the world-bridging efforts of conservative Christians, who both look backward to the biblical religion of an antique age and attempt to look forward at the same time, wanting to make their religion relevant to the modern world. The television program is helping to give birth to a new version of the conservative Christian religion as it adapts religious conservatives to the wider world and to secular, mainstream American society. As the telecasts make a foray into the wider secular world, the ritual features of the telecast performances help viewers put themselves in the position to make the adjustments along with the telecast.

As ritual transition away from the everyday world, in which the con-servative Christians must keep up their defenses while fending off a threatening and hostile secular world, the telecasts offer viewers the opportunity to relax their tight grip on their religion as they make a transition to an alternative context. Here they are invited to open them-selves to the wider world, if tentatively. With the immediate threat removed, from the safe distance provided by the ritual telecast, viewers can familiarize themselves with social issues and political developments within the wider world, and with those opinions and positions that com-pete with their own. News reports and interviews with government legislators, professionals, and others appearing as guests on the show introduce viewers to new developments in politics and social issues, as well as to legal and technical terminology and jargon.

The alternative, ritual context also invites viewers to experiment with the outlook and sensibilities of the wider, secular society. The entertain-ers and sports personalities who appear as guests introduce viewers to current lingo in popular American culture, new styles in dress, as well as new outlooks and attitudes. Leaving behind a world in which they do not quite fit in invites viewers to experiment with a new identity and lifestyle, with a new way of looking at themselves in relation to the rest of the world, that of a people who fit right in. Viewers are invited to explore the new identity of confident citizen of the wider world. The ritual context transports viewers to a brave new world where they can recast themselves as they plunge into the modern world. Conservative religion remains in view throughout the telecast. But the identity of citizen of the world stands in tension with that of conservative Christian.

### Broadening Horizons

The opening of the "700 Club" instantly grabs viewers' attention with its upbeat musical theme, played by a prerecorded band, complete with trumpets and drums,[280] and its state-of-the-art, computer generated graphics. An announcer welcomes viewers to the show and introduces the news items and topics for discussion on this edition of the program. As he speaks, short videotaped clips on news items coming up later in the program are shown. The opening is the same each day. "All this and more on this edition of the '700 Club!'" The opening sets the tempo for the remainder of the show. It moves quickly from one segment to another. Videotaped spots announcing an upcoming feature on the pro-gram keep things moving along, as do the commentaries, short medita-tions, and other segues made by Robertson and his co-host. The show starts out on a high, and stays on a high, even when Robertson or a co-host or guest becomes very serious.

The announcer then introduces Robertson: "And now here's your host, Pat Robertson!" The viewer hears the studio audience applaud as Robertson greets his audience: "Thank you, Ladies and Gentlemen, and welcome to this edition of the '700 Club'! We're delighted to have you with us!" He opens each show with prayer. Robertson plays several roles as host of the show. He is a news reporter and newscommentator, an interviewer, an entertainer, and a modern television preacher.

At the top of every program is a news segment in which Robertson reports on current news events, both national and international. The news segment makes use of videotaped clips produced by the television staff and by CBN news correspondents reporting on site. They report back to Robertson and viewers from all over the world. Robertson frequently follows a report on an item or incident with commentary from the biblical perspective. He often points out how the Bible addresses or would address the events or issues reported.

The reports focus on current social issues and significant political developments at the national, state, and local levels. They introduce viewers to the different players or different sides engaged in the issues or events. Robertson began one program with live coverage of the assassination of Anwar Sadat, who had been shot just minutes earlier.[281] While Robertson provided details of the assassination, he gave viewers background information on Sadat and Egypt, on former hostilities between Egypt and Israel, and on the Egyptian-Israeli peace accord Sadat had helped to craft. A photograph of Sadat flashed onto the screen while Robertson spoke. He noted that the Egyptian leader was shot while attending a commemoration of the 1973 war with Israel. He pointed out that Egypt had then launched an attack on Yom Kippur when Jews in Israel were in the midst of observing the religious holiday. Robertson went on to inform viewers that Vice President Mubarak had become President of Egypt, and that the U.S. government's news department would "give us an update." He then cut to a CBN reporter on the spot.

The correspondent reported on The Independent Order for the Liberation of Egypt, identified as a "fanatic" Muslim movement in Egypt opposed to the government's liberal policies. The suggestion was made that the extremist group had carried out the assassination as reprisal for the peace treaty Sadat had negotiated with Israel. The reporter gave a brief history of developments and made use of a map of Egypt put up on the screen. He announced that the White House was alarmed by the situation. Robertson thanked the correspondent and told viewers they would be kept "up to date on this program." Several times during the program, Robertson introduced an "update" from the correspondent in the field.

Robertson then discussed an effort by the United States government to put together a policy that would promote harmony among Egypt, Israel, and Saudi Arabia out of concern that the sale of AWACs to Saudi Arabia had had an adverse effect on relations among these parties. He then cut to "our reporter in Sinai. We are in touch with him." Later in the program Robertson suggested that the sale could be a "destablizing factor" in a region in which, he suggested, no leader is safe, and in which some have been called "madmen." He reported that CBS and NBC had just announced that Sadat had died, but that there were conflicting reports and that viewers would be apprised of developments. He then speculated on the new President, reminding viewers that Mubarak had been Vice President only ninety days. Robertson speculated that there was no Egyptian leader powerful enough to unify the country. He noted that Sadat had just cracked down on extremist Muslims as well as Christian Copts, who had been fighting against one another.

Robertson treated the assassination of Sadat as fulfillment of biblical prophecy concerning the end times. How events in the Middle East "tie in" to "what's going on in the Bible" is an ongoing interest of the program.[282] The report reinforced the conservative Christian belief that the world is in its final days and that the events taking place in the Middle East are signs of the last days as foretold in the book of Revelation. According to the millenarian view of conservative Christianity, the Middle East will be the staging ground for the battle of Armageddon, which will be fought in Israel. Although the presentation on developments in the region was delivered in a straightforward, no-nonsense way, mention of the apocalypse added a sinister dimension to the events which was designed to make the viewers feel anxious. The anxiety produced would reinforce the belief that Satan is alive and well and has already begun playing his hand in world events in his plan to defeat God's purposes for the world as foretold in the book of the apocalypse. The Soviet Union was also mentioned, adding another element of anxiety for the conservative Christian viewer. (Conservative Christians believed the Soviet Union would play a major role in the final battle as Satan's ally.)

The program airing the report on the Middle East focused on events back home in the United States. Getting special attention were reports on federal court decisions striking down prayer in public schools as well as religious sponsorship of Bible study in these schools in several places around the country. The reports were presented as part of the topic of discussion for the week: freedom of religion. The programs being telecast that week had been given the theme "Seven Days Ablaze." The reports were presented along with discussion of the issue of separation of church and state, of standing legal pronouncements on the issue, and the conservative Christian interpretation of the First Amendment. Other telecasts had informed viewers on other judicial and congressional decisions.

The program made use of a prerecorded video tape on religious freedom and on the nation's "Christian" beginnings. The video clip began with a cartoon typewriter pounding out the words, "policy forbidding teachers showing films depicting religious happenings in history or religious teachings." Computer generated stars then swirled into place to form an American flag, on which appeared the words, "The American Vision." The flag moved to the lower left quadrant of the screen and was replaced by a picture of George Washington and later a picture of Revolutionary War figures. As the visuals ran, drums played in the background in the military style of the colonial period. The picture was replaced by a drawing of an historic document on which the words, "We Must Pray!" were superimposed. As the images appeared on the screen, a narrator told viewers that as the Second Continental Congress prepared for further conflict during the war with England, delegates declared a day of public fasting and prayer before God. The narrator noted that "...early patriots sought God's aid and intervention on their behalf." He read from the historic document represented on the screen and then continued his commentary. "The colonial leaders knew the critical need to weld their spiritual faith in God to their conviction of liberty to preserve their freedom. So it was on July 20, 1775."

Robertson returned to the screen and reported that he was hearing from the viewing audience on the religious freedom issue and was hearing that they had been unaware of "massive attacks" on religious freedom. He told viewers that the recent court decisions were evidence of a new "threat to our religious freedom." The decisions underscored the "secular purposes" of the state, he said. Arguing that the effect of the court decisions was to replace Christianity with the new religion of "secularism," he claimed that the federal judiciary had been "sanctified" by "secular humanism." He argued that the courts had gone beyond the intent of the "founding Fathers," pointing out that the Constitution holds that the state was "not to advance *or* retard religion." The recent court decisions were insupportable, he told viewers, since there was nothing in the Constitution or in the nation's historical tradition that rules that government ought to have an overwhelming secular purpose.

To underscore the dangers of a public education lacking religious influence, Robertson read from a newspaper article reporting on an education program sponsored by the federal government under Title Ten. The article quoted a psychiatrist who had said the education program would bring about sexual promiscuity, homosexuality, changing sex roles in marriage, and incest. Robertson went on to observe that the Supreme Court had removed religious groups from public schools but had not prevented socialist, feminist, or homosexual groups from holding meetings in public schools.

Robertson then introduced a special report from another CBN correspondent on a court case concerning religious sponsorship of Bible-study groups meeting on a state college campus in Kansas. The correspondent opened her report by pulling a law book from a library shelf and quoting from it a regulation banning religious groups from meeting in public schools. The report ended with her comment that the First Amendment on the free expression of religion had far-reaching implications that needed to be considered seriously.

Robertson returned, addressed the audience, and announced that even as he spoke, lawyers were arguing a case before the Supreme Court concerning the freedom of religious expression. He told viewers he wanted them to join him in prayer for the lawyers. "In this country" it was "unlawful" to teach children about religion, he commented. He predicted that Christian schools would be closed next, because they were a threat to the secular state. He worried aloud that America might see the establishment of an official church, as in the Soviet Union. He told viewers that the current study of the Bible in public schools from the perspective of the comparative study of religion was inadequate, because the Bible was taught from an historical and literary perspective and not from a perspective that was "life-changing." "Ladies and Gentlemen, let's pray. I'm going to besiege heaven right at this moment," he said. When Robertson prayed for the lawyers again later in the program he told viewers that the Supreme Court had stepped outside God's laws, banning the Ten Commandments, which he identified as "the basis of our law." The country had turned away from "Judeo-Christian" morality, he told viewers.

Robertson then interviewed a Christian lawyer, who stated that Christians were not informed on the issue of restrictions against the free expression of religion. The lawyer made the case that what was really at issue in the court cases was Christian speech. He argued that in reality, the state was hostile to Christian speech. He reiterated the point that the Soviet system was coming to pass in the United States. "Do Christians get a chance to share in our pluralism?" he asked. He then told viewers that American society was "valueless" and ruled by "secular humanism." Robertson then joined in to decry pluralism, arguing that it lacked a basis for consensus on societal values. He led viewers in another prayer for the lawyers arguing before the Supreme Court.

The cameras then cut to Robertson's co-host, Ben Kinchlow, praying before the "prayer clock." The clock, standing just above head height, held cards mailed in by viewers indicating their pledge to pray fifteen minutes every day, seven days a week during the week of special programming. (On a later show, Robertson described the prayer clock as segmented into "regiments" that made up an "army" of prayer warriors.)[283]

The remainder of the show pursued other court cases addressing the freedom of religion issue. There were other special videotaped presentations on the "Separation Illusion" and "The American Vision: To Preserve Liberty." One of these portrayed Abraham Lincoln and Thomas Jefferson as Christian leaders who interpreted the separationist issue broadly. "America's Heritage Is Under Attack," read the headline in another video clip advertising an upcoming program. The clip showed a gavel pounding down on an American flag, which then broke into pieces.

Paul Weyrich, founder of the Heritage Foundation and Committee for a Free Congress, also appeared as a guest on the program. He urged viewers to get involved in the political process in light of the threat to "our right to worship as we please." He, too, told viewers that the United States was moving to the Soviet position on the separation of church and state in the effort of the state to prohibit the church from interfering in the affairs of state.

Robertson issued a call for a Christian "revolt" in the face of the "warfare" going on against Christians, "a very persecuted minority." In a program broadcast later still, Robertson told viewers that conservative Christians must claim "the Promised Land" in the face of opposition to God's people assuming public office and moving into public life. The "intent of the Lord," he told viewers on that occasion, was that "his people should reign and rule with Jesus Christ. That's what the Bible says."[284] "The Evangelical Vote" was the topic of another broadcast.[285] Later in the show Robertson's co-host prayed for a "ground swell" among God's people, who would build themselves into an "army" for freedom. Robertson told viewers he did not want freedom in order to impose Christian views on others, although he would like everyone to love God. Nor did he want government to impose the Christian view, he said. He just wanted religious freedom, he told his audience.

As Robertson prayed, he asked God "to roll back this tide of evil," which, he said, was not accidental, but part of a plan. "We do have the victory in his name!" "God is going to win!" Robertson shouted as he ended his prayer. He reminded viewers that what was at stake in the battle for religious freedom in America transcended politics. What was at issue was spiritual revival in America, becoming a "land and a people of righteousness," who would sweep away all that is evil in God's sight. The move away from the nation's "Christian" beginnings was evidence of the emergence of "demonic" movements, Robertson told viewers. Along with pluralism, the telecast condemned "humanism," "Marxism," and "socialism." (What was at stake, Robertson told viewers on a later program, was the very "Kingdom of God.")[286]

Throughout the program, which was dedicated to a fundraising drive—Robertson asked viewers to phone in pledges and join thousands of other viewers in becoming part of a massive movement. The cameras showed volunteers seated on another stage taking calls from viewers. As viewers phoned in, Robertson read off of pledge cards the names of cities from which viewers were calling. He reminded viewers that their effort was part of a larger effort to set the world on fire for God and part of God's pouring out his Holy Spirit, symbolized by the giant flame symbol that appeared in front of the volunteers taking calls. A light board kept track of pledges coming in. Robertson asked for a trumpet blast or a drumroll when pledges reached a certain goal. There were similar fundraising efforts on broadcasts airing later.

Robertson ends every show with a prayer in which he asks God's blessings on the viewer. He announces that the program has run out of time and says, "We'll see you tomorrow. Until then, good-bye, and God bless you." The camera shows Robertson shaking hands with guests and then pans the audience while it applauds. The logo for the show reappears on the screen. The announcer invites viewers "to join Pat Robertson and the '700 Club'" in reaching the world with the gospel and gives information on how to join in the effort. He ends by announcing the topics for discussion on upcoming programs. "For these facts and more, don't miss the next edition of the '700 Club!'" (When the format of the show was expanded, and Robertson bowed out about halfway through the one-and-a-half-hour program, the co-host signed off, inviting viewers to tune in the next day.)

As the "700 Club" reports on social issues and political developments within the wider world, viewers' horizons are broadened. But the reports reinforce conservative Christian belief by presenting issues and events within the framework of its millenarian world view, which sees the world as threatening and as opposed to God and his people. Presenting catastrophic world events and the incursion on religious liberty at home as fulfillment of millenarian prophecy reinforces conservative Christian belief. The anxiety produced by the suggestion that behind these can be seen the hand of Satan and the relief and hope created by the reassurance that God and his people will win in the end give further reinforcement to the millenarian view. The program continues to present the world as a threatening place.

There is a great disjunction between the way in which the message is presented—through the production values and technology of secular television—and the religious message presented. The presentation borrows from the wider, secular world. But the religion presented is a biblically based religion that opposes the secular world. The disjunction raises the question of whether or not the commitment to the brave new outlook and attitude adopted by the program is only skin deep. The great effort sometimes taken to present conservative religion as fitting right into today's society raises the question of whether conservative Christians sense that they do not fit into the modern world, whether they do not still see it as threatening and incompatible with their religion and must continue to insist on condemning and remaining separate from all things secular. As the program helps viewers adapt to the wider world, it also encourages them to hold onto their religion.

# ⊰ 11 ⊱

## "Jimmy Swaggart":
## Ritual Community on the Offensive

### *A Community in Solidarity and on the Counterattack*

The "Jimmy Swaggart" show is a prerecorded, old-fashioned Pentecostal worship service, complete with speaking in tongues, dancing in the Spirit, shouting, gospel singing, and hellfire-and-damnation preaching. The telecasts are edited versions of a much longer worship service, held at Family Worship Center at the headquarters of the Jimmy Swaggart World Ministries. Many of the telecasts are edited broadcasts of evangelistic crusades held around the country by Swaggart and his staff. The television audience does not see the proceedings leading up to the sermon, which opens the service. The preliminaries last as long as two hours, with plenty of gospel singing—soloists, a select singing group, a large choir, and the congregation are accompanied by piano, organ, trumpets, and drums—plenty of praying, an occasional anointing service, and a testimonial period.[287] The unseen events charge up the audience. By the time viewers tune in, there is electricity in the air.

Like the format of the program, the production and production values make very little effort to mimic commercial television. There is little interest in exploiting the full range of possibilities of television technology. Certainly Swaggart's program is a long way from the broadcasts of tent revivals and healing services of other Pentecostal preachers a couple of decades back. The program does make use of technology that did not exist earlier. The production values are very plain. The program, however, is not. The simple approach taken with television technology allows old-fashioned, unadulterated Pentecostalism to burst through. The program refuses to continue to update while other Pentecostals make improvements that are considered to water down the Pentecostal message and experience. The format and production of the program also reflect the uncompromising position taken toward the secular world by Swaggart and his followers. The program is unapologetic in promoting Pentecostalism, and in condemning the world. The format and production reflect the harsh judgment against the world made by Swaggart and his followers, as well as their disinterest in gaining the world's approval.

There is little of the secular world in the telecasts. The music has a jazz and blues quality to it, although it is Gospel music. The dress of Jimmy and Frances Swaggart, Swaggart's spouse, and that of the ministry's staff, soloists, and others appearing on the show is sometimes flashy. These are Pentecostals who have made some accommodations to secular dress, music, aesthetic sensibilities, and attitudes.

The religious message of the telecast, however, offers harsh condemnation of the secular world. The rhetoric is confrontational. It is the message and rhetoric of an uncompromising, anti-worldly and world-opposing millenarianism, which anticipates the overthrow of the "principalities and powers" identified by Christian scripture as currently ruling the world. The greater part of the telecast, the sermon, is given to judging and condemning the secular world as well as calling it to repentance. Swaggart speaks on average about forty-five minutes.

Swaggart's condemnation is fiery. He calls down God's judgment upon the news media—which, he points out, have always been critical of Pentecostals—the state, the courts, the entertainment industry, and civil libertarian groups, all of which are said to have mistreated Pentecostals. There is no discussion of issues. There is scant identification of players by name. There is no discussion of the opposing political ideology. Discussion is pointless from Swaggart's perspective. "Secularists" are simply dead wrong, he holds. And they are on the wrong side. They are said to be allied with Satan in a demonic plan to defeat God and God's purposes for the world. As he condemns secularists, Swaggart looks directly into the television cameras as if the secular world were tuned in and listening, along with Satan himself, the real enemy, who although invisible is engaged fully in the attempt to defeat God's people. Secularists are repeatedly called to repentance before it is too late.

Swaggart routinely refers to Pentecostals as the object of mistreatment and attack by the world. He continually defends Pentecostals and their unconventional practice of "speaking in tongues" and ecstatic style of worship. What the world looks down upon as the inferior practice of uneducated and backward people is, in reality, "baptism in the Spirit," which is itself a sign of favor with God, says Swaggart. God is on the side of holy people, Swaggart reminds his audience. God comes to their defense in the midst of persecution and will sustain them until the end of time, he observes, when God will defeat Satan and his ally and give his righteous people victory over the world. Satan will be cast into outer darkness and the lost world judged severely, Swaggart promises. The televangelist takes up the role of prophet. He defends the righteous, condemns the wicked who persecute them, and foretells the doom of the wicked in their day of reckoning with God Almighty himself. As prophet, calling down God's judgment upon the nation, Swaggart stands up to Satan himself. Swaggart also calls the wicked to repentance, like the biblical prophets of old, and like Jesus.

There is palpable communication between Swaggart and his hearers gathered in the worship hall. The cameras attempt to include viewers watching the telecast at home by repeatedly showing the gathered congregation as well as individual members of the congregation, creating a sense of identification. Cameras continually cut back and forth from Swaggart to members of the congregation, recording the responses of his listeners. They applaud, jump to their feet, shout "Amen!" and lend other forms of support to the preacher in the pulpit. The camera often cuts to a member of the audience in deep concentration on the message, or as she or he turns to a passage in the Bible and follows along as Swaggart reads from scripture.[288] The congregation joins Swaggart in condemning the world and in defending Pentecostals. Critical to going on the counterattack is the coming together of Pentecostals as a community united in support of one another and united in purpose as a community of the saved, namely the purpose of calling down judgment upon the secular world and calling it to repentance.

The format chosen for the telecasts—a revival meeting or worship service—provides the perfect opportunity for these Pentecostals to strengthen their community in the face of attacks by the secular world and, having done so, to mount a counterattack. The worship service provides an occasion to come together, join forces, rally in their own defense, and mount a counteroffensive. As a ritual performance, the worship service and the television program strengthen community among the Pentecostals, which is vital to mounting their counterattack. The telecasts help viewers make a ritual transition away from the hostile, everyday secular world, in which they are attacked for their beliefs, to an alternative, safe context in which they can gather with other Pentecostals, lend mutual support and renew their confidence in their religion as well as reaffirm their religious community. Ritual transition invites viewers to open themselves to one another, and to seek and give support. As ritual performance, the telecasts also provide legitimation of Pentecostals as a religious group. Mutual support and renewed confidence as a religious community together enable these Pentecostals to stand up to the secular world.

The counteroffensive launched takes the form of judging the world, calling it to repentance, and winning lost souls. It does not take the form of programmatic and highly organized political action. The "Jimmy Swaggart" telecast does not have as its stated purpose mobilizing viewers politically. The program may motivate certain viewers to support the "pro-life" movement, vote a certain way, or lobby. The program's main purpose and effect is mobilizing viewers to change the world through evangelization, through calling it to repentance, reminding it of God's judgment, and then winning it for God. The program encourages individual Pentecostals to witness to the lost world. Evangelization is most forceful as the Pentecostals gather together as a religious community in defense and celebration of their religion and religious community.

### Protest and Counteroffensive

The opening segment of the "Jimmy Swaggart" show helps viewers shift their attention to the Pentecostal community and begin to join in the effort to strengthen community among those who look to Swaggart as their spokesman. Upbeat music greets viewers as the words, "Jimmy Swaggart Ministries Presents," roll up the screen.[289] The logo for the ministry, a red cross and white dove, also appears on the screen. A lapel pin bearing the logo is offered free of charge to viewers who call the toll-free number provided in a commercial that airs just before the telecast. "The friends and partners of the Jimmy Swaggart Ministries invite you now to join with them for an unforgettable hour of praise and worship with evangelist Jimmy Swaggart," says an announcer who greets viewers. A cameo of Swaggart appears at the edge of the screen, while

Swaggart's signature appears across it, as if to say the televangelist is engaged in direct correspondence or communication with the viewer.

The announcer continues: "This ministry is fulfilling God's great commission to take the gospel to the far corners of the world through the work of spirit-led missionaries, worldwide crusades, by building churches and Bible schools in many countries, through the daily and weekly television programs, well-rounded children's outreach, and the printing and distribution of literature." As the announcer speaks, the various aspects of the ministry he describes are illustrated through short videotaped segments. The video segment includes a shot of a spinning globe superimposed upon flags of various nations of the world blowing in the breeze. The flags stand outside the ministry's headquarters and represent the countries where the ministry has its work.[290] A missionary is shown speaking to children in an African village. Hundreds responding to an altar call at a crusade are shown coming forward. Workers are shown laying concrete blocks for a school. Swaggart is shown with a guest panel of pastors appearing on his other television program, "A Study in the Word." Various publications put out by the ministry are shown. "Our prayers are that through this program you'll draw closer to the Lord Jesus Christ," the announcer concludes, while Swaggart is shown praying.

The announcer then gives the name of the city where the crusade being recorded for television is being held. A recent show taped in Milwaukee is typical. "Today from our Saturday evening service in Milwaukee, Wisconsin, evangelist Jimmy Swaggart delivers a prophetic look into this nation's relationship with God in his message entitled 'The Future of the United States of America.'" The title of the message was spelled out on screen under the words, "Today's Message." The sermon title appears within an outline of the United States. The colors used are red, white, and blue. Swaggart's signature was superimposed upon the Milwaukee skyline as the words, "In Crusade from Milwaukee, Wisconsin," appeared below. The visuals underscore Swaggart's role as prophet of God who judges the nation itself, calling the nation to repentance as God's faithful people gather in revival across the land. "So come along with us now to the Mecca arena as we present evangelist Jimmy Swaggart," said the announcer.

Cameras immediately took viewers inside the huge arena where the crusade was being held. An overhead shot from the back of the vast hall showed thousands gathered to hear Swaggart. On screen appeared the words, "The Mecca, Milwaukee, Wisconsin." The shots of the various cities, arenas, and huge crowds create the impression that Swaggart and his followers make up a huge, militant army on the march across a godless nation supported by the hand of God.

The cameras closed in on Swaggart, who was shown standing on the podium. He held the Bible in his right hand while he clutched a microphone stand with his left. He moved about the platform freely, in the style of a revival preacher. He was wearing a suit and tie. Also on the podium was the band that travels with him. The large podium was draped in blue and decorated with greenery. "Thank the Lord!" Swaggart called out to the congregation. "If you have your Bibles tonight, turn with me to the book of Matthew, chapter 11, the words of Jesus, starting with verse 28." As Swaggart announced the Bible passage and read from it, it was displayed on the screen, inside another outline of the United States. "Come unto me, all ye that labor and are heavy laden, and I will give you rest," he read aloud.

Swaggart told his hearers that while the text was comforting, there were harsh words for those who did not obey God. He told them that he would speak tonight on a prophetic subject: "The Future of the United States of America." As he repeated the title of his sermon, the screen showed the United States' flag flying in the center of an outline of the U.S. The word "Next" appeared above the sermon title. At the bottom of the screen appeared the words, "Today's Message," followed by the sermon title. The camera cut to a shot of the audience shown from the rear of the auditorium as it faced the podium from which Swaggart addressed it.

The importance of Swaggart's message of prophetic judgment was underscored in a prerecorded appeal for funds that immediately followed. Frances Swaggart appeared in it to tell viewers that she did not know how much longer her husband could continue to carry the burden of the ministry alone under added financial pressures. "My husband is laboring for souls with his last ounce of energy." The cameras closed in. "You know, in reality it's a spiritual battle. Satan is doing everything within his power to stop the work of this ministry. He doesn't want you to watch this program each week. He doesn't want you to be ministered to. And what better way than for Satan to drain Jimmy's strength with unnecessary financial pressures. You see, that's why I've come to you today to ask for your help. /.../ I know you love him and have been blessed by this ministry." As she spoke, Swaggart was shown preaching before thousands in a short video clip. "The Lord has been using this ministry like no other ministry in the history of the gospel. I can say that with all honesty. The money touches, now listen to me carefully, it touches the lives of some 70 million people in over 70 countries." A spinning globe was shown as graphics spelled out the figures she gave on the dollars spent on building Bible schools and churches around the world. There were shots of missionaries surrounded by African children, workers pouring concrete, a needy child, and thousands coming forward during an altar call given by Swaggart. "God bless you," Frances said as she winked at viewers. "We love you." The ministry's address was then flashed onto the screen.

"We now return to Milwaukee," said the announcer. On the screen appeared the words, "Today's Message," with the sermon title spelled out again within the now familiar outline of the United States.

Swaggart immediately launched into the sermon. "I do not believe God is through with this nation of America yet." The camera showed an overhead shot of the thousands gathered in the arena. It then zoomed in on Swaggart. He held an open Bible in his hand and was wearing the cross and dove Swaggart Ministries logo pin in his suit lapel. The camera then caught a member of the audience listening intently. "In the last twenty years, the United States has suffered an invasion...," Swaggart told his audience. "It has come in the spiritual realm. Satan is laying a diabolical plan to destroy the citadel of democracy in the world." The camera showed the crowded arena and then moved back to Swaggart. He paced back and forth across the podium, holding the microphone stand in one hand. "We set the moral standard. God knows we've not set a very good one in the past decade." Swaggart went on to tell his audience that God had given him the message that America deserved God's harsh judgment, but that God was delaying judgment in order to use America one more time, unlike God had ever used America. Much was expected of America, because the nation had been given much, he added.

God's judgment upon the secular world was spelled out in an earlier sermon titled "If the Footman Have Wearied Thee, How Will You Contend with Horses?"[291] The sermon drew on the prophetic, apocalyptic scenario of judgment against ancient Israel found in Jeremiah 12. Swaggart began by taking his hearers back to Jesus' time, which he characterized as an age of "apostasy." The people had drifted off their "moorings," Swaggart told his listeners. Jesus was chafed by Israel's "waywardness" or "sin," he said. Swaggart drew a comparison between ancient Israel and the United States. The nation had been great, he told his audience, because it had made God and "the holy Word of God" its foundation. He held up a Bible. America was blessed with religious freedom, he told his hearers. He drew a contrast between America and China, which, he noted, placed restrictions on preaching the gospel and on distributing Bibles. As he spoke, a video tape showed Swaggart distributing Bibles there.

There was opposition to the gospel in this land of America, however, Swaggart went on to tell his audience. He loosened his tie. And America was about to have God's judgment fall down upon it, for which the nation was not prepared, he said. "The nations of the world are headed to judgment, America included! And there is nothing that can stop it! God doesn't intend to stop it." Jesus was about to return "to catch his people away," he said. The audience stood and broke into applause, waving their arms overhead. "You can almost hear the rumble of Armageddon!" Swaggart said dramatically, drawing up his right hand and screwing up his face in anticipation of the horror of that final battle between the forces of Satan and the forces of God. "The world is headed toward the great judgment!" "I sat across the table the other day from one of the influential Congressmen from Washington," Swaggart told the audience, "and he said, 'Brother Swaggart, if certain things can be done...maybe, just maybe, we can stem the tide a few years.' Maybe we can pull it back from the brink with the help of God just a few years."

Jimmy Swaggart was a "voice" for God, Swaggart told his audience. "I'm not here to win a popularity contest! I'm here to preach the word of God! Whether you like it or not I can't help that!" The audience broke into applause. Swaggart repeated the Bible verse. He then addressed his critics. "Do you hear me? Today I'm told as a preacher of the gospel that I cannot do so. They say I'm involving myself in politics. I care not for your politics!", he said angrily, scowling into the camera. The audience applauded wildly. "I'm interested in the morals of this nation!" Swaggart then broke into the cadence of a revival preacher, growing more and more animated and shouting as he spoke. "And if it offends you, Mister, I am sorry but I am not planning to shut up! I'm not planning to sit down...to quit! I'm planning to preach this gospel as long as God gives me voice to speak, as long as he gives me lungs to shout!" The audience responded with sustained applause.

Swaggart then launched an attack on the media. "I, along with other preachers, have been caricatured, ostracized, criticized, lambasted, lampooned, laughed at, leered at. They have been increasingly, sarcastically critical because this ministry and others have raised large amounts of money for the work of God." Swaggart looked directly into the camera and sneered. "You call American people that give their money to the Swaggart ministry 'hicks, imbeciles, unlearned, unknowledgeable, unknowing products of the Bible belt.'" He gave the dollar amounts, in the millions, spent by the ministry to build Bible schools and churches around the world and spent on food relief. "I'm sure that bothers you, sir!" The audience applauded. "We did something good with that money! You newsmen, you hypocrites! Why don't you write about abortion?" In the previous year $500 million was spent on abortion in America, Swaggart told his audience. "Hypocrites!" he shouted.

"My eighty million bothers you, but I don't hear you saying too much about the five billion dollars spent on rock and roll, the sadistic, horrifying, hellish, demonic, music that's damning and destroying untold millions...you generation of vipers! You hypocrites!" As he spoke, uttering Jesus' own words of condemnation, Swaggart slammed his fist into the air. Ten billion dollars were spent on pornography, and $4 billion on entertainment, "causing this nation to become a sore," he told his listeners. "Why don't you write about that, you generation of vipers?" The audience broke into applause. Swaggart reported that $5 billion was spent on alcohol, but that the press had not written about "the broken homes, broken lives, and the broken dreams, and the broken hearts, and the wasted souls" that resulted. "You've not written one single, solitary word about it, you journalists. Hypocrites!" Swaggart reported that $100 billion was spent on the drug business, which, he said, "rapes this nation." "Write what you want to write about, but I will continue preaching this gospel!" he shouted as he strode across the stage with an open Bible in hand.

Swaggart went on to report the recent jailing of a director of a Christian school before attacking judges. "You let the pornographers go free, you judges...you let the Communists go free, but you will put in jail a Baptist preacher!" "Mr. Judge, I want you to hear me a minute if you happen to slide across this channel on your set. No secular humanist judge would be caught dead hearing a Pentecostal minister!" The audience applauded. "Mr. State has no right to tell me how to educate my children, has no right to tell me that I have no right not to teach evolution...! The state has no right to take the Ten Commandments down from our school walls, for this nation is a nation under God, of God, and by God Almighty, and this is the Constitution of the United States, the Word of Almighty God!" He held the Bible in his hand. "The state has no right, sir, to force atheism, secular humanism, materialism, socialism, Communism down the throats of our children!"

The United States was founded on the Bible, Swaggart told his audience. "'What creed should form the foundation of American law?'" he asked, quoting Patrick Buchanan. "'Whose beliefs should serve as blueprint for governance of American society? Should the United States be a Christian or pagan country?'" The question was no less momentous, as Buchanan asserted, in regard to school prayer, Swaggart observed. Swaggart continued, quoting Buchanan. It was "'time to separate the sheep from the goats.'" For 180 years, the creed of law in the United States had been Christianity, and "'a rather stern Christianity,'" he said. America had been a Christian country, Swaggart continued. He told the audience that twenty-five years ago, the Warren Supreme Court, without the support of democratic people, began to "dechristianize" America by allowing secular humanism into the public schools through values clarification and sex education. Abortion, crime, pornography, drugs, prostitution had now destroyed families and neighborhoods, Swaggart said.

"You hear what I'm saying?" Swaggart asked. He repeated the scripture passage for the hour, which was again flashed onto the television screen. "A systematic attempt to destroy the American way of life has been about its business now for over two decades. And I want to tell you something. The way they want to do it is destroying public schools and destroying the freedom of preaching." Swaggart told his audience he had something shocking to say. Communists had laid out a blueprint to take over America, he told them. The plan, he said, called for nuclear disarmament, free trade with Communist countries, the recognition of "Red China," as well as support of the United Nations' "one-world government" policy. The plan also called for gaining control of the Democratic Party, and gaining control of the schools by teaching socialism and humanism, he added. "Mister, they've done it!" In addition, he said, the plan called for infiltration of the press, infiltrating the churches, replacing "revealed religion" with the social gospel, and the elimination of laws that violate a free press. The last plan would enable the press to promote homosexuality, promiscuity, and pornography as normal behavior. The plan also called for the elimination of prayer in public schools as violation of the law of separation of church and state, he added.

"They have come perilously close to doing just that! We are about to contend with the beasts of the field who have come to devour [us]." Swaggart returned to the passage in Jeremiah, while the Bible verse was again displayed on the television screen. "And this is exactly what's happened! I want to tell you this. If you think this is just the rantings and ravings of another preacher, just another problem in American society, you are wrong! Satan is playing for keeps to destroy this United States of America!" Satan was destroying our freedom to worship God because the United States was "the missionary center of the globe," Swaggart told his audience.

Swaggart then told his listeners the "shocking truth" of why America was in its present position. He quoted Jeremiah 12:10: "Many pastors have destroyed my vineyard." There were preachers, he observed, who no longer believed the Bible or preached it, and who no longer believed or preached the Virgin Birth, Jesus as Son of God, etc. Many preachers were atheists, he said. Homosexuals were being ordained, he went on to say. Homosexuality was "the most vile, hellish sin this nation has ever known" and was one of the three sins of a fallen nation, Swaggart told his hearers. The other two mentioned were incest and the sexual abuse of children, "pedophilia." As Swaggart uttered the word, it was superimposed on the screen.

America's fall could not be stopped by political powers, Swaggart observed. Only one thing would stop it, he said. Every church "must preach the Word as they've never preached it before, until the pews literally shake and tremble, until the power of God falls." Every church must preach that "sin is black, hell is hot, and heaven is pure!" Swaggart shook the Bible in his upraised right hand for emphasis as he spoke, breaking into cadence. "For God is still able to save our sons, and save our daughters, and save our families, and save our nation!" God was able to "hold back the tide of destruction a while." The audience applauded. "God said, 'If they will not obey, I will destroy them.'" He quoted a Bible passage, which was displayed on the screen. America was great, if there was any greatness, if it remained faithful to the Bible, Swaggart observed, holding up the Bible for all to see. "'America, America, God grant his grace on thee!'" he said in closing.

In his sermon on "The Future of America," Swaggart told his audience that, while judgment and the destruction of the secular world were certain, God had delayed both in order to bring more lost souls into the fold and bring victory to his people.[292] The nation was beginning to return to "traditional values," to "the old-fashioned Word of God that I hold in my hand today," Swaggart said. He held up the Bible. The return baffled the news media, news reporters, politicians, and the political parties, Swaggart added. "I believe this is God stepping in." The gospel would "cover the face of the earth" if Jesus' Second Coming was delayed,

Swaggart promised. "I believe that God Almighty is going to pour out his Spirit and send a Holy Ghost revival that's going to result in multiplied multiplicities of multitudinous millions being swept into the Kingdom of God!"

"God has given me a message I must give you. /.../ God spoke to my heart." The first message was to the church, Swaggart pointed out. "God is coming back to the glorious church!" Swaggart smiled broadly as he made his point. The audience applauded. "Some ask, 'Who are you?' I'm nobody. I am nothing. I'm just 'a voice crying in the wilderness. Prepare ye the way of the Lord,'" Swaggart continued, quoting Christian scripture. The words are those of Isaiah, used by gospel writers to describe John the Baptist, who preached about the coming of the messiah, judgment, and repentance. "I'm just a voice, a mouthpiece. If you don't like what I say, talk to my boss!" The audience responded with thunderous applause. "I get my order from the highest!" As Swaggart looked out over the audience, the camera looked out over his shoulder at the crowd. The camera moved back and forth from Swaggart to the crowd. The camera then followed Swaggart from behind as he paced across the stage, looking out over the audience. An overhead shot of the audience was then shown.

Next, Swaggart delivered his message to the nation, directing his initial comments to the news media. "If perchance you think you have it in mind that this is some passing fad, and you're here to cover the show and to use your terminology, the 'Far Right' and the 'religious kooks'—you've made your statements that the religious Far Right, the fringe, fanatics have taken over the nation—you better go back to your Bible somewhere and look up who we are! We've been around a long, long time!" "After you're dead and gone, Communists, secular humanists, we will still be here!" The audience applauded wildly. Many raised their hands in the air. Swaggart paced the podium. "What you see is what you get!" "You better bone up on what's happening," he told members of the news media, "because for the next two or three decades, if Jesus tarried, this [Bible] is the way the ball's gonna bounce, the river's gonna flow, and the grass is gonna grow! These Bible thumpers, Bible wavers..., call us fanatics if you want to, but I'm here to tell you that the next decade, the next two decades, the next three decades, until Jesus comes, belongs to the saints of Almighty God!" Swaggart shouted. The media, politicians, and government wondered what was shaking the nation "to its core," Swaggart told his hearers. The gospel would go out from the

United States and would penetrate the Soviet Union, China, and "the whole world. I know what I'm talking about!" he shouted.

"I have a message not only to the news media but to the educational infrastructure," Swaggart continued. "We are sick and tired, sick and tired up to here! Sick until we cannot stomach it anymore of your teaching our little boys and girls that men came from monkeys and there is no God and no heaven and hell! We are sick to our stomach of it!" "Hallelujah!" Swaggart exclaimed. "I'm simply telling you what the Word of God says."

Swaggart returned to the podium. "This nation was founded on the principles of this book I hold in my hand," he declared, holding the Bible up to be seen. "Our founding fathers founded it on the Word of Almighty God. *Time* magazine said some time ago the true Constitution of the United States is the Bible." "We're coming home!" Swaggart shouted. He then broke into speaking in tongues. "We're coming back to the God of our fathers, to one nation, under God, indivisible, with freedom and liberty for all!" The camera showed an excited member of the audience bouncing up and down in her seat.

"I've got a message to the entertainment business." "[We are] sick of long-haired, smelly, stinky, beer-guzzling, coke-snorting, marijuana-smoking freaks! These rock, so-called rock stars that are held up for models for our young people. Sick of it!" "This is not the rock age but the age of the King of kings!" "CBS, ABC, NBC, I'm sick of your no morals. You denigrate the God of this Bible." He held up the Bible. A generation of "throwaway kids" had been lost to drugs, alcohol, and rock music, Swaggart told his audience.

"I have a message to the Communists," Swaggart continued. "The future of this world is not going to be Communist, not Red, not belonging to totalitarian, dictatorial slavemasters! [You are]...morally bankrupt, spiritually bankrupt and you don't have any sense! You're just about to find out there is a God who rules in the affairs of men! You are about to find out the he is a God of judgment!" The audience applauded. "This old United States is sick and in need of God. I raise it up. /.../ Uncle Sam is saying, 'I've been away a long time, but I'm coming home! I'm coming home!' 'America, America, God shed his grace on thee!'" Swaggart shouted in closing.

Swaggart also reminded his hearers of their final victory over the world with the return of Christ. In a sermon titled "Come Up with Me," delivered after his sex scandal, Swaggart reminded his audience that they would be rewarded for remaining faithful.[293] "God gave me tonight's sermon," Swaggart told his audience. The sermon compared Christians to Judah, the ancient Hebrew tribe. With God's help, it defeated the Canaanites, a pagan people, Swaggart reminded the audience. For Judah's faithfulness, God rewarded it with the land of Canaan. The story, found in Judges 1:1-3, laid out God's "plan" for "the entirety of the human race," Swaggart said. The Hebrew tribe was targeted for defeat by Satan, who knew that from this "motley group of poor human flotsam that a redeemer would come," he said. "He's come. But he's coming again!" Swaggart proclaimed. "Glory!" "Hallelujah!" he shouted.

Satan had now targeted for defeat Jesus' people, Swaggart continued, but God continually defeated Satan's efforts to thwart the plan of God. The gates of the heavenly city described in the book of Revelation toward which all Christians were destined bore the names of the sons of Jacob, Swaggart reminded his hearers. The "heavenly Judah," like Judah, inherited more land than needed, and had said to us, "Come on up into my lot. And we'll take the Canaanites together!" Jesus' kingdom would have no end, Swaggart reminded listeners. Members of the congregation shouted, "Glory!" Swaggart joined in.

Swaggart closed the sermon, as he closes every sermon, with a prayer for those in need of repentance and redemption, asking those in the congregation and those watching at home to bow their heads in prayer with him. "Heavenly Father, these words I have spoken take to the hearts of people," Swaggart said at the close of the sermon on the coming apocalypse.[294] "I know we're about to contend with forces, dark days ahead. Help me tell them to come back to the God of our fathers. /.../ A storm is coming. I hear the rumbling of thunder. Pull toward the light. For Jesus is the light." As Swaggart prayed, the cameras closed in on various individuals praying along with him. An organ began to play a hymn.

Swaggart then gave the altar call, which closes each of the telecasts. The large number of people responding to the altar call gave the impression that God was at work through Swaggart, winning lost souls, bringing backsliders back to the fold in God's effort to build up the Christian forces through which God does battle with Satan and the world. Swaggart asked members of the audience to stand. He then asked for a show of hands of those who would say, "I've lost my way." "Hundreds and hundreds of godly Christians" were praying for them, he told those lifting their hands. He told them the Spirit of God was going to touch them shortly. He then asked those raising their hands to come forward to the podium. As he spoke, he stretched his open hands out over the auditorium and then brought them toward himself. The cameras looked out over the auditorium from the platform as people began to move forward. The choir sang, "Just as I am without one plea but that thy blood was shed for me and biddst me gently come to thee. Oh Lamb of God, I come. I come." Swaggart then spoke directly to the television audience tuning in from "your living room, family room, hotel room, wherever you may be." The cameras pulled in tight as he spoke.

Dozens of people were shown coming forward and crowding around Swaggart on the podium. Those who had come forward were greeted by the staff of the Swaggart ministry and by dozens of followers who had gathered with them down front. As he often does, Swaggart asked followers to gather around those who had come forward. Followers laid their hands on those who had come.

"Those kneeling here, I want you to look at Brother Jimmy for just a moment," Swaggart continued. "I want you to look at me by TV as well. The Lord asked me to tell you he loves you, and you, and you." Swaggart asked those who had come forward and those watching "by television" to pray with him the "Sinner's prayer." "Repeat...after me please," Swaggart said, looking into the camera. He smiled, nodded his head, and gestured with open hands. Those gathered at the front were heard as they prayed in antiphonal response: "Dear God in heaven, I'm a sinner. I'm lost. I need your help. I need it badly. Have mercy on me." Person after person who had come forward was shown repeating the words.

Swaggart declared forgiveness and invited those watching by television to call the toll-free number shown on the screen for a free copy of his book, *There's A New Name Written Down in Glory*, a book devoted to the Christian life. He told viewers that those who called would also receive the cross and dove lapel pin, symbol of the Jimmy Swaggart ministry. The book and pin were shown. "Congratulations!" Swaggart said. He smiled and nodded his head. "You've found the answer! You've found the Lord. /.../ We love you so very, very much!" Those who had come forward and the followers who had moved forward to support them applauded.

The information on how to receive the free booklet and the cross and dove pin was repeated by the program announcer, who returned and brought the telecast to a close. (On one telecast the announcer pointed out that the pin is "a symbol of your faith to all.")[295] "Operators are standing by now." The announcer continued, "More than 500,000 people received this book [this year]...alone. So you can join the many thousands of believers who've received this book by writing us today." Swaggart then appeared in a short video clip to invite viewers to tune in to the next week's broadcast. "You don't want to miss it. I think it's going to be a tremendous service. I know that it will be," he said confidently.

The "Jimmy Swaggart" program unites its Pentecostal viewers in support of one another and in purpose in its role as ritual transition to the alternative world of Pentecostalism. Ritual transition to the safety of the Pentecostal world invites viewers to open themselves to other Pentecostals, to seek and give support, and build community. As ritual performance, the television program strengthens community among these Pentecostals as it provides legitimation of their religion and of their religious group. The Pentecostal view of the world and millenarian vision of the future are reinforced as the religious message is presented in a dramatic performance. Belief is further reinforced as Satan is brought alive through the experience of anxiety and fear created by the dramatization of his diabolical threat. God's presence is made equally real through the relief and sense of triumph elicited by the dramatic presentation of God's imminent deliverance of his people. The telecasts strengthen community among these Pentecostals as they create experiences that underscore the view that God is on their side. Ritual legitimation of their religion and of their religious group as God's righteous people strengthens the community of Pentecostals to withstand the criticism and opposition of the secular world, and to go on the attack by calling the world to judgment and repentance. Strengthening the community of the saved and their opposition to the world, however, invites continued attack by it.

# ⊰ 12 ⊱

## The "PTL Club" and "The Jim and Tammy Show": Ritual Community As Refuge

### Community As Refuge

Rejection and "persecution" of conservative Christians and of the Bakker ministry by the secular world were running themes of the "PTL Club" and "The Jim and Tammy Show." The second program replaced the earlier program following the Bakkers' departure from the PTL ministry. Played out over and over was the "conspiracy" to bring down the Bakkers organized by the secular press, which was portrayed as falsely critical of their television ministry and its operations. The programs included viewers in the struggle. As followers of the Bakkers, and as Pentecostals, they, too, were hounded by the world, viewers were reminded. The telecasts continually refered to the shabby treatment of Pentecostals as well as harsh treatment by the world. They also continually emphasized the need of Pentecostals, and especially the Bakkers' followers, to band together and stand up for themselves. And there was continual mention of the trials and tribulations of life in this world—illness, financial burdens, loss of a job, domestic problems, and other crises—and of how overwhelming these become. The Bakkers offered many prayers for healing—physical, emotional, and spiritual. Jim Bakker even prayed over the telephone with viewers who called in, while Tammy held up the receiver to his ear.[296] The need for mutual love and support among the Bakkers' followers was also a running theme. The television programs attempted to provide support for viewers. "You can make it!" the Bakkers reminded them. The Bakkers got "up close and personal" with their viewers. Jim Bakker took up the role of "pastor." "We're here for the viewer. Our whole purpose is to minister to people, to touch hurting people, to make a difference in their life, to show them that they can make it."[297] The Bakkers' viewers were the "down and out," the little people of the world.[298]

The Bakkers devoted a great deal of air time appealing to viewers for funds to support the television program and the ministry. And viewers gave. They also got a great deal back. Through their financial gifts, viewers became part of the effort of the television ministry to witness to the world. Viewers also funded a program that stuck up for them as it stood up to the hostile secular world, provided nurture and support, and extended to them the nurture and support of the wider Pentecostal community of Bakker followers.

The telecasts offered viewers support in standing up to the secular world by registering a protest against its hostility and mistreatment. They offered viewers the support of Pentecostal people needed to stand up to the world. The telecasts also offered the safe haven of Pentecostal religion and of Pentecostal community. There was a strong emphasis on Pentecostal community as refuge. "The [Christian] church is a sanctuary, safety, a place where the weak feel safe," Jim Bakker told his viewers.[299] He reminded viewers that Heritage, U.S.A., too, was a "Christian retreat Center,"[300] where Pentecostals could come together to play and worship together freely, unencumbered by the world. The emphasis on refuge had the effect of turning the focus of these Pentecostals inward and away from standing up to the world, which only took the form of lodging a protest against persecution. The telecasts had the effect of promoting community as a refuge from the world.

The ritual nature of the telecasts helped these Pentecostals attempt to create community among themselves as a refuge. As ritual, the telecast performances helped viewers remove themselves from the menacing and hurtful outside world where they were treated poorly, and move themselves to an alternative world or safe haven of Pentecostal religion and Pentecostal community. As ritual, the telecasts invited viewers to open themselves to one another and to provide mutual support. As the telecasts reaffirmed the Pentecostal religion and Pentecostal community in their role as ritual legitimation, they turned viewers' focus inward, promoting Pentecostal community as a retreat from the world.

From the safe distance of the ritual context, these Pentecostals were free to protest against a hostile world, call down God's judgment upon it, and speak of its pending defeat and of their vindication with the return of Christ. There was little mention of standing up to the world within the political arena, and little mention of organizing politically. Having closed themselves off from the world, their protests and bravado become muted.

### Persecution and Retreat

The opening of the "PTL Club" helped its beleaguered viewers leave the weary world behind. The program's opening song, an ebullient, pop-style tune, was played by a live stage band, which included snazzy trumpets and drums, set up on a side stage just off the main stage.[301] A singing group that appeared regularly on the show took another stage. The opening musical theme served notice to the world that these Pentecostal Christians were sick and tired of being "persecuted" by the world, and deserved better. It served notice that they are a significant people, since they were the people of God. "Enough is enough!" go the words. "I won't sit down. I won't sit down. In God I'm standing strong and tough. /.../ I'm taking back what's rightfully mine. Watch out, Satan, I'm calling your bluff. Enough is enough is enough!" As the music played, a video tape showed pictures of new buildings going up at Heritage, U.S.A., including the reconstructed boyhood home of Billy Graham.

"Welcome to our 'Enough is Enough' telethon hosted by Jim and Tammy Bakker," announced the program's emcee, Doug Oldham, a Christian singer. The audience applauded. He was seen on the screen with the Bakkers, who were milling with some of the volunteers positioned at telephones on the large stage where they took calls from viewers who phoned in pledges during the telethon. A large banner hung above the phone bank announcing the telethon's theme: "Enough is Enough!" "Hi-oooh!" the emcee called out, imitating the famous introduction of Johnny Carson by Ed MacMahon, the emcee on "The Tonight Show." The rest of the program also mimiced the talk-show's format. There were guest interviews, music specials, commentaries by the hosts, etc. The show's format, production values, and music looked and sounded like secular television. The show's production values were first-rate, equaling those of commercial and public television. They were produced by state-of-the-art technology. The Bakkers were smartly dressed and groomed, as were many of their guests. Their speech was friendly and informal. They spoke often about the right of Pentecostal people, too, to enjoy the finer things in life and about God's desire to see his people go first-class.

The Bakkers then greeted the audience. "Oh, you're a nice group! Hello everybody! Welcome to our annual telethon coming to you from Heritage, U.S.A.," Jim Bakker said to the large audience in an animated, cheerful voice. The program was one in a series of programs running over a six-week period devoted to raising financial support for the growing PTL ministry. The cameras showed the audience applauding heartily. The camera shots of the audience helped the viewer feel a part of the action. The cameras cut back and forth from the Bakkers and their guests to the audience throughout the program, registering the audience's response. The Bakkers spoke directly to viewers throughout the show. "[This is ] the place to be!" "Such nice people!" Tammy Bakker joined in. "There is something so exciting happening!" Jim Bakker said enthusiastically. The quick-paced and upbeat opening produced an immediate high.

Straight off the bat, Jim Bakker told viewers that "The Devil came against PTL. Thought he could destroy it." On another telecast aired one week later, Bakker told viewers that the Devil wanted PTL because it was "the largest full-time [twenty-four-hour] Christian network in the world."[302] He referred to the television congregation as the largest Christian church in the world. PTL declared the gospel to an enormous number of people, he said. That was why the Devil was trying to discredit PTL, as he was trying to "discredit everything Christian today," Bakker told viewers. "But I've got news," Bakker said, "No weapon formed against me shall prosper." This was the "inheritance of the children of the most high God," he said. Tammy raises her right hand and quietly uttered an "Amen" in response as she nodded her head.

Jim Bakker then asked that a telephone number be put up on the screen "right away" in order that viewers could help fight back by phoning in their pledges of financial support for the ministry. There were "friends all over the land standing with us," Bakker told viewers. This was "the greatest rally I've ever seen in my life," he said. "People are saying, 'Enough is enough! We're gonna keep PTL on twenty-four hours a day.'" The telephone lines were "jamming," Bakker told viewers. (On a telecast aired the following week Bakker reported that the telephone company had logged 6,000 calls coming in during a single hour.)[303] "All over America people are calling. The [PTL] Partners are saying, 'We want Jim and Tammy in our home. We want the PTL satellite in our home.'" Partners were saying they want to be a part of a television ministry broadcasting "around the world for Jesus," part of the Heritage, U.S.A. Christian retreat ministry, and part of the other ministries of PTL, Bakker added.

Jim Bakker offered those who pledge monthly support to the ministry as "Partners" a copy of his book, *Showers of Blessing*, and a bumper sticker reading "Enough is Enough!" Tammy handed Jim a copy of the book to display. She also held pledge cards collected from volunteers answering the calls of viewers who phone in to make a financial pledge. Volunteers were shown answering the phones. There were several dozen of them. A light board kept track of the thousands of viewers who had phoned in pledges. Bakker also offered viewers who made a pledge a PTL membership card that read: "I'm a member of a worldwide team that is trying to win the world for Jesus Christ."

Jim Bakker told viewers he wanted to send them the book and bumper sticker to remind them that "We're not going to put up with the Devil any more," that "We're not going to give up our dreams...we're going to take back what the Devil took away." The camera showed a close-up shot of Bakker's book, the bumper sticker, and the membership card. Bakker urged viewers to phone and say, "'Jim and Tammy, you can count on me.'"

The Bakkers then joined their guests who were seated on a smaller stage in front of the main stage. The telephone number remained on the screen. Bakker said he was exhausted after the telethon effort "to beat back the Enemy," who had "thrown in everything but the kitchen sink." "He even threw the kitchen sink in, Honey," Tammy added, jumping in. As Jim Bakker sat down with his guests he pointed out that by sitting he was breaking a rule of the telethon. But "God said he's running the telethon," he added. "Amen," Doug Oldham responded. Bakker continued to run the telephone pledge campaign from his seat. "God's spirit has spoken to me," Bakker told viewers. He quoted Christian scripture: "'It's not by might, it's not by power, but it's by my spirit sayeth the Lord.'" There were already signs that God was victorious, he said. "Jesus is coming soon." He told viewers he believed they were going to call to say, "'Jim and Tammy, you can count me in. I want to be part of PTL, Christian television.'"

"Our enemies worry about the power of Christian television ministry," Jim Bakker continued. "If they don't stop, we'll come together and become the biggest army on the face of the earth." There were responses of "Amen." "In persecution, the church stands together." The enemy was going "to drive millions and millions and millions of Christians together for survival," producing a "unity" among them, as on the day of Pentecost, Bakker told viewers. There were already signs and miracles that showed that "Jesus is coming soon," he added. "It's time we shouldn't have to beg Christians to do the work of the Lord," Tammy Bakker joined in. Jim Bakker continued. "We need a miracle. Something is happening across this land. People are saying, 'Enough is enough.' /.../ The Lord is moving. Together we stand strong. Divided we fall." Bakker then asked viewers to pray with him. "God bring healing. God, speak to those needing healing."

Doug Oldham commented on the large number of calls coming in response to the fundraising campaign. "The Lord is vindicating his people." There were so many calls coming in that someone might wonder if the calls were rigged, he said. "God's people are saying, 'Enough is enough. I'm tired of the way I've been treated. I'm poor, but I have had enough. The Devil is walking on me.'" Jim Bakker reminded viewers that giving opened up the "floodgates of blessing." Vestal Oldham, seated on the platform with the others, suggested that pledges were "seed offering(s)": God would bless those who gave in order that they might give even more. Tammy Bakker passed along the report from a viewer who had phoned in from Rockhill, South Carolina, that he had received a financial miracle after sending in a pledge. She passed along another, similar report from a viewer in Knoxville, Virginia. We're becoming an "army," Vestal Oldham responded, "because we're tired of being pushed around." She pointed out that the PTL Partners were pushed around all the more easily because they did not make up a denomination and lacked the clout of one.

Jim Bakker then read off the number of pledges phoned in, as well as the number of pledges given under different categories of membership as a PTL Partner. "Life-time" memberships promised three nights of free accommodations at Heritage, U.S.A. "We need to hear from everyone. It's time to get on board. If you don't do right, it's a sin, the Bible says. It's also a sin to sit back and let Christian television be raped by Satan's cohorts," he told viewers. As he spoke, a short video tape showed the theme park, as well as the new water park about to open. "Campmeeting twenty-first century style!" Bakker commented. He pointed out that the view of the water park was from the hotel that was in the process of going up. The cameras then showed a typical room in one of the completed hotels, named the "Grand Hotel." Bakker described the accommodations as "Waldorf-Astoria-style rooms. When you come, you're a King's kid." Later in the show Bakker told viewers that Heritage, U.S.A. was a place that could help Pentecostals get over feeling apologetic. ("Just because you're poor doesn't mean you have to be tacky," he said on another telecast aired around the same time, winning laughter from the audience.)[304] He reported that memberships had sold out for the Grand, but were still available for the then unfinished "Towers Hotel." "That tower is going up and the Devil can't stop it," he said on the other telecast. On the same telecast, Bakker pointed out that at Heritage, U.S.A., PTL Partners could go on a "Jesus holiday." On that occasion he pointed out that the theme park had a prayer room, "dedicated as a house of prayer 'til Jesus comes," which was open twenty-four hours a day, with a pastor on duty.[305]

"'Give and it shall be given,'" Jim Bakker said, quoting Christian scripture. "'Give in order to receive. Faith without works is dead,'" he said, continuing to quote scripture. "You've got to give to receive. As we stand together we'll see the greatest move of God in the world." Bakker reported that 70,000 people had become PTL Partners. As he spoke, the cameras showed individual telephone volunteers taking calls. "People are saying, 'Enough is enough! We're gonna stand with Jim and Tammy not out of emotion...[but] because we're going to be obedient to the call of God in our lives.' And that's what's happening," he told viewers.

Jim Bakker went on to report that there had been a "demonstration of the spirit and power of the Lord" at Heritage, U.S.A. during the period of the telethon, then in its fourth week. He told viewers that many had received a "word of knowledge" and many had received healings. "Jim, I feel like the Lord is just moving all over," Tammy Bakker responded. "I believe the power of the Lord is being loosed throughout this earth and you can have it if you want it in your soul." "You," she said, pointing directly into the camera. Her voice broke. As she testified, she raised her right palm and clinched her hand several times as if claiming power. The studio audience broke into applause. The telephone number reappeared on the screen.

"Amen!" Jim Bakker replied. "I want to tell you something," he said. "Man can't hold back what God is going to do." He told viewers that they were entering "a new era. God is going to begin a wave of the Spirit." The "slandering of God's people is going to come to an end!" he shouted. The Oldhams responded with shouts of "Praise God!" and "Amen!" "The enemies of the gospel will fall on the right and the left.

/.../ We're entering, ushering in the coming of the Lord Jesus Christ," Bakker declared. He pounded the air with both fists. The audience broke into applause. "People are either going to be on God's side or Satan's. There are groups out now to destroy Evangelicals." There were "campaigns against God," Bakker told viewers. He mentioned abortion rights groups, groups opposed to prayer in public schools, and groups opposed to Bible reading in the schools. "People, God said he will separate the sheep from the goats. The Bible says, you must choose this day whom you will serve. I believe millions of people are saying, 'Enough is enough. We are not going to side with the Devil.'" The audience applauded.

The ringing telephones were a "roll call from the saints of God," Jim Bakker told viewers. People were phoning to pledge and say, "'Jim and Tammy, enough is enough. We're standing with you.' This is our twenty-fifth year of ministry, and [the secular press] is writing as if we're the new kid on the block." Bakker again mentioned the Christian retreat center and other programs of the PTL ministry: the food distribution center, the prison ministry, the home for unwed pregnant mothers, and PTL in Japan. The telephone volunteers were shown answering calls. "You phone and say, 'We're not going to let the Devil have a heyday anymore. /.../ We are here to refire, not retire, to be a part of a worldwide ministry to one another.' The best is yet to come, if you believe it. Let's take the territory!" Bakker shouted. "The best is yet to come!" he declared as he introduced a song by Doug Oldham which included these same words: "The best is yet to come before this life is done. So hold on. We've just begun. The best is yet to come." "This ministry is under attack by the press and other agencies," the singer stopped to tell viewers. "We've walked to the edge [of having to close]. But God holds on. His miracles still happen." The telephone number remained on the screen while the volunteers continued to answer calls.

The musical interlude was followed by a video tape on the PTL ministry. It was accompanied by upbeat, light-rock music. The video clip moved quickly from one scene to another. There were scenes of visitors at Heritage, U.S.A. They were seen playing ball, attending an outdoor cookout, swimming, riding a miniature train ride, walking through "Winter Wonderland," weeping in a prayer service in the "Upper Room," a recreation of the biblical location of Jesus' last meal with his disciples, attending a Passion play, listening to Jim and Tammy sing, and "dancing in the Spirit" at a campmeeting service. There were also shots of personalities who had come to visit: "Mr. T," the television star; Mickey Rooney; and Billy Graham.

The video segment included pictures of other projects carried out by the PTL ministry, some of which were worldwide in scope: food relief— food was shown being distributed to homeless people; clothing, shelter, health, and education programs, and a prison ministry—Tammy was shown visiting prisoners; a home for unwed expectant mothers—Tammy was shown holding a newborn baby; and the PTL television ministry— the television ministry's satellite dishes were shown.

"I'm not building this for Jim Bakker. I'm building this for the people of the Lord till Jesus comes," Bakker told viewers. He and Tammy were shown standing in front of architectural drawings of future buildings to go up at the retreat center.

Tammy Bakker then reported that her sister had phoned in a pledge and adds, "This is the most exciting thing, PTL." She and Jim had moved among the telephone volunteers. "Callers are saying, '[Jim and Tammy] you can minister on your television program to America without having to face this [financial] burden every day,'" Jim Bakker told viewers. A telephone volunteer reported that calls were coming in from Michigan, Virginia, and elsewhere. "I just want to cry for sheer relief!" Tammy exclaimed. "I just love new Partners, Jim."

"Everyone is doing what they can," Jim Bakker said. "I believe if we do, then God can do what he can." "I believe in…what we do at this place," Tammy declared. Bakker told viewers that the response to the telethon was "a witness to this ministry. This is the greatest response in the history of the ministry. People are not going to buy the trashing of the work of the Lord."

A volunteer from the telephone bank called out the names of other places from which viewers were phoning in: Nova Park, California! Columbus, Ohio! Mississippi! The helper reported that she had received a one-time gift of 10,000 dollars. Jim made a surprise announcement, "I have in my hand a check for 100,000 dollars from Memphis. It is verified." The audience let out a whoop and broke into applause. The cameras showed the audience from the rear of the auditorium, looking forward toward the stage. They were going to see "victory in this camp," Bakker assured his listeners. "We as God's people are not going to put up with it anymore. Enough is enough!" Bakker offered viewers who phoned in a "PTL Partner pin." He again mentioned the PTL Partner membership card, pointing out that the card identified a contributor as an "official partner."

A volunteer telephone staffer read the names of other places: Little Rock, Arkansas; New Jersey; Munford, Tennessee. Another volunteer gave other cities: Dallas, Texas; Uniontown, Ohio; Pearl River, Louisiana. The volunteer again mentioned the food relief project. He added that when PTL Partners came to Heritage, U.S.A., they would be "refreshed and renewed...[to go out on] the fighting line."

Bakker then asked how many in the audience were there for a workshop. Those who were stood. The audience applauded them. He reports that 200 Partners were there to attend one or another of the ministry's workshops. Bakker asked people in the group how they were coming along. He reached out and touched one of the couples. "God has changed my life," the male member of the couple testified. He reported that he had been called back to his job after being laid off. Bakker pointed out that those who have stood are participating in the ministry's workshop for drug and alcohol counseling. He asked someone else about his progress. The man said he "got delivered from alcohol."

Jim Bakker specified other enemies of the PTL ministry in other telecasts aired during the fundraising telethon. They were by and large the news media making allegations of financial impropriety. Bakker said he regarded these as "smear campaigns" designed to "discredit" and "slaughter" the ministry. He portrayed the press as "very powerful" and heavily bankrolled.[306] On one of these telecasts Bakker told viewers the allegations of financial impropriety made by the *Charlotte Observer* were part of a "conspiracy to destroy PTL" by discouraging pending bank loans.[307] (The newspaper won a Pulitzer Prize for its investigation of the ministry.) "They tail Tammy and I like criminals everywhere we go," Bakker told viewers. The newspaper was trying to get the United States government to investigate the ministry and "to close PTL down," he added. "They have tried for ten years and have not been able to do it," he noted, drawing applause from the audience. He reminded viewers that the U.S. Justice Department, "the highest investigative branch of government," had already cleared PTL of any wrongdoing. He issued a "challenge" to the newspaper "to document" the accusations of financial illegality and welcomed the opportunity to speak the truth.

"There's a war people!" Jim Bakker shouted. Some members of the press were "out to kill religion," he told viewers. There was an effort, he declared, "to literally bring down Christianity in this country!" It was "time for Christians to stand up and say, 'Jim and Tammy, we hold dear our religious freedom.' Liberty today means freedom for everyone except evangelical Christianity," Bakker continued. This nation was built on the principle of the "founding Fathers" of "freedom for all," Bakker told viewers. He reported that the program had been banned from some television stations. "We're literally letting them rape Christianity today and we're not doing a thing about it!" There were scattered "Amens!" from the audience.

"The Devil is trying to cut off money from the ministries, to destroy them." Bakker told viewers that stories carried in the *Charlotte Observer* led some banks to stop loans that had already been approved to finance new construction at the ministry's "campground." "Don't you think the Devil wants to close the largest Christian retreat center in the world? /.../ I'd be worried if he didn't.... If we're not careful, we're going to wake up and you're gonna find out it's all gone, people. /.../ You're gonna find out that because we did nothing, evil took over."

Jim Bakker reminded viewers that Christians were living in the final days. He told them that they were undergoing the great conflict of "the Church of Jesus Christ" with the secular world as foretold by the Bible. He suggested that the derision of the ministry by the talk-shows on commercial television was another example of the conflict. "It's time to stand up people. They're laughing at us. The world is mocking the Church like never before. I think it's time that we stand together and say, 'Enough is enough.'" Some who called themselves Christians would fall away as the Bible said, Bakker told viewers, "cause they can't stand the heat."

"I believe you need to know this is more than a battle between a newspaper and a church," Jim Bakker said of the fight with the *Charlotte Observer* on another telethon telecast.[308] He read a quote from an interview with the editor of the newspaper: "I don't think there is a God, but I really don't know." He repeated the quote. "This is...a spiritual battle." "There are only two powers in the world [God and the Devil], the Bible says." He read pejorative headlines from other newspapers and urged viewers to "Tell us how you feel, how you want us to do. /.../ I can talk to you. /.../ We need your help. We need your prayers."

Someday these buildings would crumble, Jim Bakker told viewers. The newspaper presses would fall silent. "I want to tell you there's only one thing according to the holy Word of God that's gonna survive from this world into eternity, and that's the Church of Jesus Christ." There were "Amens!" from the audience. "Jesus said...I will build my church and the gates of hell shall not prevail against it!" Bakker exclaimed, jabbing the air with his fist, thumb extended upward, signaling victory. The audience broke out in thunderous applause. "'Greater is He [God] that is in you than He [Satan] that is in the world,'" Bakker declared, quoting scripture.[309] "We win!" he reassured viewers.

Jim Bakker ended many of the telecasts with his familiar farewell, "Remember, God loves you. He really does!" offering support and encouragement.[310] "Good things are happening. God is on your side," he said at the conclusion of another broadcast.[311] Tammy blew a kiss to viewers and waved her fingers at the conclusion of some of the shows. "Praise the Lord, for the battle has been won. Together we can make it. Together we can face the world," sang the choir in closing.[312]

Following the Bakkers' departure from the "PTL" show in the wake of scandal, the program made a concerted effort "to close ranks and prevent the enemy from having a field day."[313] Jerry Falwell made the declaration on a PTL program introducing him as the new advisor to the troubled ministry. He had been invited to serve as advisor by Bakker himself. Along with Falwell, the program introduced the new board of directors to PTL followers. Richard Dortch, PTL staff member newly appointed by Falwell as PTL "pastor," made the introductions. Recognizing that the Bakkers' Pentecostal followers had reservations about the fundamentalist televangelist, who had been among the religious figures who had criticized the Bakkers, Dortch asked him to tell viewers about "Falwell the man," emphasizing that "PTL is about relationships," about a "bond." Falwell reassured viewers they could expect the PTL ministry to remain Pentecostal, ministering to "the family of God." He went on to make the point that at that time, there was a real need to demonstrate to the national media that Christians would remain united. "The world and the press will take note" of members of "the body of Christ" helping one another, he said.

Falwell asked viewers to join him in praying for "Jim and Tammy." He also offered prayers for the Bakkers' followers. "We're going to pray for you. We care about you," he said. He prayed that the Bakkers would know that they "are wrapped up in love and prayer and concern" and that God would give followers "strength and courage." He referred to the "field day" Satan had had in recent days. "We claim the promise...that 'All things work together for good ultimately for them that love you [God],'" he prayed, invoking the well-known and comforting passage in Christian scripture.

The telecast closed with a show of unity and support as Dortch and Falwell clasped hands. The audience also joined hands and raised them overhead as the PTL chorus sang "Holding on Together." Dortch closed the program by repeating the familiar farewell with which Bakker had ended the telecasts, "Remember, God loves you! He really, really does! Bye-bye for today." While the show was going off the air, there was an "update" on the PTL ministry "from Heritage, U.S.A." The report was given by "Uncle Henry," a regular on the program. An announcement also notified PTL followers of opportunities for them to engage in "intercessory prayer" with "prayer warriors" in the "Upper Room" at the retreat center, along with opportunities for a Bible seminar, devotional and anointing services, a communion service, a healing service, and a "praise" service at the retreat center.

Pentecostal community in the face of persecution took on new meaning on the new "Jim and Tammy Show," which aired following the Bakkers' departure from PTL and just ahead of Jim Bakker's going to trial, and then to prison. The new show aired from the Bakkers' makeshift studio in a converted, partially unfinished strip shopping center in Orlando. The musical theme for the new show, "You Can Make It," an upbeat pop-Gospel tune, provided comfort to those followers who could catch the show on one of the dozen or so stations still carrying the Bakkers: "You can make it. God will show you just what to do. /.../ I don't care what's going on. You're not in this thing alone. You can make it."[314] The Bakkers themselves were living proof, the song seemed to say. Whatever their trials, God would see them through, the song reminded viewers.

Missing from the new show were the big stage, huge audience, singing group and band—replaced by prerecorded, "Christian music"— and flashy production values. The Bakkers sat close together on the new, small set. Their conversations with viewers were low-keyed and very personal. They spoke openly about the trials they had gone through and about Jim Bakker's impending court trial. Tammy sang a great deal more than she had on the old show. She sang about mercy and forgiveness: "The just are forgiven, a new name is written, for mercy rewrote my life." Their guests, many of them Pentecostal pastors, defended the Bakkers. "Forgiveness" and "restoration" of the Bakker ministry were the themes of the new show. There was also a great deal of talk about the ministry's critics, including unnamed televangelists, and their unjust judgments against the ministry. There were prayers for forgiveness and healing. There was a great deal of talk of rebuilding the ministry. And there was a great deal of talk by Jim Bakker of building a new Christian retreat center, "where people can get together..., congregate." "I believe the best is yet to come," Tammy Bakker told viewers. "I believe the Devil would dance with glee if Jim Bakker lost influence. God won't let that happen," Bakker told viewers. The new show also devoted a good deal of time to raising funds to start up the new television ministry.

"What kind of people will Jesus use?" Jim Bakker asked at the beginning of another telecast from the new headquarters.[315] He read a passage from Christian scripture, which he identified as 1 Corinthians 3: "'Not many who are wise or noble are called. God chooses the foolish. I take pleasure in my persecution. When I am weak, then I am strong.'" Bakker told his audience that because they were weak, they would eventually defeat the powers of this world as well as Satan. He reminded them that God had sided with them. "The enemy uses our own failure to destroy us...[but] the enemies of God will be confounded." "The higher man walks, the more demonic" the activity against him, Bakker told his audience. "When the enemy smashed PTL, they did not just smash Jim and Tammy. They smashed thousands of ministers..., [and] millions of Christians and supporters." The attack on him and Tammy was an attack on the Church, Bakker said. "We've got a warfare [going on]. The Church is always open to the evil powers in the world." If the people of God stood together during these last days of "warfare," they would "defeat Satan," Bakker reminded viewers.

He continued in the same vein on another telecast of "The Jim and Tammy Show."[316] Again he read from the Bible after identifying the scripture passage (1 Corinthians 21:36-41): "'God has chosen the lowly, weak, base things to confound the wise.'" "The world says these are foolish people," Bakker told viewers. "God says these are the real people. ...Jesus says, you are complete in me, no matter what the world says." God poured out his grace and wisdom upon the lowly, Bakker added. He read another verse from the Bible (2 Corinthians 12:9), which lay open in his lap: "'My strength is made perfect in weakness.' God says, 'I choose to use the weak.' 'My power shows up best in weak people,'" Bakker reminded viewers. "Hallelujah!" some in the audience shouted while they applauded. Bakker again quoted Christian scripture: "'If God be for us, who can be against us?'" "'We know that all things work for good for those that love the Lord.'" As Bakker signed off, he repeated his old, familiar farewell: "And remember, God loves you! He really, really does!"

The Bakkers' telecasts offered their followers a refuge or retreat from the weary world, where they could come together as a beleaguered group. The telecasts offered an opportunity for these Pentecostals to come together as a supportive community to help one another nurse the wounds and hurts inflicted by a hateful world. The broadcasts also offered these viewers the support of a community of Pentecostals needed to stand up to the world and voice a complaint about their mistreatment. As ritual transition away from the everyday world, in which defenses must remain high, to the safe haven offered by Pentecostal religion, the telecasts invited viewers to open themselves to one another, and to ask for and receive support. As ritual legitimation of Pentecostalism, the telecasts validated and strengthened Pentecostal community. The emphasis on Pentecostals, and on the Bakkers' followers as God's persecuted people encouraged viewers to stick to themselves. In the end, retreating amongst themselves invited further derision and rebuff by the larger world.

# -⊨ 13 ⊨-

## Conclusion:
## The Recent Shift in Ritual Roles:
## Televangelism's New Emphasis on
## Community

### *Supportive Christian Community*

The emphasis given televangelism's roles as ritual self-legitimation and ritual adaptation by viewers and programmers has shifted, following the Bakker and Swaggart scandals and following the political defeats or set-backs suffered by Robertson, Falwell, and the Religious Right. There is a new emphasis on televangelism's role as ritual community. The shift reflects the shift in the social fortune of televangelism's conservative Christian viewers and promoters. Ahead of the crises, televangelism played a major role in the aggressive foray of religious conservatives into American politics. Televangelism gave legitimacy in the eyes of the conservative Christians to their religion as well as religious group. This was vital to their efforts to mobilize themselves politically. At the same time, televangelism played a major role in another kind of foray by the conservative Christians into American life. It helped religious conservatives familiarize themselves with and adopt features of the more secularized outlook and lifestyle of mainstream American society. Televangelism also helped them make a foray into secular American society.

The aggressive entry into the political arena, along with the display of worldliness, has won religious conservatives the opposition and rebuff of mainstream society. Defeat and rebuke have led them to ease their combativeness toward secular society and to take a more inward focus. While conservative Christians have continued to look to televangelism to legitimate and adapt themselves, defeat and reproach have led them to look to it even more to help them strengthen community among themselves, feeling the need for mutual support.

Robertson and Falwell have redirected their energies toward pastoring their flocks and overseeing their ministries. Robertson had taken a leave of absence from his program when he set out on the Presidential campaign trail in order to satisfy federal election laws. Falwell had devoted a great deal of time to running the Moral Majority while he continued to preach to viewers from the pulpit of his Thomas Road Baptist Church.

To underscore his return home following his long absence from the air, Robertson had his son interview him about his shift in direction and about his plans to tend more to the needs of his television ministry and television viewers in a kind of reversal of the story of the return of the prodigal son. Back from his stinging defeat in his Presidential bid, Robertson said he had put politics aside, or at least his own political ambitions. He spoke of the need to nurture the Christian community and to build it up through a return to "Bible basics." Robertson stepped out of the high-tech newsroom set, from which he continues to report on political events and social issues, and stepped up to a humble chalkboard, where he illustrated a Bible lesson. He returned to the study of "the Word" in order to nurture and build up the community of followers and provide encouragement to them.

In a cameo spot coming just ahead of one of his telecasts Falwell told viewers that God had instructed him to redirect his "priorities" away from devoting the majority of his time to involvement in politics and in campaigns, and back toward the pulpit.[317] He gestured toward the pulpit in the church auditorium that would soon be filled with his flock from where he was speaking. "I am now listening to God's voice and cutting back to basics." "It's back to basics with Jerry Falwell," back to "The Old-Time Gospel Hour," and back to "soul winning." Falwell announced his plans to devote more time to Liberty University and to training Christian young people to evangelize America. He predicted his announcement would make headlines the next day. Falwell had not yet shut down the Moral Majority, which he would do a few years later for lack of adequate support. The political lobby had also come under heavy criticism and opposition.

With passion, Falwell spoke about his reasons for shifting his priorities. He acknowledged that since founding the Moral Majority in 1979 he had devoted most of his time to it. He had spent day and night, he told viewers, organizing millions of Christians "to stand up and be counted," and crying out against "America's sins" "trying to save America," which had been on the verge of "collapse." He said he truly believed he had "fought a good fight" and that America was "beginning to turn around." He spoke openly of the burden on his heart. He reported that his ministry was on the verge of financial default and appealed to "friends like you who are still behind me" to show a "miraculous outpouring of financial support," $5.8 million to pay off a loan falling due shortly. "I'm asking for a vote of confidence from you and every one of my friends." He told viewers that he had never needed a vote of confidence like he needed this show of support. Without the money, he explained, "everything we've worked and prayed for" would be in "jeopardy." "Let's stand together." "My soul has been agonizing," he told viewers. He had gone "down to the valley," he said, and had cried himself to sleep. He compared himself to a soldier returning home from the frontlines to see the home front in shambles. "I am back home for good. Let me repeat that to you. I am back in Lynchburg for good."

Falwell's announcement was followed by several hymns sung by the "The Old-Time Gospel Hour Choir" on the theme of following God's leadership. "God leads his dear children along. Some through the waters, some through the flood, some through the fire, but all through his blood. Some through great sorrows, but God gives a song, in the night season and all the day long," went one of the songs, an old, traditional hymn. The sermon that followed was given to "Christian Crises." Falwell spoke of the crisis of being called into Christian service. He spoke of crises faced during the humble origins of his preaching ministry and the thirty-year-old television and radio ministry, and of those faced while leading the Moral Majority. And he spoke of the immediate financial crisis facing the Thomas Road church and its ministry. He spoke of a church at the "crossroads" and of plans to build a larger church building and build up Liberty University as part of a plan to expand the ministry of world evangelization. He closed the service by asking the congregation and viewers at home to pray for the "reconsecration" of the ministry to the service of God. "Let's just join hearts right now" to pray for reconsecration he asked his audience. Members of the congregation were shown falling down upon their knees at the altar and were overheard praying aloud in small groups gathered in the aisles of the church. "If God's people pray, we can make it," Falwell said in closing.

Following his sex scandal, Swaggart was taken back in by his fold. In a tearful, televised confession, Swaggart asked the forgiveness of his congregation, who were later shown encircling and embracing their fallen and forgiven brother.[318] Swaggart made another confession in another telecast.[319] "To my knowledge I've never asked a man to pray for me. I thought I didn't need you to pray for me," he told his faithful followers. Swaggart reached out and took the hands of a male member of the congregation as he confessed to his "pride" of believing he did not need their support or admonition. He confessed to the pride of not allowing himself to be touched by sister and fellow Christians while he touched nations. He reached out to yet another man in the congregation. Taking the hand of a woman seated nearby he confessed, "You see, a year ago I would have never come to you to ask your prayer for me." "When finally...pride is broken, when you're so weak you reach out to anybody. You don't care who it is and say, 'Would you lay your hand on my head and pray for me.'" He reached out for the hand of someone else in the congregation. As the program closed, members of the congregation were shown streaming forward to the altar to pray. They placed their arms around one another, held hands, and cried together.

The new "The Jim and Tammy Show," aired from the Bakkers' makeshift broadcast center in Orlando, provided comfort and support to the extended Bakker family who were able to view them on the few remaining stations carrying them. Viewers of the new show were comforted by a new theme song: "You can make it. God will show you just what to do. /.../ I don't care what's going on. You're not in this thing alone. You can make it." Viewers of the new program were given a cozy welcome by a grandmotherly senior citizen who appeared regularly on the new show, affectionately called "Grandma Gruber": "Welcome to Sunny Florida!" "Grandpa Gruber" sometimes appeared alongside her. Adding to the cozy feel of the new show was a new set that resembled a family sitting room. The Bakkers, their guests, and Grandma and Grandpa Gruber sat gathered in tight around a coffee table piled with Bibles the Bakkers were selling to contributors. The Bakkers sat in twin wingback armchairs. The group was shown holding hands while they prayed together. Just over the couple's shoulders was a large portrait-studio photograph of the Bakker family. The cozy set and the family gathering created the impression that viewers were visiting the Bakkers in their own living room. Jim Bakker repeated the point, over and over, that the extended Bakker family needed one another.

In the middle of one program, Jim Bakker invited an ordinary guest in the small studio audience to join him and the guest pastors and evangelists on the set to give his testimony.[320] Bakker explained to the audience that the young man had reintroduced himself to him before the show. He told viewers that the two had met earlier after the man identified himself as the individual for whom Bakker had prayed on a broadcast of the "PTL Club" after receiving a "word of knowledge" about someone suffering from a disabling back disorder. The man had made a trip to see Bakker following his healing. The guest, a professional golfer, testified about his healing and about the support he had received from the program, without which he said he would not have made it through his ordeal or through the painful surgeries and therapy. The golfer, who reported that he had returned to playing the game as a professional, went on to defend the Bakker ministry as one that God continued to support. He reported that the support he had received during his own ordeal had led him to continue to follow the Bakkers in spite of controversy. A family visiting the new Bakker headquarters expressed its support off the air. The family had given up a vacation and had driven all the way from Michigan to the new home of the television ministry to help do carpentry work, paint, and make repairs.

Bakker ended the new show with words of encouragement. "You can make it. You can make it. You. You. Right now. God is on your side," he reminded viewers.

## Conclusions

Christian community is televangelism's new theme for the moment. Human community is its unstated emphasis. Televangelism cannot satisfy either interest completely, given the indirectness forced upon the communication and interaction among viewers by the medium. Televangelism does not allow conservative Christians to embody community with one another, even though it helps to create a sense of community among them. The prominence of the television ministers in the various telecasts, together with the authoritarian structure of the television ministries, also place limits on televangelism's capacity to create community among its followers. Televangelism nevertheless remains attractive for the masses of conservative Christian viewers scattered across the country who find in it the support of sister and fellow Christians in the extended community of conservative Christians.

What televangelism's future emphasis will be depends in large measure on the unfolding of the ongoing social drama of tension and conflict between televangelism's conservative Christian viewers and promoters and secular, mainstream American society. Televangelism will continue to play an important role in the playing out of this conflict, and in the shaping of it in its several roles as ritual. In its role as ritual legitimation for conservative Christians of their religion and religious group, televangelism helps mobilize religious conservatives as confident and militant warriors to undertake the moral regeneration of American society through political activism. In its role as ritual adaptation, televangelism helps conservative Christians accommodate themselves to some of the demands of secular society. In its role as ritual community, televangelism provides its followers, if in limited ways, with the support of human community in their ongoing struggle for greater inclusion in mainstream American society. As ritual, televangelism will continue to help its conservative Christian followers respond to mainstream society and produce a response from it. It will also continue to help its conservative Christian viewers take action that helps to shape the larger social drama in which they are engaged and remain active subjects of their own lives.

# ⊰ Appendix ⊱

## Survey of Viewers

*Background on the Survey and Its Design*

As a proviso, I note that my survey of viewers is not offered as a scientific measurement. Respondents were self-selected, after all, which is reflected in their overwhelmingly positive response to the television programs. The survey was intended to gather responses that would be illustrative of viewers' general attitudes toward the programs, their reasons or motivations for watching, their viewing habits, and the extent to which they participate in the programs. The survey results are in keeping with those of the scientific survey undertaken jointly by the Annenberg School of Communications at the University of Pennsylvania and the Gallup Organization, the most extensive study to date of viewers of religious television, their attitudes, and viewing patterns.[321] My survey was made during the period of May 27 to June 3, 1990.

The scope of the survey as well as the number of respondents—336 viewers participated—was restricted by "shoestring" research funds. In order to maximize the pool of responses, the survey targeted viewers in the top television markets identified by the Arbitron Ratings Service in February 1990 for the "700 Club," "The Old-Time Gospel Hour," and Jimmy Swaggart's telecasts. The Bakkers were no longer broadcasting the "PTL Club." Nor were they broadcasting nationally. I attempted to get some of the viewers who had watched the Bakkers by targeting former viewers in the top markets for the "PTL Club" in February 1988, when they last appeared on the program.

The top markets for each of the programs were: Los Angeles, where Robertson drew 37,800 individual viewers, and the Bakkers drew 23,800 viewers; Philadelphia, where Falwell drew 30,800 viewers; and Atlanta, where Swaggart drew 50,400 viewers. In order to get a national represen- tation of viewers, the top markets for each of the programs were clustered together to determine which cities were the top markets for all of the programs combined. Viewers of the various programs living in these cities were then targeted. This brought in the Detroit area. Detroit was Robertson's third largest draw (16,800 viewers). It shared with two other cities the rank of fifth largest market for the Bakkers (7,000 viewers). It was the twentieth largest market for Falwell, a rank shared with several other cities (5,600 viewers). And it was Swaggart's twenty- second largest market, tied with a few other cities (8,400 viewers).

Los Angeles was Swaggart's ninth largest draw. The only ministry for which Los Angeles was not a top draw was Falwell's. Los Angeles did not even fall within Falwell's top thirty markets. Philadelphia was the Bakkers' second biggest market (18,200 viewers). It was Swaggart's third biggest market (30,800), and the fourth largest for Robertson (14,000). Atlanta was Falwell's fifth biggest draw, a rank shared with a few other cities (12,600). It was the eighth largest market for the Bakkers, at the same rank as two other cities (5,600). Atlanta was the eleventh largest market for Robertson, ranked there with two other cities (5,600).

Viewers in these markets learned about the survey through a 30- second television spot that ran just before or just after the various programs aired there. In some cases the television spot ran adjacent to other religious broadcasts. The spot was professionally produced. It invited viewers to participate in a national telephone survey of viewers of religious television by calling a toll-free number. The spot explained that the survey was not a fund drive, and to satisfy FCC requirements, it identified the university with which I was affiliated at the time as the survey sponsor (Southern Methodist University). The University had provided funds for the survey.

The spot aired on two different weekends, one week apart, in Los Angeles and Atlanta. It was aired over a Memorial Day weekend in hopes of drawing even more viewers. It ran three times during that week in Philadelphia, and five times during the week in Detroit. The times for which the spot was scheduled as well as the number of times it was aired were determined by the times when the various programs were scheduled to air (Robertson's show aired on weekdays) and by the costs for air time set by each station.

Viewers reached telephone operators provided *pro bono* by International Telecharge, Incorporated (ITI), a Dallas-based communications technology business. The survey was ITI's first 800 service application and served as a trial run to test their new technology and operations. Callers were asked a series of questions by operators who took their calls. Twenty-six operators took calls immediately after the television spots were aired and throughout the day up until late evening.

Many of the telephone operators reported that they were struck by the seriousness and sincerity of the callers. The operators reported that callers gave some thought to the questions as well as their responses. Callers were very eager to elaborate their answers. Instead of simply giving the requested short answer, callers would often explain their responses: "That's not in the Bible." "It's not in God's Holy Book," "not in God's plan." "It's a sin." One operator reported that only one caller reaching his terminal stuck to yes and no responses. Many callers had to be cut short in order to keep the survey questions and responses moving. Operators reported that dozens of callers began to share their personal stories. Some callers testified about how they had benefited from the television ministry. Others gave testimonies about God at work in their lives. Callers were enthused about the programs as well as the television ministries.

A few final details about the way the survey was conducted call attention to callers' enthusiasm about the programs watched. Callers heard a recorded, 25-second greeting before operators came on the line. The robotic opening thanked callers, informed them that an operator would come on the line shortly, oriented them to the nature of the survey, and invited them to make comments at the completion of the survey. Callers held the line an additional thirty seconds on average before an operator came on. One stalwart caller waited nine-and-a-half minutes for an operator to come on the line.

The operators then thanked the callers for waiting and introduced themselves by first name to help break the ice. The survey took eight minutes to complete on average. Initially, the communications firm staff and I had wanted to keep the survey to three minutes in order to encourage callers to stay on the line. Sixty-two additional people phoned in but abandoned the call before the survey could be completed, three-and-a-half minutes into the survey on average. Fourteen additional people phoned in but abandoned the call before an operator could come on the line.

### Survey Questions

The questions put to callers and their responses are found below. Questions are listed in the order in which they were put to viewers. Responses given by the different viewing audiences for each of the television shows are given after each question. The different program audiences are identified by the first letter of each host's last name: R (Robertson—the "700 Club"), F (Falwell—"The Old-Time Gospel Hour"), S (Swaggart—"Jimmy Swaggart"), and B (the Bakkers—the "PTL Club" and "The Jim and Tammy Show"). The Bakkers' programs are treated together, since there were only eight callers who had watched their latest show, which replaced the old "PTL Club." The last figure given is the average of all of the responses combined, designated by the letter "C," for "combined." The percentages given have been rounded off. No response or multiresponses account for discrepancies in totals.

One-hundred-and-ninety-four of Robertson's viewers took part in the survey. Forty-eight of Falwell's viewers took part. Sixty-two people who watch Jimmy Swaggart participated. And 32 people who watched the Bakkers took part.

As operators took the first few questions, the caller's sex was recorded. My sample is more divided along gender lines than samples of viewers in other studies. Seventy-five percent are female, and only 25% are male. The Annenberg-Gallup poll shows that 56% of the total audience for religious television is female, and 44% is male.

### Female:

R 75% (out of 194); F 69% (out of 48); S 81% (out of 62); B 66% (out of 32); C 75% (out of 336)

### Male:

R 24%; F 31%; S 19%; B 34%; C 25%

### 1.   What state do you live in?

California (the Los Angeles market):
R 24%; F 10%; S 27%; B 41%; C 24%

Pennsylvania (the Philadelphia market):
R 21%; F 21%; S 15%; B 3%; C 21%

New Jersey (Philadelphia):
> R 19%; F 21%; S 24%; B 9%; C 18%

Delaware (Philadelphia):
> R 8%; F 13%; S 6%; B 0; C 7%

Georgia (the Atlanta market):
> R 4%; F 10%; S 11%; B 13%; C 7%

Michigan (the Detroit market):
> R 22%; F 13%; S 11%; B 19%; C 18%

**Other states represented:**

Florida:
> R .5%; F 0; S 0; B 0; C .3%

Maryland:
> R .5%; F 0; S 2%; B 0; C .6%

New York:
> R 0; F 0; S 2%; B 0; C .3%

Ohio:
> R 1%; F 0; S 0; B 0; C .6%

Tennessee:
> R 0; F 0; S 2%; B 0; C .3%

Virginia:
> R 1%; F 0; S 0; B 0; C .8%

**2.  How many hours a week do you watch Christian television programs?**

*Less than 1 hour*:
> R .5%; F 2%; S 2%; B 6%; C 2%

*1–3 hours*:
> R 21%; F 27%; S 15%; B 22%; C 21%

*3–5 hours*:
> R 22%; F 29%; S 31%; B 16%; C 24%

*5–7 hours*:
> R 14%; F 10%; S 13%; B 3%; C 13%

*More than 7 hours*:
> R 43%; F 29%; S 39%; B 44%; C 41%

**3.  How many hours a day do you watch commercial television?**

*Less than 1 hour*:
> R 23%; F 29%; S 19%; B 31%; C 24%

*1–3 hours*:
> R 42%; F 40%; S 34%; B 38%; C 40%

*3–5 hours:*
  R 21%; F 19%; S 24%; B 22%; C 21%

*5–7 hours:*
  R 4%; F 4%; S 5%; B 0; C 4%

*7 hours or more:*
  R 7%; F 2%; S 11%; B 3%; C 7%

### 4.   What program do you primarily watch?

*The "700 Club":*
  C 58% (194 callers)

*"The Old-Time Gospel Hour":*
  C 14% (48 callers)

*"Jimmy Swaggart":*
  C 18% (62 callers)

*The "PTL Club" and "The Jim and Tammy Show":*
  C 10% (32 callers)

*The "PTL Club":*
  C 10% (32 callers)

*"The Jim and Tammy Show":*
  C 2% (8 callers)

### 5.   Do you watch another of these programs?

Viewers tend to watch and support more than one program.[322] Just over half of the viewers who participated in my survey watch several of the telecasts, although they have their preferences. And they watch both fundamentalist and Pentecostal programs. Fifty-three percent of those who phoned in watch more than one of these shows. Two percent watch all of these shows.

Fourteen percent of the callers who watch Robertson also watch Falwell. Fourteen percent of this group watches Swaggart. Six percent used to watch the Bakkers. One of these callers watches all four programs. Five percent watch Robert Schuller's "The Hour of Power." Schuller, pastor of the Crystal Cathedral and a minister in the Dutch Reformed church, draws more of the callers who watch Robertson than any other religious programs watched, after the other three programs are counted.

Forty-eight percent of the callers who watch Falwell also watch Robertson. Twenty-five percent watch Swaggart. Eight percent used to watch the Bakkers. One caller watches all of the programs. And 17% watch Schuller.

Fifty-two percent of those who watch Swaggart also watch Robertson. Twenty-three percent watch Falwell. And 11% watched the Bakkers. One of these callers watches all of the programs. Three percent watch Schuller.

Forty-one percent of those who watched the Bakkers watch Robertson. Twenty-two percent watch Falwell. And 19% watch Swaggart. One watches every one of the programs. Three percent watch Schuller. Only among respondents who used to watch the Bakkers is Schuller not the top draw, outside the other four programs. More watch Paul and Jan Crouch of the Trinity Broadcast Network. Schuller is tied with Charles Stanley and Larry Lea among callers who watch Swaggart.

### 6. Do you watch any other Christian television programs?

Listed below are the other programs watched by those participating in the survey. The number that follows indicates the percentage of callers among all of those who took part in the survey. The most watched programs are listed first.

Robert Schuller (C 16%)

Paul and Jan Crouch (5%)

Charles Stanley (3%)

Kenneth Copeland (3%)

Billy Graham (2%)

Larry Lea (3%)

"Project 90" with Sheila Walsh, on Robertson's Christian Broadcasting Network (3%)

Fred Price (2%)

Oral Roberts (2%)

James Kennedy (2%)

James Robison (2%)

**Other shows watched but watched by less than 2% of callers are listed below:**

Mother Angelica

Ben Armstrong's "World of Tomorrow"

"Capital Life"

Ron Embree

"Great Life Today"

W. B. Grant

Pastor John Hagee

Marilyn Hickey

Huckabee

"It is Written"

Jordon

"Liberty"

Manning

"Morning Chapel"

Mario Murillo

Lloyd Ogilvie

John Oldstein

James Robison

Morris Sellars

Pastor Chuck Smith

"Plain Truth"

"Power Team"

Dan Reeves

Richard Roberts

"Psychiatry: A Christian Point of View"

"Straight Talk with Scott Ross," on Robertson's Christian Broadcasting Network

Robert Tilton

George Vandeman

Jack van Impe

"Voice of Prophecy"

Five percent of those who took part in the survey watch programs that were not specified.

**7.    How often do you watch this program?**

*Every time aired*:
R 48%; F 48%; S 55%; B 53%; C 51%

*Most of the time it airs*:
R 42%; F 40%; S 34%; B 34%; C 40%

*Sometimes*:
R 10%; F 10%; S 8%; B 13%; C 10%

*Rarely*:
R 0; F 0; S 0; B 0; C 0

**8.    How much of this program do you watch?**

*All of it*:
R 73%; F 81%; S 87%; B 69%; C 76%

*Most of it*:
R 21%; F 13%; S 8%; B 16%; C 17%

*Some of it*:
R 7%; F 8%; S 5%; B 16%; C 8%

**9.    Do you think the program host cares about you personally?**

*Yes*:
R 93%; F 92%; S 84%; B 78%; C 90%

*Don't know*:
R 4%; F 0; S 2%; B 0; C 3%

**10.    Do you think of the host as a worship leader, newscommentator, friend, entertainer, other?**

*Worship leader*:
R 58%; F 65%; S 63%; B 59%; C 60%

*Newscommentator*:
R 16%; F 8%; S 5%; B 6%; C 12%

*Friend*:
R 23%; F 15%; S 13%; B 13%; C 19%

*Entertainer*:

> R 7%; F 8%; S 3%; B 3%; C 6%

*Other*:

> A few of the callers who watch Robertson indicate they think of the host as combining the role of worship leader and newscommentator. A few view Robertson as a teacher or educator. A few see him as a religious counselor. And a few see him as a pastor. A few callers who watch the other programs also see the host or hosts as a teacher and religious counselor (the Bakkers), or teacher and pastor (Falwell and Swaggart).

**11. Do you feel that you belong to a community of viewers of the TV ministry and television program?**

*Yes*:

> R 80%; F 69%; S 81%; B 81%; C 79%

*Don't know*:

> R 5%; F 13%; S 6%; B 0; C 6%

**12. Do you think about other viewers of the TV ministry and television program when you watch?**

*Yes*:

> R 82%; F 71%; S 73%; B 72%; C 78%

*Don't know*:

> R 4%; F 0; S 3%; B 3%; C 3%

**13a. Have you been to the TV ministry's headquarters or studios?**

*Yes*:

> R 27%; F 27%; S 27%; B 44%; C 28%

**13b. Plan to go?**

> R 7%; F 8%; S 8%; B 0; C 7%

**13c. Want to go?**

> R 5%; F 2%; S 3%; B 13%; C 5%

**14a. Have you had a religious experience while viewing the program?**

*Yes*:

> R 62%; F 54%; S 81%; B 59%; C 64%

**14b. Which of the following?**

Salvation:

> R 16%; F 10%; S 37%; B 13%; C 19%

Rededication:
R 25%; F 29%; S 29%; B 13%; C 25%

Physical healing:
R 25%; F 23%; S 32%; B 6%; C 24%

Word of knowledge:
R 19%; F 6%; S 24%; B 28%; C 19%

Gift of tongues:
R 4%; F 0; S 3%; B 0; C 3%

Gift of prophecy:
R 4%; F 0; S 5%; B 0; C 3%

Gift of dancing in the Spirit:
R 6%; F 8%; S 8%; B 9%; C 7%

A few callers reported they had experienced all of these (R .5%; B 3%).

### 15a. Do you pray before you turn on the program?

*Yes*:
R 39%; F 48%; S 53%; B 41%; C 43%

*No response*:
R 2%; F 4%; S 0; B 0; C 2%

### 15b. During the program?

R 84%; F 77%; S 79%; B 81%; C 82%

*No response*:
R .5%; F 2%; S 0; B 3%; C 1%

### 15c. After you turn off the program?

R 65%; F 67%; S 68%; B 75%; C 77%

*No response*:
R 3%; F 4%; S 3%; B 0; C 3%

### 16a. Do you read a Bible before you turn on the program?

*Yes*:
R 43%; F 31%; S 39%; B 38%; C 40%

*No response*:
R 3%; F 2%; S 3%; B 3%; C 3%

### 16b. During the program?

R 30%; F 40%; S 47%; B 50%; C 37%

*No response*:
R 3%; F 2%; S 0; B 3%; C 1%

### 16c. After you turn off the program?

*Yes*:
> R 61%; F 46%; S 60%; B 56%; C 58%

*No response*:
> R 2%; F 4%; S 6%; B 3%; C 4%

### 17. Did you purchase your Bible from the TV ministry you watch?

*Yes*:
> R 18%; F 15%; S 37%; B 41%; C 23%

*Don't recall*:
> R 1%; F 2%; S 0; B 0; C 1%

### 18a. Do you participate in the worship format of the telecasts: praying, singing, reading the Bible, humming along, etc.?

*Yes*:
> R 76%; F 81%; S 94%; B 94%; C 82%

### 18b. How often?

*Frequently*:
> R 49%; F 52%; S 53%; B 53%; C 51%

*Occasionally*:
> R 27%; F 29%; S 32%; B 38%; C 29%

### 19a. Do you phone in prayer requests during the show?

*Yes*:
> R 53%; F 50%; S 47%; B 50%; C 51%

### 19b. How often?

*Frequently*:
> R 11%; F 17%; S 13%; B 9%; C 12%

*Occasionally*:
> R 42%; F 29%; S 34%; B 44%; C 39%

### 20a. Do you phone in pledges during the show?

*Yes*:
> R 55%; F 33%; S 47%; B 41%; C 49%

### 20b. How often?

*Frequently*:
> R 10%; F 10%; S 3%; B 3%; C 8%

*Occasionally*:
> R 43%; F 23%; S 44%; B 44%; C 40%

**21a.  Have you purchased study materials or notes or other mementos from the TV ministry?**

*Yes:*

R 62%; F 67%; S 61%; B 60%; C 63%

**21b.  How often?**

*Frequently:*

R 14%; F 17%; S 18%; B 9%; C 15%

*Occasionally:*

R 48%; F 50%; S 47%; B 56%; C 49%

**22a.  Do you do other things while you watch?**

*No:*

R 45%; F 54%; S 55%; B 53%; C 49%

**22b.  What kind of things do you do?**

*Household chores:*

R 39%; F 38%; S 29%; B 25%; C 35%

*Business tasks:*

R 7%; F 6%; S 2%; B 25%; C 7%

*Other:* Callers reported the following:

*Robertson:*

Five percent eat. Four percent sew. Three percent get ready for work. One percent cook. One percent take care of children. One exercises. One works on hobbies. One works on puzzles. One reads.

*Falwell:*

Two percent eat.

*Swaggart:*

Five percent eat. One viewer reads.

*Bakkers:*

Six percent eat.

**23.  Whenever possible, do you include your family in viewing the show?**

*Yes:*

R 61%; F 60%; S 63%; B 78%; C 63%

**24a.  Do you discuss the show with your family?**

*Yes:*

R 81%; F 79%; S 85%; B 91%; C 82%

### 24b. Your friends?

*Yes:*

R 88%; F 81%; S 81%; B 94%; C 86%

### 25a. Do you watch the program instead of going to church?

*Yes:*

R 19%; F 15%; S 31%; B 19%; C 26%

*No response:*

R 3%; F 0; S 0; B 0; C 2%

### 25b. In addition to going to church?

R 81%; F 75%; S 69%; B 81%; C 78%

*No response:*

R .5%; F 2%; S 0; B 0; C .6%

### 26. Do you watch the program because it helps you understand today's changing society and/or lifestyle?

*Yes:*

R 78%; F 60%; S 23%; B 62%; C 63%

*No response:*

R 3%; F 6%; S 3%; B 3%; C 3%

### 27. Because it helps you fit your lifestyle into today's changing society and lifestyle?

*Yes:*

R 59%; F 44%; S 48%; B 44%; C 54%

*No response:*

R 4%; F 6%; S 2%; B 3%; C 3%

### 28. Because it helps increase the political influence and power of Bible-believing Christians?

*Yes:*

R 58%; F 44%; S 37%; B 44%; C 51%

*No response:*

R 4%; F 6%; S 3%; B 3%; C 4%

### 29. Because it stands up for Bible-believing Christians who are not taken seriously in America today?

*Yes:*

R 80%; F 63%; S 69%; B 66%; C 74%

*No response:*
    R 2%; F 4%; S 3%; B 0%; C 2%

## 30a. Do you watch to get answers to personal problems?

*Yes:*
    R 61%; F 69%; S 48%; B 47%; C 59%

*No response:*
    R 1%; F 2%; S 0; B 0; C 1%

## 30b. Which did you seek answers concerning?
## *Marriage counseling/advice?*

*Yes:*
    R 14%; F 15%; S 17%; B 16%; C 15%

*No response:*
    R 2%; F 2%; S 5%; B 0; C 2%

*Financial counseling/advice?*

*Yes:*
    R 24%; F 19%; S 27%; B 38%; C 25%

*No response:*
    R 2%; F 2%; S 5%; B 0; C 7%

*Family counseling/advice?*

*Yes:*
    R 40%; F 35%; S 35%; B 47%; C 39%

*No response:*
    R 3%; F 2%; S 5%; B 0; C .3%

*Job counseling/advice?*

*Yes:*
    R 18%; F 12%; S 16%; B 38%; C 19%

*No response:*
    R 2%; F 2%; S 3%; B 0; C 2%

## 31.  Choose from the following statements the one that best describes your main reason for watching the program:

To get the biblical position on moral or political issues
    R 45%; F 33%; S 27%; B 34%; C 39%

To have a religious experience and not just to worship
    R 7%; F 6%; S 15%; B 3%; C 8%

To worship or get a spiritual boost
    R 51%; F 58%; S 53%; B 53%; C 35%

To get answers to personal problems or crises
    R 15%; F 13%; S 15%; B 16%; C 15%

For companionship or company
> R 11%; F 17%; S 15%; B 0; C 11%

Many callers chose several reasons. Four percent of Robertson's viewers reported they watch for all of these reasons.

## 32. Did you vote in the last Presidential election?

*Yes:*
> R 86%; F 88%; S 81%; B 84%; C 85%

*No response:*
> R 1%; F 0; S 0; B 0; C .6%

## 33. In the last state election?

*Yes:*
> R 74%; F 83%; S 63%; B 66%; C 73%

*No response:*
> R .5%; F 2%; S 0; B 0; C .6%

## 34. In the last local election?

*Yes:*
> R 68%; F 75%; S 56%; B 66%; C 67%

*No response:*
> R 2%; F .3%; S 0; B 0; C 2%

## 35. Do you consider yourself a:

*Republican?*
> R 59%; F 69%; S 27%; B 44%; C 53%

*Democrat?*
> R 18%; F 10%; S 34%; B 22%; C 20%

*Independent?*
> R 19%; F 13%; S 23%; B 28%; C 20%

## 36. Do you object to:

### Abortion?

*Yes:*
> R 88%; F 90%; S 94%; B 84%; C 89%

*No response:*
> R 3%; F 0; S 0; B 0; C 1%

### Homosexuality?

*Yes:*
> R 85%; F 88%; S 87%; B 84%; C 86%

*No response:*
> R 4%; F 0; S 0; B 3%; C 3%

### Divorce?

*Yes:*
R 68%; F 71%; S 71%; B 56%; C 69%

*No response:*
R 6%; F 2%; S 6%; B 0; C 5%

### Women's rights?

*Yes:*
R 31%; F 21%; S 32%; B 38%; C 32%

*No response:*
R 13%; F 10%; S 21%; B 9%; C 14%

### Sexual freedom?

*Yes:*
R 78%; F 71%; S 84%; B 78%; C 78%

*No response:*
R 6%; F 8%; S 5%; B 13%; C 7%

### Women clergy?

*Yes:*
R 34%; F 35%; S 37%; B 28%; C 34%

*No response:*
R 8%; F 6%; S 3%; B 6%; C 7%

37. **Do you support:**

### Prayer in public schools?

*Yes:*
R 97%; F 94%; S 90%; B 94%; C 95%

*No response:*
R 0; F 0; S 2%; B 0; C .3%

### The traditional family?

*Yes:*
R 97%; F 90%; S 94%; B 94%; C 95%

*No response:*
R 0; F 2%; S 0; B 3%; C .6%

### Separation of church and state?

*Yes:*
R 56%; F 58%; S 58%; B 56%; C 57%

*No response:*
R 10%; F 13%; S 8%; B 19%; C 11%

### A Christian oriented government?

*Yes:*

R 88%; F 71%; S 84%; B 91%; C 85%

*No response:*

R 3%; F 6%; S 5%; B 3%; C 4%

### A militarily strong America?

*Yes:*

R 91%; F 90%; S 84%; B 97%; C 90%

*No response:*

R 2%; F 0%; S 0; B 0; C 1%

### Financial success?

*Yes:*

R 84%; F 79%; S 77%; B 88%; C 82%

*No response:*

R 6%; F 6%; S 5%; B 6%; C 6%

### 38. What is your denomination?

More Pentecostals took part in the survey than members of any other denomination, representing 29% of the callers, a larger representation than that found among the total audience for televangelism. See Chapter Two on the number of Pentecostal as compared to fundamentalist viewers. Eighteen percent of this group are members of independent Pentecostal churches or unspecified groups. Eight percent are Assembly of God. Two percent are Church of God. And one is Full Gospel (.3%). The next largest denominational group of callers is Baptist. They make up 17% of the callers. Fifteen percent of this group are members of independent Baptist churches. And 2% are Southern Baptist. The denominational affiliation of the total audience of televangelism's viewers is given in Chapter Two. The denominations represented by those who participated in the survey are listed below:

*Independent Pentecostal:*

R 14%; F 10%; S 32%; B 25%; C 18%

*Assembly of God:*

R 9%; F 4%; S 8%; B 3%; C 8%

*Church of God:*

R 2%; F 0; S 2%; B 6%; C 2%

*Baptist:*

R 15%; F 27%; S 10%; B 9%; C 15%

*Southern Baptist:*

R 2%; F 2%; S 5%; B 0; C 2%

*Methodist:*
R 8%; F 10%; S 2%; B 0; C 7%

*Presbyterian:*
R 4%; F 8%; S 0; B 3%; C 4%

*Church of the Nazarene:*
R 2%; F 6%; S 6%; B 3%; C 3%

*Church of Christ:*
R 2%; F 2%; S 5%; B 0; C 2%

*Christian:*
R 3%; F 2%; S 6%; B 6%; C 4%

*Lutheran:*
R 3%; F 0; S 0; B 0; C 2%

*Episcopal Church:*
R 3%; F 0; S 0; B 0; C 2%

*Roman Catholic:*
R 7%; F 0; S 2%; B 0; C 4%

*Nondenominational or independent:*
R 15%; F 2%; S 5%; B 3%; C 11%

**Other:**

*Seventh-day Adventist:*
R .5%; F 2%; S 2%; B 2%; C 1%

*Dutch Reformed:*
R .5%; F 0; S 2%; B 3%; C .9%

*Missionary:*
R .5%; F 2%; S 0; B 0; C .6%

*Mormon:*
R .5%; F 0; S 0; B 0; C .3%

*Evangelical Free Church:*
R 0; F 0; S 0; B 6%; C .6%

*Judaism:*[323]
R .5%; F 0; S 0; B 0; C .3%

*Islam:*
R .5%; F 0; S 0; B 0; C .3%

Two callers introduced the category "fundamentalist" (.6% of the callers). They watch Robertson and Falwell. Two identify themselves as "charismatic" (.6%). They watch Robertson. Four place themselves among "other, unspecified" groups (1%). And four report that they do not belong to any denomination or church (1% of the callers). Two of these watch Robertson. One watches Falwell. And one watched the Bakkers.

Several callers felt compelled to improve upon categories found in the survey. They gave themselves the following labels:

"Born-again" (1%)
"Christian-born" (.6%)
"A Christian that loves the Lord" (.3%)
"Self-religion" (.3%)

Responses by those who do not like to be pigeonholed underscores the fact that televangelism's conservative Christian viewers come from outside the mainstream of the Christian Church and denominational life. This point is clearly illustrated by a tendency of several callers to point out that they "used to be" brand x within the Christian Church, but are now "a Christian." Some callers hedged when selecting a category of denominational affiliation.

Only 20% of those who took part in the survey are members of mainline Christian churches. If the seven Southern Baptists were removed—as some analysts would do in light of the recent move of the nation's largest Protestant denomination to the extreme right—the number of callers who belong to mainline churches falls to 18% of all of the viewers taking part in the survey.

### 39. What age group are you in?

*Below 20:*
R 2%; F 0; S 0; B 0; C 1%

*20-30:*
R 5%; F 10%; S 3%; B 6%; C 6%

*30-40:*
R 11%; F 6%; S 13%; B 3%; C 9%

*40-50:*
R 25%; F 29%; S 19%; B 47%; C 27%

*50-60:*
R 21%; F 19%; S 32%; B 28%; C 11%

*60-70:*
R 32%; F 27%; S 19%; B 16%; C 27%

*70-80:*
R .5%; F 2%; S 0; B 0; C .6%

*Over 80:*
R 2%; F 2%; S 2%; B 0; C 2%

The average age of those responding to the survey is just over 50 years old. Most of those who watch nonreligious television are under 49 years old.[324]

40.  **What was your last year of school?**

*Elementary*:
R 3%; F 4%; S 2%; B 3%; C 3%

*High school*:
R 32%; F 35%; S 48%; B 44%; C 37%

*College*:
R 44%; F 29%; S 31%; B 28%; C 38%

*Graduate school*:
R 18%; F 25%; S 11%; B 25%; C 9%

41.  **How would you best describe your household salary range?**

*Under $5,000 a year*:
R 8%; F 4%; S 6%; B 3%; C 8%

*Under $16,000 a year*:
R 16%; F 10%; S 21%; B 6%; C 15%

*Under $20,000 a year*:
R 10%; F 8%; S 13%; B 13%; C 11%

*Under $30,000 a year*:
R 20%; F 19%; S 15%; B 19%; C 18%

*Under $50,000 a year*:
R 17%; F 21%; S 8%; B 28%; C 17%

*Over $50,000 a year*:
R 16%; F 19%; S 13%; B 16%; C 16%

Callers have an average household income of well below $30,000 annually, 34% with annual household incomes of under $20,000, and 23% below $16,000. ($13,000 is the poverty line established by the federal government for a family of four.) The caller who has a household income greater than $30,000 is the exception (10%). Sixteen percent report household incomes of $50,000 or greater.

42.  **How would you describe your ethnic background?**

*European-American/White*:
R 73%; F 88%; S 66%; B 75%; C 74%

*African-American/Black*:
R 19%; F 2%; S 17%; B 16%; C 13%

*Hispanic-American*:
R 2%; F 0; S 2%; B 6%; C 2%

*Asian American/Asian*:

> R 2%; F 2%; S 0; B 0; C 1%

*Native American/Indian*:

> R 6%; F 2%; S 6%; B 0; C 5%

*Other*:

> One of Robertson's viewers is African-European, and one is Middle Eastern (1% of the respondents who watch Robertson). Two-percent of those who watch Falwell did not specify a category. One of Swaggart's viewers is European-Indian (representing 2% of those participating in the survey who follow Swaggart). Three percent of the callers who watched the Bakkers did not specify their ethnic background. The group of "other" makes up 5% of all of the viewers taking part in the survey.

# ⊰ Endnotes ⊱

## Chapter One

[1] Gerbner *et al.* 1984. See also, Fore 1987 and Horsfield 1984.

[2] See Hoover 1988 for some of viewers' stated personal and religious reasons for watching the telecasts.

[3] Gerbner *et al.* 1984.

[4] *Ibid.* In discussing the religion of viewers I will use masculine pronouns and imagery to refer to God and Satan in order to reflect viewers' practice of using noninclusive language.

[5] *Ibid.*

[6] Gerbner *et al.* 1984 report crossing over by viewers. My survey of viewers also shows crossover. See the Appendix.

[7] Roof and McKinney 1987.

[8] Gerbner *et al.* 1984.

[9] I visited the headquarters of Robertson's Christian Broadcasting Network in Virginia Beach, Virginia, in July 1988 and again in July 1989. I also visited Falwell's Liberty Broadcasting Network in Lynchburg, Virginia, in July 1988 and July 1989. Also in July 1989 I visited the Bakkers' new headquarters in Orlando, Florida. I visited Swaggart's Baton Rouge, Louisiana, headquarters in July 1990. I attended live broadcasts or tapings of all of these shows.

[10] Driver 1991, 112.

[11] Schechner 1977, 65.

[12] Driver 1991, 80.

[13] *Ibid.*, 114.

[14] Turner 1986b, 190 and 201.

[15] Turner 1986a, 43. See also Turner 1985, chapters 8 and 9.

[16] See Geertz 1973.

[17] See Turner 1974.

18    See Goethels 1981 and Carey 1975. See also Carey 1989.
19    See Goethels 1981 and Kottak 1990.
20    Goethels 1981.
21    See Hoover 1988.
22    See Turner 1974.

## Chapter Two

23    *The Dallas Morning News*, September 29, 1990.
24    *Electronic Media*, January 30, 1989.
25    *Ibid.*
26    *The Atlanta Journal*, February 5, 1989. Figures are based on the viewer count made by the Arbitron television ratings service. Figures were not given for the "PTL Club." See Bruce 1990 for an overview of the difficulty of gaining an exact count of viewers and of the different methods used to count viewers. The decline in Robertson's audience has been attributed by one observer to his long absence from the program while campaigning for President, more than to anything else (Winzenburg 1988, 25).
27    *Electronic Media*, January 30, 1989. In November 1988, the "PTL Club," without the Bakkers, was aired on only 32 stations, down from 67 stations in November 1987. Swaggart was aired on 179 stations, down from 194. Robertson was aired on 57 stations, down from 87. And Falwell was seen on 125 stations, down from 156 (*ibid*).
28    Swaggart's contributions fell by more than half between 1987 and 1988, from 150 million dollars to 60 million. Falwell's dropped by 6.5 million dollars. Robertson's fell by 30% over a two-year period (*Christianity Today*, February 3, 1989). Three other television ministers, all among the seven most watched TV ministers, saw their contributions increase in 1987 (Winzenburg 1988, 25). Part of the decline in donations can be attributed to the ceilings on tax deductions for charitable gifts established by new tax laws, the bite into contributors' pocketbooks by the declining American economy, and the deaths of older viewers, who provide the bulk of the donations that keep the ministries going (*Christianity Today*, February 3, 1989).
29    Between January 1988 and January 1989, the number of religious television programs of all forms fell slightly, from 42 to 39, as did the number of commercial television stations carrying them, from 2,208 to 2,161. But the number of Christian television stations airing religious television climbed from 259 to 336, an increase of 30%. The number of organizations producing religious programming climbed from 447 to 476. The market share also grew, from 52.6% of all TV viewers tuned in during the times the programs aired to 55.4%. Figures are from the A.C. Nielsen ratings. Donations held at two billion dollars annually (*Electronic Media*, January 30, 1989). Programs generally air during the Sunday morning "ghetto" hour, off-peak times, when the cost of air time is significantly lower and when stations need filler (Hoover 1988).
30    It is argued that much of the growth is a result of the recent expansion of religious television into the cable television market (*Electronic Media*, January 30, 1989).
31    William Martin's foreward to Hoover 1988, 11.
32    Winzenburg 1988, 25.
33    Horsfield 1984.

34 For a discussion of controversy, see Bruce 1990, Hadden and Shupe 1988, Hadden and Swann 1981, Horsfield 1984, Martz and Carroll 1988, and Young 1982.

35 On the role played by the televangelists in the overall operations of the television ministries, see Frankl 1987, Fore 1987, and Horsfield 1984. All are good sources on the structure and operations of the television ministries.

36 For a revealing discussion of how viewers think for themselves and how they receive and evaluate the message of televangelism in light of their own faith and opinions, see Hoover 1988.

37 Gerbner *et al.* 1984; Korpi and Kim 1986; and Hoover 1988.

38 Stacey and Shupe 1982, 299. See also Gerbner *et al.* 1984 and Korpi and Kim 1986, 412–413.

39 Gerbner *et al.* 1984; Stacey and Shupe 1982.

40 Gerbner *et al.* 1984; Korpi and Kim 1986.

41 Wuthnow 1989, 121–123.

42 Hoover 1988, 65. Hoover discusses viewers' involvement in the television ministries and the place of the telecasts in their daily lives. See also Gerbner *et al.* 1984.

43 Gerbner *et al.* 1984.

44 Durfey and Ferrier 1986, 115.

45 Gerbner *et al.* 1984. The Annenberg-Gallup study was conducted jointly by the Annenberg School of Communications at the University of Pennsylvania and the Gallup Organization in 1983. It is the most exhaustive study of viewers of television religion to date. The study was undertaken in cooperation with more than thirty religious organizations, including the National Council of Churches, the Southern Baptist Convention, the United States Catholic Conference, the conservative National Religious Broadcasters association, and leading television ministries, including Robertson's, Falwell's, the Bakkers', and Billy Graham's. The purpose of the study was to determine whether religious television competes with local churches for members and contributions. The continuing decline in membership of mainline churches helped prompt the study. The study was based on a national survey sample as well as regional surveys of viewers in ten television markets in the Northeast and ten in the Southeast. For a discussion of how the survey was conducted, see Hoover 1987. (Hoover was a member of the design team.) Other results of the survey are given in other chapters in this book.

46 Gerbner *et al.* 1984; Barwise and Ehrenberg 1988.

47 Gerbner *et al.* 1984. See also Stacey and Shupe 1982.

48 Gerbner *et al.* 1984.

49 *Ibid.*; Korpi and Kim 1986.

50 Thirty-eight percent of televangelism's viewers only completed grade school, and 39% only completed high school. Thirteen percent had some college education, and only 10% are college graduates. Those who do not watch religious television are college-educated for the most part (Gerbner *et al.* 1984).

51 Twenty-three percent of televangelism's viewers have incomes under $15,000. Twenty-five percent have incomes between $15,000 and $25,000. Twenty-two percent have incomes between $25,000 and $35,000, and 30% have incomes over $35,000. TV viewers who do not watch religious programs have higher incomes (*ibid.*).

52 Forty-eight percent of televangelism's viewers are 50 years old or over, 35% are between 30 and 49 years old, and 17% are under the age of 30 (*ibid.*). The average age

of conservative Christians is 48.4 years. The average age of the American population is 43.9 (Hunter 1983, 51).

Viewers are female by and large. They make up 56% of the audience (Gerbner *et al.* 1984). This is in keeping with the percentage of females among conservative Christians: 60% (Hunter 1983, 51). And most viewers are European-American: 81% (Gerbner *et al.* 1984).

Today's audience, like viewers of an earlier era, live primarily in the South (37%) and Midwest (29%) (*ibid.*). These are the most religious regions of the country (see The City University of New York, The Graduate School 1991). Eighteen percent live in the East and only 16% in the West. Twenty-nine percent live in cities, 35% in suburbs, and 36% in rural areas (Gerbner *et al.* 1984).

On viewers' social profile, see also Buddenbaum 1981 and Gaddy and Pritchard 1985.

53   Gerbner *et al.* 1984.

54   See the famous study made in the 1950s by Parker, Barry, and Smythe (Parker, Barry, and Smythe 1955). The study, sponsored by what is today the National Council of Churches, found that viewers of religious television in the New Haven, Connecticut, sample were predominantly undereducated, lower middle-class, conservative Protestants.

55   Gerbner *et al.* 1984.

56   *Ibid.* See also Fore 1987 and Horsfield 1984.

57   See Buddenbaum 1981, Gaddy and Pritchard 1985, and Stacey and Shupe 1982.

58   Gerbner *et al.* 1984. See also Gaddy and Pritchard 1985.

59   Fore 1984, 104. Fore was a member of the Annenberg-Gallup survey (Gerbner *et al.* 1984) research team.

60   See the Appendix for the denominational affiliation of viewers in my survey.

61   Gerbner *et al.* 1984. Viewers' position on social and political issues is given in Chapter Four. See also the Appendix for the position of viewers in my survey.

62   *Ibid.*

63   Abelman 1988.

64   Hoover 1988, 63.

65   Hoover 1987.

66   See Hoover 1988, 183–185, 197, and *passim*, for a discussion of viewers' discomfort about their low social standing within American society and of televangelism's role in raising viewers' self-image as it adapts them to the wider society.

67   Bruce 1990, 236.

68   Hoover 1988, 104; see also 99, 108, and 151. Hoover draws from the observations of McLoughlin 1978.

69   Hoover 1988, 113.

70   *Ibid.*, 108 and 99. Hoover draws from McLoughlin 1978.

71   Bruce 1990, 126.

## Chapter Three

72   Hadden and Swann 1981, 203, 85, 87, and *passim*; see also Hadden and Shupe 1988 and Bruce 1990.

73   Hadden and Shupe 1988, 286.

74 For sources on the role of televangelism in the rise of the Religious Right, see Hadden and Shupe 1988, Hadden and Swann 1981, Bruce 1990, and Bruce 1988.

75 Hoover 1988, 20. See Frankl 1987, Fore 1987, and Horsfield 1984 on the role of mass media religion in communication among conservative Christians.

76 Four percent of air time is given to politics in the narrow meaning of the word. When politics is discussed, the issues presented are very general, for example, religious freedom and prayer in public schools. More time is given to social issues, about 25% of air time. Most of the air time is given to religious topics, especially salvation and evangelization (Abelman and Neuendorf 1987).

77 See Frankl 1987.

78 See Fore 1987 and Hadden and Shupe 1988.

79 Carpenter 1985, cited in Hoover 1988, 49.

80 See Hadden and Shupe 1988 for an account of the growth.

81 Hoover 1987, 142.

82 *Ibid*.

83 The figures come from the Annenberg-Gallup study (Gerbner *et al*. 1984). See note 45 in Chapter Two on the study and its sponsors. The study was undertaken to determine if television religion were taking away members and funds from local churches. The study shows that it does not. Other estimates of audience size range from 10 to 20 million (Hoover 1988, 63). Hoover cites W. Martin 1981, Hadden and Swann 1981, and Gerbner *et al*. 1984.

Discrepancy among figures for televangelism's audience grows out of differences among methods used to estimate audience size. For an overview of difficulties encountered in estimating the number of viewers, undercounting and overcounting, see Bruce 1990, 98–107. He refers to the Annenberg-Gallup study, the Nielsen/Christian Broadcasting Network study, made in 1985, and other studies. See also Fore 1987.

For a detailed discussion of the problem and the problem as treated by the Annenberg-Gallup count, see Hoover 1988 and Hoover 1987. Hoover was a member of the Annenberg-Gallup study research team. He reports that the audience count is based on the number of viewing households. Only those viewers previously identified as regular viewers by the Arbitron ratings service were surveyed by the study. The goal was to avoid self-styled religious viewers, a problem encountered in earlier surveys. The study counted only once those viewers who watch different television shows, and those who watch a television show that airs more than once a week. Seventy-five percent of viewers watch more than one program regularly, according to the study. When people who watch a show more than once a week are counted, Hoover notes, the count for the weekly audience climbs to 24.7 million viewers. (The study showed that cable television had not enlarged the size of televangelism's audience, since viewers were not any more likely to have cable than nonviewers.) Nor do local programs enlarge the audience, according to the study. The same people who watch the local programs also watch the nationally syndicated programs. Hoover points out that Sunday morning programming attracts larger audiences than weekday programming because more people are free to watch at that time. The weekend audience is not the same audience as the weekday audience, which tends to be more conservative. Weekday programming tends to be the more conservative programming. The audience tuned in on weekends is made up of members of traditional denominations—Presbyterian, Baptist, Catholic, etc. They are better educated than weekday audiences. The weekday audience belongs to independent denominations, and comes from the lower end of the socio-economic spectrum, challenging the claim of the television ministries to have attracted more upscale viewers (Hoover 1988, 63–65, 67, and 91).

For a critical assessment of the Annenberg-Gallup study, its methods, and results, see Hadden and Frankl 1987a and Hadden and Frankl 1987b.

[84]    Gerbner *et al.* 1984.

[85]    Roof and McKinney 1987, 81–82. Catholics make up 25% and Jews 2.3%.

[86]    McKinney reports that seven mainline denominations suffered a 20% loss between 1965 and 1985—5.6 million members (McKinney 1991, 153).

[87]    Hutchison 1991, 136–137. See also Roof and McKinney 1987, 23.

[88]    Bruce 1990, 22–23 cites Greeley 1972; Carroll, Johnson, and Marty 1979; and Gallup 1985.

"Mainline" is a problematic term. It glosses over differences in theology, doctrine, church polity, and outlook on social issues among the various historic denominations: the Episcopal Church, the United Church of Christ, the Presbyterian Church, the United Methodist Church, the Lutheran Church, the Christian Church/Disciples of Christ, American Baptists, the Southern Baptist Convention, the Reformed Church, etc. Neither does it convey the fragmentation and decline of denominations identified with the mainline. Most, but not all mainline churches are affiliated with the National Council of Churches. The Southern Baptist Convention, the largest Protestant denomination in the country, is not. It is the most conservative of mainline churches. The term "mainline" is used here in its conventional sense, referring to those historic Protestant denominations that are intermeshed with the dominant, European-American society, having influenced values that are central to American public life. Not all members of mainline churches are European-Americans. For a discussion of mainline Christianity, see Roof and McKinney 1987.

[89]    Bruce 1990, 170.

[90]    Horsfield discusses the limited power of the Religious Right during the Reagan era (Horsfield 1984), as do Johnson and Tamney (Johnson and Tamney 1982), and Bruce (Bruce 1990).

[91]    *The Dallas Morning News*, December 9, 1992.

[92]    *The New York Times*, November 21, 1992.

[93]    Johnson and Tamney 1985.

According to a survey recently made by *The New York Times* in conjunction with CBS, 43% of those polled believe homosexuals cannot make a choice about their homosexuality. Forty-four percent believe they can. Thirteen percent were undecided. Of the first group, 62% believe homosexual relations among consenting adults should be made legal, and 57% believe homosexuality should be acknowledged as an acceptable lifestyle. Of the group who believe homosexuality is a choice, only 32% believe homosexual relations among consenting adults should be legalized. Only 18% of this group believe homosexuality should be acknowledged as an acceptable lifestyle (*The Dallas Morning News*, March, 5, 1993).

[94]    Bruce 1990, 184–189 cites Sigelman and Presser 1988 and Ferguson and Rogers 1986.

[95]    Johnson and Tamney 1985.

[96]    Bruce 1990, 168, 179–189, 196–197, 238–239, and *passim*. See also Bruce 1988. For a detailed discussion of diversity, fragmentation, and the splintered vote among con-

servative Christians, see Bruce 1990. On Robertson's failed bid for the Presidency, see Bruce 1990 and Bruce 1988.

[97] Bruce 1990, 181 cites Johnson and Tamney 1985.

[98] Hoover 1988, 178–179.

[99] For discussion of the Religious Right in historical perspective, see Marsden 1983a and Marsden 1983b.

[100] See Bruce 1990 and Hunter 1987 on political activism among conservative Christians, and on the historical shift in emphasis from inner piety to activism.

[101] Steve Bruce makes the observation. For a discussion of friction between the two groups, see Bruce 1990 and Bruce 1988.

[102] On the limited power of the Religious Right, see Bruce 1990, Bruce 1988, Johnson and Tamney 1982, and Stacey and Shupe 1982.

[103] Bruce 1990, 239. See also Bruce 1988.

[104] Bruce 1990, 239.

[105] "Mainstream" is made a slippery term by the complex mix of multiple, inter-linked, and changing societies in which Americans hold membership. Here the term is used in its traditional application to refer to those identified with the dominant base of power in American public and political life. The mainstream is made up of those who hold to democratic values at their root, which leads them to subscribe to the separation of church and state, even though the majority of them identify them-selves as religious, having been influenced by the nation's Christian and Judaic heritage through its early and continuing denominational history, especially Protestantism. Most of the members of mainstream society are affiliated with main-line Protestant denominations, while many others are affiliated with Roman Catholicism and other religions, especially Judaism. While the social mainstream is made up of a variety of racial and ethnic groups, it is dominanted by those of European-American ancestry.

[106] 113,000 Americans of diverse socio-economic backgrounds were surveyed dur-ing 1989 and 1990 on their religious affiliation and their religious and political out-looks in a poll conducted by the Graduate School of The City University of New York (The City University of New York, the Graduate School 1991). The poll was the largest such survey ever undertaken. For a summary of the survey, see *The New York Times* April 10, 1991. See also Roof and McKinney 1987.

[107] On the continued influence of religion and religious values in shaping American society, see Roof and McKinney 1987 and Bellah *et al.* 1985.

[108] On this point, see Bruce 1988.

[109] Wuthnow 1989, 158. See also Hoover 1988, 64–65.

[110] Wuthnow 1989, 140.

[111] Moore 1986.

[112] Bruce 1990, 126.

[113] Gerbner *et al.* 1984.

[114] Bruce 1990, 40 and 48. See also Hoover 1988, 178.

[115] Horsfield 1984, 154–155.

[116] Hadden and Swann 1981, 203.

[117] Hadden and Swann 1981. See also Hadden and Shupe 1988 and Fore 1987.

[118] Bruce 1990, 240.

[119] William Martin in his foreward to Hoover 1988, 11.

[120] Hadden and Swann 1981. See also Fore 1987.

121    Horsfield 1984, 154–155.

122    Bruce 1990, 236. See also Hoover 1988.

123    William Martin in his foreword to Hoover 1988, 11.

124    Seventy-seven percent of viewers of religious television in all of its forms, televangelism included, report that they voted in the 1980 Presidential election (Gerbner *et al*. 1984). Eighty-five percent of the viewers who took part in my survery indicated that they voted in the 1988 Presidential election. Seventy-three percent reported voting in the last state election, and sixty-seven percent in the last local election. See the Appendix.

125    James Davison Hunter reports on significant changes made in the conservative Christian lifestyle, especially among younger conservative Christians. See Hunter 1987 and Hunter 1983.

126    Bruce 1990. Bruce gives a discussion of changes in conservative Christian theology since the nineteenth century.

127    Hunter 1987; and Hunter 1983.

128    See Bruce 1990 on the new attitude toward pleasure, psychological gratification and health, and that toward financial prosperity among conservative Christians.

129    Gerbner *et al*. 1984.

130    Bruce 1990.

131    *Ibid*., 95.

132    *Ibid*., 68.

133    *Ibid*., 45.

134    Hoover 1988, 126.

135    For a discussion of the conservative Christian position on "secular humanism," see Bruce 1988.

136    See Bruce 1990, 70–71 for a discussion of the trend toward the generalizing or the homogenizing of televangelism's religious message, particularly in the communication of doctrine. The trend, Bruce argues, is bound up with the accommodation of conservative Christians to the modern world. See also Gerbner *et al*. 1984. There the point is made that the need to draw a mass audience to cover production costs forces a "middle of the road" message produced for the masses. In addition, demands of the medium along with the television market help force a more generalized approach.

137    Bruce 1990.

138    Fore 1987. Fore borrows the concept of a morality play from Real 1977.

139    Gerbner *et al*. 1984.

140    Efforts to identify the message of television religion by making a content analysis are fine as far as they go. See Abelman and Neuendorf 1987 and Kim and Korpi 1986. Televangelism has religious meaning for viewers that goes beyond actual rhetoric. Televangelism communicates the whole of the conservative Christian message through synecdoche, imagery, and symbol.

141    Hoover 1988, 64 and 67. Hoover cites Clark and Virts 1985. See Frankl 1987 for a discussion of changes in format. Televangelism has come a long way since the early days of amateur broadcasting.

142    Hoover 1988, 69.

143    Gerbner *et al*. 1984.

144    *Ibid*.; Stacey and Shupe 1982.

145    Gerbner *et al*. 1984; Barwise and Ehrenberg 1988; and Hoover 1988.

[146]  Gerbner *et al.* 1984.

[147]  *Ibid.*; Stacey and Shupe 1982.

[148]  Hoover 1988. On the resurgence of conservative religion in response to a society and culture in crisis, see Roof 1983.

[149]  See Roof 1983.

## Chapter Four

[150]  Gerbner *et al.* 1984. See also Fore 1984, 104.

[151]  Gerbner *et al.* 1984.

[152]  See Ammerman 1987 and Marsden 1980 for an in-depth discussion of fundamentalistic belief and the historical settings that helped shape it.

[153]  For a detailed discussion of other significant differences between fundamentalists and Pentecostals, see Bruce 1990, Bruce 1988, Marsden 1980, and Wuthnow 1989. The differences run deep and help explain the concern among the Bakkers' followers upon Falwell's appointment to head the ministry in the days following the scandal in an effort to put the PTL house back in order. As one of the principal spokespersons for fundamentalists, Falwell was held in suspicion. That Falwell had openly criticized Pentecostal doctrine and the Bakkers did not help matters.

[154]  Bruce 1990, 67, 87 makes the observation about Schuller.

[155]  For a detailed discussion of fundamentalism, see Ammerman 1987 and Marsden 1980. For an overview of differences between conservative and liberal Christian theology and doctrine, see Bruce 1990, chapter 4, and Bruce 1988.

[156]  For an overview of Pentecostalism and its history, see Anderson 1979 and Hollenweger 1972.

[157]  Marsden 1980 makes the point.

[158]  "Post-millennialists" disagree with "pre-millennialists" on the sequence of events. The first group believes that Christ will return to earth and judge the unrighteous following the millennium, a thousand years of peace. The disagreement grows out of differing interpretations of the ordering of events in the book of *Revelation*. Most of the fundamentalist and Pentecostal followers of televangelism are pre-millennialists. In general both groups expect the world to become increasingly secular before Christ returns. Both hold that only those who have been saved will enjoy the millennium. Some millennialists view converting the world as a precondition of Christ's return; hence the emphasis on evangelism, as in the pre-millennialist school. See Marsden 1980 for a discussion of millennialism and of the various forms it takes.

[159]  See Chapter Three for discussion of this point.

[160]  Gerbner *et al.* 1984.

[161]  See the Appendix.

[162]  Gerbner *et al.* 1984.

[163]  *Ibid.* See Roof and McKinney 1987 for the views of moderate and liberal members of the mainline church on these issues.

[164]  Gerbner *et al.* 1984.

[165]  Women are underrepresented in religious programs, along with people of color. Women rarely, if ever, appear as clergy and rarely quote the Bible. They are rarely discussants. Women are presented as more likely to suffer physically or suffer from personal problems than men. This feature is shared with nonreligious television (Gerbner *et al.* 1984).

166   *Ibid.*

167   Bruce 1990 makes the observation.

## Chapter Five

168   Several sources trace the development of religious and conservative Christian radio and television. See Cardwell 1985, Durfey and Ferrier 1986, Fore 1987, Hill 1983, Hoover 1988, and Horsfield 1984. See also the account by the former head of the National Religious Broadcasters: Armstrong 1979. This chapter draws from all of these.

169   Cardwell 1985, 39.

170   *Ibid.*, 40.

171   Horsfield 1984, 9.

172   Hadden and Swann 1981, 55.

173   Horsfield 1984, 9–10.

174   Durfey and Ferrier 1986, 34.

175   Horsfield 1984, 9–10.

176   Durfey and Ferrier 1986.

177   Horsfield 1984, 10.

178   Durfey and Ferrier, 1986, 275.

179   *Ibid.*, 273.

180   Griswold and Schmitz 1957, 9–10.

181   *Ibid.*, 10–11.

## Chapter Six

182   Horsfield 1984, 28.

183   Programmers at Pat Robertson's television headquarters told me during a visit there that viewers comment on every conceivable aspect of the television programs, from the religious and political views expressed by hosts and guests, to format and aesthetic considerations.

184   Robertson's staff told me their information on viewers is detailed enough to construct an elaborate profile of viewers. Programs are then geared to meet the interests and needs of the average viewer.

185   Hoover 1988, 65.

186   Gerbner *et al.* 1984.

187   Hoover 1988, 126–127.

188   Korpi and Kim 1986. See also Buddenbaum 1981.

189   The results of the survey are given in full in the Appendix.

190   George Gerbner and Stewart Hoover report the figure in their foreward to Horsfield 1984, ix.

191   "700 Club," November 5, 1984.

192   Robertson's ministry has a massive phone counseling program, with 5,000 volunteer telephone counselors scattered throughout the country, 1,500 of them stationed at CBN headquarters, between 600 to 700 of them active at any given time (Hoover 1987, 74).

193   Chapter Four spells out televangelism's millenarian message in detail.

194   See Hoover 1988 on the way in which televangelism's viewers filter what they take in through their own religious views and opinions.

195  See Goethels 1981 and Kottak 1990.

196  On the production of meaning relevant to the wider social context by television viewers, see Fiske 1987. For discussion of the production of meaning relevant to the wider social context by participants in ritual, see Geertz 1973 and Turner 1974.

## Chapter Seven

197  Cardwell 1985, 46–47.

198  Kottak 1990.

199  See Goethel 1981.

200  Fore 1987.

201  *Ibid.*, 57–61.

202  See Kottak 1990.

203  See Stacey and Shupe 1982, for example.

204  On the varieties of messages communicated by religious television, see Frankl 1987. While there is variety, televangelism communicates the basic message of conservative, millenarian Christianity.

205  See Chapter Four for a discussion of conservative Christian belief, especially millenarianism.

206  Hoover 1988, 185, and 203–204.

207  I am drawing on Clifford Geertz's observations of the communication and reinforcement of a world view and style of life made possible in ritual performance (Geertz 1973).

208  See Geertz 1973 on the experiential support provided by ritual performance.

209  The "700 Club," July 21, 1988.

210  The "700 Club," July 19, 1988.

211  The "700 Club," July 20, 1988.

212  See Kottak 1990 and Goethels 1981. Barwise and Ehrenberg argue that television viewing does not change people's outlook by and large. They argue that new content that does not fit viewers' world view is simply ignored (Barwise and Ehrenberg 1988).

213  Hoover 1988, 150–152. See also 136 and 186. Hoover reports, for example, that the programs have made viewers aware that the Bible has contradictions, which is not acknowledged by their fundamentalist churches (*ibid.*, 142–143).

214  *Ibid.*, 152.

215  *Ibid.*, 229–230.

216  *Ibid.*, 103–104, 108, and 151.

217  *Ibid.*, 99; see also 99–103. On the universalizing of faith, Hoover draws from Fowler 1984.

218  Hoover 1988, 104; see also 108. On the response to cultural dissonance, Hoover draws from McLoughlin 1978.

219  Hoover 1988, 102 and *passim* cites Turner 1974 and Turner 1969. Hoover cites a later edition of Turner 1969. Hoover also draws from commentators who have drawn from Turner in their observations on television's role as ritual in innovation: B. Martin 1981; Newcomb and Alley 1983; Silverstone 1987; and White 1986. See also Goethels 1981 on this point. Hoover is of the mind that all mass media, including television religion, are ritual sources of innovation or potential sources.

220  See Turner 1969, Turner 1974, and Turner 1982. For an extended discussion of Turner's observations, see Alexander 1991.

221   Cardwell 1985, 48–49; see also Hoover 1988.

## Chapter Eight

222   See Wuthnow 1989, 119–122.
223   Gerbner *et al.* 1984.
224   See Hoover 1988 for an account of personal problems and interests provided by viewers themselves.
225   See Hoover 1988 for extended comments from viewers on their sense of community with other viewers.
226   Wuthnow 1989, 122–123.
227   Hoover 1988, 210 and 206.
228   *Ibid.*, 206. Hoover cites Bellah *et al.* 1985. See also 243.
229   Hoover 1988, 206. Hoover cites P. Berger, B. Berger, and Kellner 1973.
230   Hoover 1988, 29 cites Bellah *et al.* 1985. See Chapter Seven on the role played by televangelism as ritual adaptation in broadening viewers' horizon to include a larger view of the wider society.
231   See Turner 1982, 48, 51, 55 on millenarian or utopian visions of community.
232   Kottak 1990. See also Goethels 1981 and Fore 1987, 57–61.
233   Hoover 1988, 103. See also 102.
234   The discussion of Turner's observations of ritual and its role in creating community draws from Turner 1982, Turner 1974, Turner 1969. For an extended discussion of Turner's theory of ritual community, see Alexander 1991.
235   Turner 1982, 48. See also 44.
236   *Ibid.*, 84.
237   Turner 1974, 13. See also 47, 231, 238, and 273–274.
238   Turner 1982, 85 and 49. See also 32, 44–45, 52, 54, 84; and Turner 1974, 242–243.
239   Gerbner *et al.* 1984.
240   Bruce 1990, 138.

## Chapter Nine

241   Falwell made the comment on "The Old-Time Gospel Hour," program #421 in the archives of Falwell's television ministry (December 1980).
242   *Ibid.*
243   *Ibid.*
244   "The Old-Time Gospel Hour," November 2, 1986.
245   "The Old-Time Gospel Hour," recorded July 24, 1988.
246   *Ibid.*
247   "The Old-Time Gospel Hour," program #342 (1979).
248   "The Old-Time Gospel Hour," #421 (December 1980).
249   "The Old-Time Gospel Hour," January 1, 1981.
250   "The Old-Time Gospel Hour," #421 (December 1980).
251   "The Old-Time Gospel Hour," January 1, 1981.
252   "The Old-Time Gospel Hour," #421 (December 1980).
253   "The Old-Time Gospel Hour," program #694 (1986).
254   "The Old-Time Gospel Hour," recorded July 23, 1989.
255   "The Old-Time Gospel Hour," January 1, 1981.

## Chapter Ten

256  A member of the Christian Broadcasting Network staff told me during a visit to the television headquarters that the national networks often ask to borrow film footage for a story on religion because CBN knows how to do these types of stories more effectively and is often already on the scene of a newsbreaking event of relevance to conservative Christians.

257  The "700 Club," October 6, 1981.

258  *Ibid*. See also the "700 Club," March 27, 1987.

259  The "700 Club," July 18, 1989.

260  The "700 Club," June 11, 1986.

261  See, for example, the "700 Club," November 5, 1985, and July 19, 20, 21, and 22 1988.

262  The "700 Club," May 16, 1986.

263  The "700 Club," October 6, 1981.

264  The "700 Club," July 17, 1989.

265  The "700 Club," July 18, 1989.

266  The "700 Club," March 27, 1987.

267  The "700 Club," May 16, 1986.

268  "Straight Talk," July 17, 1989.

269  "Straight Talk," July 18, 1989.

270  A member of the CBN staff told me that "Straight Talk" treats issues that are too controversial for the "700 Club."

271  The Roe versus Wade decision was discussed on the May 16, 1986 edition of the "700 Club."

272  The "700 Club," July 21, 1988.

273  The "700 Club," July 17, 1989.

274  The "700 Club," July 19, 1988.

275  The personalities appeared on the "700 Club" on May 16, 1986.

276  The "700 Club," March 27, 1987.

277  The "700 Club," June 11, 1986.

278  The "700 Club," March 24, 1987. One of Robertson's viewers who responded to my survey said about the news reports carried over the "700 Club," "That's the only place you get the truth. The others [the national television newscasters] are liars."

279  The "700 Club," May 16, 1986.

280  The program's producers, directors, and technical crew told me they use a great deal of technological know-how in order to sustain viewers' attention and interest. I was played a tape of a new version of the musical theme that introduces the show. The question being considered was whether or not the rock guitar music would turn off some of the more conservative viewers.

281  The "700 Club," October 6, 1981.

282  The comment was made by Tim Robertson, who hosted in his father's absence while Robertson campaigned for the Presidency (the "700 Club," March 27, 1987).

283  The "700 Club," November 5, 1984.

284  The "700 Club," May 16, 1986.

285  The evangelical vote was the subject of a broadcast of the "700 Club" on November 4, 1984.

286  *Ibid*.

## Chapter Eleven

287   The events described took place during a worship service I attended on July 1, 1990 at Swaggart's headquarters. The service was one of several held during a "Campmeeting" of Swaggart followers who had traveled from all over the country to the ministry's headquarters.

288   See, for example, "Jimmy Swaggart," November 11, 1984.

289   "Jimmy Swaggart," July 7, 1985. See also "Jimmy Swaggart," November 11, 1984.

290   According to Swaggart, his ministry is present in 145 countries ("A Study in the Word," June 3, 1987).

291   "Jimmy Swaggart," November 11, 1984.

292   "Jimmy Swaggart," July 7, 1985.

293   This edition of "Jimmy Swaggart" was recorded on July 1, 1990.

294   "Jimmy Swaggart," November 18, 1984.

295   See "Jimmy Swaggart," July 7, 1985.

## Chapter Twelve

296   See, for example, the "PTL Club," April 25, 1986.

297   The comments are those of the Associate Pastor for the Bakker ministry. I interviewed him during a visit to the new television headquarters in Orlando in July 1989. The Associate Pastor went on to point out that there was an "amazing empathy" for the Bakkers among viewers following the PTL scandal.

298   The ministry's Associate Pastor is quoted. According to him, 40% of the Bakkers' audience is from the lower middle class.

299   "The Jim and Tammy Show," recorded July 12, 1989.

300   The "PTL Club," April 17, 1986.

301   The "PTL Club," April 17, 1986.

302   The "PTL Club," April 25, 1986.

303   *Ibid*.

304   Jim Bakker made the comment on a program aired during the fundraising telethon in the spring of 1986.

305   See note 304.

306   The "PTL Club," March 14, 1986.

307   The "PTL Club," April 25, 1986.

308   The "PTL Club," March 14, 1986.

309   Bakker quoted the same scripture on the "PTL Club," March 14, 1986.

310   The "PTL Club," March 14, 1986.

311   The "PTL Club," April 17, 1986.

312   The "PTL Club," March 14, 1986.

313   The "PTL Club," March 26, 1987.

314   The telecast of "The Jim and Tammy Show" discussed below was taped on July 11, 1989.

315   "The Jim and Tammy Show," taped on July 10, 1989.

316   "The Jim and Tammy Show," taped on July 12, 1989.

## Chapter Thirteen

317 "The Old-Time Gospel Hour," November 2, 1986.

318 "Jimmy Swaggart," February 21, 1988.

319 "Jimmy Swaggart," July 24, 1988.

320 "The Jim and Tammy Show," taped on July 12, 1989.

## Appendix

321 Gerbner *et al.* 1984.

322 *Ibid.*; and Hoover 1987.

323 For a report from a Jewish viewer on her reasons for watching the "700 Club," see Hoover 1988, 170 and 190–192.

324 Gerbner *et al.* 1984.

# ⊰ Bibliography ⊱

Abelman, Robert. 1988. "Financial Support for Religious Television: The Impact of the PTL Scandal." *Journal of Media Economics*. Vol. 1 (Spring): 23–38.

Abelman, Robert, and Kimberly Neuendorf. 1987. "Themes and Topics in Religious Television Programming." *Review of Religious Research*. Vol. 29 (December): 152–174.

Alexander, Bobby C. 1991. *Victor Turner Revisited: Ritual as Social Change*. Atlanta: Scholars Press (American Academy of Religion, Academy Series, no. 74).

Ammerman, Nancy T. 1987. *Bible Believers: Fundamentalists in the Modern World*. New Brunswick, New Jersey: Rutgers University Press.

Anderson, Robert Mapes. 1979 (1992). *Vision of the Disinherited: The Making of American Pentecostalism*. New York: Oxford University Press.

Armstrong, Ben. 1979. *The Electric Church*. Nashville: Thomas Nelson Publishers, Inc.

Barwise, T. Patrick, and Andrew Ehrenberg. 1988. *Television and Its Audience*. London: Sage.

Bellah, Robert, R. Marsden, W. M. Sullivan, A. Swidler, and S. M. Tipton. 1985. *Habits of the Heart: Individualism and Commitment in American Life*. Berkeley: University of California Press.

Berger, Peter L., Brigitte Berger, and Hansfried Kellner. 1973. *The Homeless Mind: Modernization and Consciousness*. New York: Random House.

Bruce, Steve. 1990. *Pray TV: Televangelism in America*. London: Routledge.

Bruce, Steve. 1988. *The Rise and Fall of the New Christian Right: Conservative Protestant Politics in America 1978–1988*. New York: Oxford University Press.

Buddenbaum, Judith M. 1981. "Characteristics and Media-Related Needs of the Audience for Religious TV." *Journalism Quarterly*. Vol. 58 (Summer): 266–272.

Cardwell, Jerry D. 1985. *A Rumor of Trumpets: The Return of God to Secular Society*. Lanham, Maryland: University Press of America.

Carey, James W. 1989. *Communication As Culture: Essays on Media and Society*. Boston: Unwin Hyman.

Carey, James W. 1975. "Communication and Culture." Review of Clifford Geertz's *The Interpretation of Cultures*. In *Communication Research*. Vol. 2 (April): 173–191.

Carpenter, Joel. 1985. "Tuning in the Gospel: Fundamentalist Radio Broadcasting and Revival of Mass Evangelism, 1930–1945." Paper presented to the Mid-American Studies Association, University of Illinois, Urbana, April.

Carroll, Jackson W., Douglas W. Johnson, and Martin E. Marty. 1979. *Religion in America: 1950 to the Present*. San Francisco: Harper & Row.

*Christianity Today*. February 3, 1989.

Clark, David W., and Paul H. Virts. 1985. "The Religious Television Audience: A New Development in Measuring Audience Size." Paper delivered to the Society for the Scientific Study of Religion. Savannah, Georgia, 25 October.

Driver, Tom. 1991. *The Magic of Ritual: Our Need for Liberating Rites that Transform Our Lives and Our Communities*. San Francisco: HarperSanFrancisco.

Durfey, Thomas C., and James A. Ferrier. 1986. *Religious Broadcast Management Handbook*. Grand Rapids: Academie Books.

*Electronic Media*. January 30, 1989.

Ferguson, Thomas, and Joel Rogers. 1986. "The Myth of America's Turn to the Right." *Atlantic Monthly*. Vol. 257 (May): 43–53.

Fiske, John. 1987. *Television Culture*. London: Metheun.

Fore, William F. 1987. *Television and Religion: The Shaping of Faith, Values, and Culture*. Minneapolis: Augsburg Publishing House.

Fowler, James. 1984. *Becoming Adult, Becoming Christian*. New York: Harper & Row.

Frankl, Razelle. 1987. *Televangelism: The Marketing of Popular Religion*. Carbondale, Illinois: Southern Illinois University Press.

Gaddy, Gary D., and David Pritchard. 1985. "When Watching TV Is Like Attending Church." *Journal of Communication*. Vol. 35 (Winter 1985): 123–131.

Gallup, George, Jr. 1985. *Religion in America: Fifty Years: 1935–1985*. Princeton: Princeton Religion Research Center.

Geertz, Clifford. 1973. "Religion As a Cultural Symbol System." In his *The Interpretation of Cultures*. New York: Basic Books, Inc.

Gerbner, George, Larry Gross, Stewart Hoover, Michael Morgan, Nancy Signorielli, Harry Cotugno, and Robert Wuthnow. 1984. "Religion and Television." Philadelphia: The Annenberg School of Communications, The University of Pennsylvania.

Goethals, Gregor T. 1981. *The TV Ritual: Worship at the Video Altar*. Boston: Beacon Press.

Greeley, Andrew M. 1972. *The Denominational Society: A Sociological Approach to Religion in America*. Glenview, Illinois: Scott Foresman & Co.

Griswold, Clayton, and Charles H. Schmitz. 1957. *How You Can Broadcast Religion*. Edited by Lois J. Anderson. New York: National Council of the Churches of Christ in the United States of America, Broadcasting and Film Commission.

Hadden, Jeffrey K., and Razelle Frankl. 1987a. "Star Wars of a Different Kind: Reflections on the Politics of the 'Religion and Television' Research Project." *Review of Religious Research*. Vol. 29 (December): 101–110.

Hadden, Jeffrey K., and Razelle Frankl. 1987b. "A Critical Review of the Religion and Television Research Report." *Review of Religious Research*. Vol. 29 (December): 111–124.

Hadden, Jeffrey K., and Anson D. Shupe. 1988. *Televangelism: Power and Politics on God's Frontier*. New York: Henry Holt.

Hadden, Jeffrey K., and Charles E. Swann. 1981. *Prime Time Preachers: The Rising Power of Televangelism*. Reading, Massachusetts: Addison-Wesley Publishing Company, Inc.

Hill, George H. 1983. *Airwaves to the Soul: The Influence and Growth of Religious Broadcasting in America*. Saratoga, California: R & E Publishers.

Hollenweger, Walter J. 1972. *The Pentecostals: The Charismatic Movement in the Churches*. Translated by R. A. Wilson. Minneapolis: Augsburg Publishing House.

Hoover, Stewart M. 1988. *Mass Media Religion: The Social Sources of the Electronic Church*. Newbury Park, California: Sage Publications, Inc.

Hoover, Stewart M. 1987. "The Religious Television Audience: A Matter of Significance, or Size?" *Review of Religious Research*. Vol. 29 (December): 135–151.

Horsfield, Peter G. 1984. *Religious Television: The American Experience*. New York: Longman, Inc.

Hunter, James Davison. 1987. *Evangelicalism: The Coming Generation*. Chicago: The University of Chicago Press.

Hunter, James Davison. 1983. *American Evangelicalism: Conservative Religion and the Quandry of Modernity*. New Brunswick, New Jersey: Rutgers University Press.

Hutchison, William R. 1991. Comments in "Forum." *Religion and American Culture: A Journal of Interpretation*. (Summer): 131–137.

Johnson, Stephen D., and Joseph B. Tamney. 1985. "Mobilizing Support for the Moral Majority." *Psychological Reports*. Vol. 56 (June): 987–994.

Johnson, Stephen D., and Joseph B. Tamney. 1982. "The Christian Right and the 1980 Presidential Election." *Journal for the Scientific Study of Religion*. Vol. 21 (June): 123–131.

Korpi, Michael F., and Kyong Liong Kim. 1986. "The Uses and Effects of Televangelism: A Factorial Model of Support and Contribution." *Journal for the Scientific Study of Religion*. Vol. 25 (December): 410–423.

Kottak, Conrad P. 1990. *Prime-Time Society: An Anthropological Analysis of Television and Culture*. Belmont, California: Wadsworth Publishing Company.

Marsden, George M. 1983a. "Understanding Fundamentalists' Views of Society." In *Reformed Faith and Politics*. Edited by Ronald H. Stone. Washington, D.C.: University Press of America.

Marsden, George, M. 1983b. "Preachers of Paradox: The Religious New Right in Historical Perspective." In *Religion and America: Spiritual Life in a Secular Age*. Edited by Mary Douglas and Steven Tipton. Boston: Beacon Press.

Marsden, George M. 1980. *Fundamentalism and American Culture: The Shaping of Twentieth-Century Evangelicalism: 1870–1925*. New York: Oxford University Press.

Martin, Bernice. 1981. *A Sociology of Contemporary Cultural Change*. New York: St. Martin's Press.

Martin, William. 1981. "The Birth of a Media Myth." *Atlantic Monthly*. Vol. 247 (June): 7, 10–11, 16.

Martz, Larry, and Ginny Carroll. 1988. *Ministry of Greed: The Inside Story of the Televangelists and Their Holy Wars*. New York: Weidenfeld & Nicolson.

McKinney, William. 1991. Comments in "Forum." *Religion and American Culture: A Journal of Interpretation*. (Summer): 149–153.

McLoughlin, William G. 1978. *Revivals, Awakenings, and Reform: An Essay on Religion and Social Change in America, 1607–1977*. Chicago: University of Chicago Press.

Moore, R. Laurence. 1986. *Religious Outsiders and the Making of Americans*. New York: Oxford University Press.

Newcomb, Horace, and Robert S. Alley, eds. 1983. *The Producer's Medium: Conversations with Creators of American TV*. New York: Oxford University Press.

Parker, Everett C., David W. Barry, and Dallas W. Smythe. 1955. *The Television-Radio Audience and Religion*. New York: Harper & Brothers, Publishers.

Real, Michael R. 1977. *Mass-Mediated Culture*. Englewood Cliffs, New Jersey: Prentice-Hall.

Roof, Wade Clark. 1983. "America's Voluntary Establishment: Mainline Religion in Transition." In *Religion and America: Spiritual Life in a Secular Age*. Edited by Mary Douglas and Steven Tipton. Boston: Beacon Press.

Roof, Wade Clark, and William McKinney. 1987. *American Mainline Religion: Its Changing Shape and Future*. New Brunswick, New Jersey: Rutgers University Press.

Schechner, Richard. 1977 (1993). *Essays in Performance Theory: 1970–1976*. New York: Drama Book Specialists.

Sigelman, Lee, and Stanley Presser. 1988. "Measuring Public Support for the New Christian Right: The Perils of Point Estimation." *Public Opinion Quarterly*. Vol. 52: 326–339.

Silverstone, Roger. 1987. "Television, Rhetoric and Everyday Life." Paper presented to a symposium on "Rethinking the Audience: New Tendencies in Television Research." Blaubeuren, West Germany, February.

Stacey, William A., and Anson D. Shupe. 1982. "Correlates of Support for 'The Electronic Church.'" *Journal for the Scientific Study of Religion*. Vol. 21 (December): 291–303.

The City University of New York, The Graduate School. 1991. Survey of Religion in America 1990.

*The Atlanta Journal*. February 5, 1989.

*The Dallas Morning News*. March 5, 1993.

*The Dallas Morning News*. December 9, 1992.

*The Dallas Morning News*. September 29, 1990.

*The New York Times*. November 21, 1992.

*The New York Times*. April 10, 1991.

Turner, Victor. 1986a. "Dewey, Dilthey, and Drama: An Essay in the Anthropology of Experience." In *The Anthropology of Experience*. Edited by Victor W. Turner and Edward M. Bruner. Urbana, Illinois: University of Illinois Press.

Turner, Victor. 1986b. *The Anthropology of Performance*. New York: PAJ Publications.

Turner, Victor. 1985. *On the Edge of the Bush: Anthropology as Experience*. Edited by Edith L. B. Turner. Tucson: University of Arizona Press.

Turner, Victor. 1982. *From Ritual to Theatre: The Human Seriousness of Play*. New York: Performing Arts Journal Publications.

Turner, Victor. 1974. *Dramas, Fields, and Metaphors: Symbolic Action in Human Society*. Ithaca, New York: Cornell University Press.

Turner, Victor 1969 (1982). *The Ritual Process: Structure and Anti-structure*. Chicago: Aldine Publishing Company.

White, Robert A. 1986. "The Mass Media and the Religious Imagination." Unpublished paper. London: The Centre for the Study of Communication and Culture.

Wuthnow, Robert. 1989. *The Struggle for America's Soul: Evangelicals, Liberals, and Secularism*. Grand Rapids, Michigan: William B. Eerdmans Publishing Company.

Winzenburg, Stephen. 1988. "On Understanding TV Evangelists." *Broadcasting*. (July 18): 25.

Young, Perry Deane. 1982. *God's Bullies: Native Reflections on Preachers and Politics*. New York: Holt, Rinehart and Winston.